68/37)

Various references to
Delius & other English composers

Journey into Music

Journey into Music
(by the slow train)

An autobiography

Christopher le Fleming

REDCLIFFE
Bristol

First published in 1982 by
Redcliffe Press Ltd., 14 Dowry Square, Bristol 8

© Christopher le Fleming

ISBN 0 905459 42 3

Photoset and printed in Great Britain by
Photobooks (Bristol) Ltd.,
28 Midland Road, St. Philips, Bristol

Contents

		page
Acknowledgements		vii

PART ONE – THE JOURNEY

1.	Sounds in a Country Town (c.1910)	3
2.	Sounds into Music	7
3.	Household Music – 1. A Succession of Pianolas	11
4.	Household Music – 2. Enter the Gramophone	15
5.	Music in the 1920s – 1	19
6.	Music in the 1920s – 2	24
7.	Doctor Gradus	30
8.	'I too will something make'	34
9.	'And joy in the making'	37
10.	Some Three Choirs Festival Memories (1925–27)	43
11.	Dorset Landscape with Figures	48
12.	'That can sing both high and low'	55
13.	R.V.W.	60
14.	S.H.N.	66
15.	Songs of Summer	74
16.	A London Overture	80
17.	Da Capo	86
18.	'Drei Intermezzi'	92
19.	Forest Murmurs	99
20.	'Cool Sequester'd Vale'	105

21. In Search of Vision   113

22. Two Interludes: 1. Downland Vigil   118

                    2. What the teacup told me   123

23. The Slow Train gathers speed   127

24. About People and Places   133

25. Music in Religious Drama   138

26. Oxford and Offley   143

27. Andante and Rondo Capriccioso   148

28. Kentish Coda   154

PART TWO – 'MEDITATIONS'

29. Composers and Communication   161

30. Organists and the Clergy   166

31. Music, Places – and Silence   170

32. Music and Railways   177

33. The Piano – in Sickness and in Health   185

34. Bach's '48', Dr. Ebenezer Prout and others   187

List of Music by Christopher le Fleming   192

Arrangements and transcriptions by Christopher le Fleming   196

Index   197

Acknowledgements

Grateful thanks are due to the following: the Trustees of Michael Flanders' Estate for permission to quote from *The Slow Train*; Gerald Duckworth and Co. Ltd. for some lines from the poem *Stillness* by Harold Monro (Collected Poems); Myfanwy Thomas for a similar favour with the poem *Adlestrop* by her father Edward Thomas: Lady Bliss for an extract from Sir Arthur's autobiography *As I Remember*; Mrs. Audrey Browne for the poem *The River Stour* by R.H.B. (Roger Browne); Chatto and Windus for a quotation from *Sappho* by Bliss Carman; The Society of Authors, on behalf of the Bernard Shaw Estate, for a comment from *Music in London*, and also to the society for some lines from *Last Poems* by A. E. Housman: the Oxford University Press for excavations from early numbers of *Music and Letters*: Clare Leighton and Macmillan and Co. for permission to reproduce a woodcut from a special edition of *The Return of the Native* by Thomas Hardy: Biddie Kindersley for making it possible to include a picture of Wimborne, from a painting made nearly a century ago, in her possession.

Also to the Editor of *The Countryman* for the greater part of Chapter 1, which originally appeared in that journal; the Editor of the *Railway Magazine* for two extracts from past issues; the Governing Council of the Rural Music Schools Association and Norman Hearn for material from contributions to *Making Music*; and the Kent County Music Committee and Michael Wearne for similar quarrying from *Kent Friends of Music Bulletins*.

C. le F.

To **Mary** and my three sons
Michael, Daniel and **Antony**

"I aske nothing else alwaies but health and a purseful of monie,
for my paramour a pretty conie, and Paradice at the end of my
daies."

JOHN ELIOT
The Parliament of Prattlers 1593

"No more will I go to Blandford Forum or Mortehoe
By the slow train from Midsomer Norton and Mumby Road,
No churns, no porter, no cat on a seat
At Chorlton-cum-Hardy or Chester-le Street –
We won't be meeting again
On the slow train . . ."

MICHAEL FLANDERS
At The Drop Of Another Hat

PART ONE

THE JOURNEY

CHAPTER 1

Sounds in a Country Town (c. 1910)

To be born into this world with defective eyesight often produces an immediate and vivid awareness of the sounds that 'creep in our ears' from earliest infancy. Perhaps this is why a good many people with limited vision tend to become musicians. Many of us, from Toscanini downwards, have been stimulated by the ear rather than the eye – the latter, like the Old Superb in Newbolt's poem 'lagging all the way.' Being obliged to look hard and closely at scores can also be an aid to memory.

The Dorset market town of Wimborne Minster, where I was born towards the end of Edward VII's reign, provided a rich and varied tonal background. The visual outlines might be blurred, but the sounds were quickly assimilated into consciousness, soon placing themselves like instruments in an orchestral score.

The voices of my parents, Nanny and her cronies, the household domestic staff with their rich west country 'burr' – here was exciting material for sorting and placing. And our garden wall was flanked on three sides by roads, each of which produced a different mêlée to be sifted, analysed and registered in the mind. The West (or Straight) Borough, in front of the house, provided the main access from Cranborne and the clustered farms and villages that lay northward beyond Walford Bridge and the town boundary. Their names rang like bells – Hinton Martell, Chalbury, Witchampton, Didlington, Crichel, Wimborne St. Giles. Since my father was a doctor, the place-names on his rounds were often mentioned at meal-times and thus became quickly familiar. From them came many different forms of traffic – the sounds made more resonant by the tall houses opposite.

There was the slow clip-clop of horses bringing loaded waggons to market. Some farmers still bedecked their horses with sets of bells that jingled above the harness-collars as the animals tossed their heads. Thomas Hardy recalled these bells in *The Woodlanders:* as well as for adornment they served a useful purpose when a loaded waggon needed headway down a long narrow drove. When originally cast, the bells were tuned to the farmer's special liking: this also provided a means of identification.

Though the Borough was now a staid and ultra-respectable place in which to live, it had formerly been a haunt of smugglers, thus acquiring an aura of hidden mystery. One of the houses still bore the name of Gulliver – an exponent of the art whose ghost was said to haunt the area.

Besides the waggons, my ear made out the brisk trot of pony-and-trap, the sedate tread of horse-and-carriage, interspersed with the gradual crescendo of vintage cars, rapidly growing in number. There were still a few ancient two-cylinder veterans that chugged laboriously along, but they were giving place to four and six-cylinder motive power, most makers producing so individual a sound that they could be recognised without the effort of visual checking.

Beyond the bottom of the garden ran the East (or Crooked) Borough, from which came an even greater variety of sounds. The clink of the anvil came floating from Mr. King's forge; from Bert Joyner's workshop, the abrasive noise of sawing wood. Here were all the impedimenta of pre-mechanized farming, brightly painted in red, blue and yellow. The floor was thick with shavings through which you could 'tash' as though through fallen leaves in an autumn wood. Beyond the forge was an inn, formerly known as The Silent Woman. From the yard a dog, too long chained, would raise a mournful howl – a first intimation of misery beyond the garden wall.

Also in the Crooked Borough was a doleful institution then known as the Workhouse – with an old, gaunt and forbidding door. Occasionally I would watch a bedraggled figure shamble up to that door – and knock. After a pause it would open to admit yet another victim of poverty and despair. On Sunday afternoons the Warden, Mr. Wareham, could be heard singing hymns in the front room, discreetly accompanied by his spouse. Years later my father, visiting a sick inmate, found a set of hand-turned sycamore plates thrown on a rubbish-heap: officialdom had decreed enamel hardware as a replacement. For years we used the discarded treasure-trove as side-plates; they were greatly admired by us all and coveted by friends.

Best of all, the Crooked Borough was a favourite haunt on Sundays for the Salvation Army to mount extended bursts of Evangelizing. And on every Easter Sunday, early in the morning, they played a tune that we all waited to hear, and found ourselves singing for the rest of the day. Recent enquiries have revealed it as *Low In The Grave He Lay*, though from the *brio* created it is evidently more concerned with subsequent events! Invariably it stirred a nearby and dissonant chapel bell into petulant protest, thereby producing a bitonal effect later to be associated with the music of Charles Ives.

From the lane connecting the two Boroughs came the sound of a steam bakery, followed by an alluring aroma of farthing buns. Also from the lane came frequent sounds of merry-making, the young intent on hop-scotch, maternal scoldings, paternal aftermaths of overlong pub sessions in the days before 'permitted hours' reduced the frequency, and intensity of such scenes.

All these sounds were diffused according to the prevailing wind. Often they would be filtered through rustling leaves on the garden trees. Floating serenely above them all came the voice of the Minster bells. Day and night the ding-dong from the Quarter-Jack sounded, while the deep tenor bell tolled the hours. On Sunday the full glory of a peal of ten, rung with unfailing skill and certainty, never failed to lift our spirits. Every evening at eight o'clock the Curfew would echo through the emptying streets: the Death-Bell would sound the passing of a soul from the world – one pull for each year of the life then ended.

These Wimborne bells seem exceptionally well tuned and toned. The Minster archives record their being taken down and repaired 'in the yard of the George Inn 1227'. That Quarter-Jack provided my first music lesson. Its insistence on repeating the notes C-G (Tonic-Dominant) and, by adding the lower C at the hour, taught me the most basic of all intervals in music – the octave (within which are contained all the available notes that can be used).

But there was yet another – and a more distant – sound that aroused my deep curiosity. The south-east wind would bring the tantalizing noise of trains coming towards the station by way of Leigh Common. Then, after a pause, the trains would start the climb to Merley, the note changing as they rumbled over the iron bridge spanning the river. Sounds of shunting provided an effective descant. These operations were carried out in the unfailingly seemly manner that characterized the London and South Western line, that, unlike its neighbours the Brighton and the South-Eastern, was not given to frequent whistlings or violent bursts of surplus steam. But when the south-west wind came, bringing rain, we would hear in the night an altogether deeper note as a Somerset and Dorset freight train laboured up the gradient from Corfe Mullen towards Broadstone – at the head of it a locomotive from a very different stable – that of Derby, whose products emitted a deep and throaty sound. This would fade as the train reached a sandy cutting, much beloved of martens.

Elsewhere in this book I have written of the almost mystic fervour that many musicians have experienced for steam railways in the days of pre-grouping, prenationalized splendour. In my own case the virus was caught from my elder brother, whose railway paintings still adorn the walls of the room in which I write.

An awareness of sound must surely carry with it a sense of distance. Even in those early years I was fascinated by the vast canopy of space and silence in the sky above our house and garden. Sometimes, as in Walter de la Mare's 'steep blue sky' the trees seemed almost to touch it. On other days it would appear like a great sea through which sailed clouds that, to my limited vision, recalled the sailing ships in children's picture books. Always this infinity – away and beyond, above the sound of the wind in the trees, street noises, voices, the Quarter-Jack and the trains. Soon they would all merge into the ordered harmony of music.

CHAPTER 2

Sounds into Music

The Minster bells set a seal on the sounds recalled from early childhood. From them came a clear intimation of another world awaiting discovery. And then, on a memorable day, my father appeared with something that looked like a speaker unit that had been left out in the rain. It proved to be a musical box of quasi-organ vintage, with bellows worked by turning a handle. There were six tunes that, for me, were the music of the spheres. They were played incessantly (except to eat, sleep or to go for a daily walk) until my father gently but firmly removed the magic box and returned it to the rightful owner. The infinite kindness of this loan was repaid several years later when, during school holidays, I would go to Miss Kaye's house to play the piano pieces acquired during the previous term. By then she had become a permanent invalid. And so a very small boy began a lifelong journey into music.

In our drawing-room there was a Broadwood grand piano with a shining black ebony case. On it my mother would play, in the magic hour before bedtime. At first she plied me with nursery rhymes, but these did not 'strike on my box' as Jack Moeran used to say. We had two books of nursery rhymes: one an ever-so-delicate affair that seemed strangely lacking in vitamins. In later years, despite childish sales-resistance, some of the tunes found their way into my cantata *The Echoing Green*. They also provided a basic ingredient to music for Kay Baxter's mime *Pull Devil Pull Baker*, later revised as *The Silver Dove*.

The other book, German in origin (memory suggests Wilhelm Busch as illustrator) contained less attractive music, but terrifying illustrations. There was one picture of The Spider and The Fly that I used to dare myself to look at – and quickly turn the page with a shudder of fear. From the spider came an obsession about bogey-men, ghoulishly fostered by my erstwhile little playmates. I became aware that music, like the other arts, has a dark and sinister aspect. The two pieces, however, that never failed to dispel the ogre were the Barcarole from *Tales of Hoffmann* and 'A Regular Royal Queen' from *The Gondoliers*.

Both parents, when young, had lived in West Kent, and had been able to attend most of the vintage productions of Gilbert and Sullivan opera at the Savoy Theatre. For many people at the time these unique manifestations represented the alpha and omega of

musical experience. This was certainly so for my father, though
he later added two or three storeys to this bungaloid concept.
From the first, Sullivan's music held me spellbound, though
Gilbert was harder to accept. From early days I found his ill-bred
jibes at spinsters hard to take: unmarried women abounded in
those days, many arousing in me a sympathetic and protective
response. A good deal of the humorous content of the Savoy
Operas still seems pawky and dated, though the sheer dexterity
and expressive eloquence of the lyrics – and Sullivan's settings –
remains an unfailing source of delight, particularly when heard
after a fairly long abstinence.

My mother, in her playing, covered a rather wider field. She
had acquired a good deal of the gentler and easier Chopin who, in
common with many people at the time, she bracketed with
Schumann. She also revealed 'a little' Beethoven, Schubert and
Grieg. Of Bach nothing, since to her his music was 'mathematical
and unfeeling,' – a point of view that had something in common
with Beecham's 'Too much counterpoint – and Protestant
counterpoint at that!' Mozart was still in the half-shade, along
with Hummel, Clementi and others of the period. He was
summarily dismissed as 'quite pretty but rather tinkly!' For me,
both heresies were to be sunk without trace, though my mother
held on to them for life. Meanwhile I set about discovering the
keyboard and soon acquired (by ear) large dollops of Sullivan's
tunes to do-it-yourself harmonies, unhampered by the presence of
Gilbert.

Apart from the Salvation Army, already encountered in the
Crooked Borough at the bottom of the garden, there was a
Children's Service at the Minster, to which I was firmly taken.
Here the more soupy aspects of Hymns A & M (unrevised)
predominated. Blandishments such as 'Homes for Little Children
Above The Bright Blue Sky' evoked even less response than
nursery rhymes – and the suggestion that bliss might be obtained
by 'Leaning On His Breast' positively repelled. Still, we were
given brightly coloured stamps to be stuck in albums week by
week, that partly compensated for an atmosphere of over-
righteous and decorous tedium. We were also indoctrinated with
the idea that The Rich Man In His Castle etc. existed by Divine
Ordinance; young though we were, we instinctively rejected such
subversive evasions of reality. On one glorious occasion there was
a new curate who produced a superb – and entirely unintentional
– comic turn. But alas! he was considered 'most unsuitable' and
hastily replaced by a successor, who toed the party line by
continuing to hand out muted platitudes. Occasional visits to the

Congregational Chapel (during a parental absence from home) revealed something very different – a warm and outgoing friendliness, an absence of starched gentility and a singing from the heart that warmed us as though we had been sitting by a fire.

When later I was promoted to Matins at the Minster (and thankfully unleashed before the Sermon) the choir did most of the singing. In the boys' voices the familiar Anglican hoot predomin- ated, while the rugged individuals who provided the other parts were all too easily recognized. There was also a diverting tendency among the congregation, when those who claimed to be 'musical' attempted to sing the part most suited to each voice, leaving the tune to those less cultured.

Echoing 'Rich Men In Their Castles', there is a Deed of Sale in my possession for a house acquired by a forebear in 1843. Among the attractions mentioned is the following: 'The Property carries with it accommodation for Worship in the Parish Church, but with separate accommodation for Servants'. They at least could sing the tune! And in 1908 when a clerical uncle moved into a vicarage in the Isle of Wight, he found a notice that read: Confirmation Classes – Ladies, 6.30 in the Drawing Room: Females, 7.30 in the Kitchen.

So much for first impressions. A few years later the mists obscuring the splendours of music composed *Ad majorem Dei gloriam* were to lift in an unexpected fashion. The first intimation came after a visit to Wimborne by Canon Edmund Fellowes during a search for missing parts needed to complete his edition of Tudor Church Music. The Minster, under a Charter granted by Elizabeth I, is placed in the care of twelve worthy citizens of Wimborne, duly elected, of whom my father was one. As he was deeply interested in anything historical or antiquarian, unusual queries were generally passed to him. The Canon arrived to discover, among other treasures, missing parts of music by Byrd and other composers of the period, locked away in a chest in the Chained Library. Delighted with the success of the day's revelations, he came to our house for tea. With him, as an assistant, was a young university graduate – Sylvia Townsend Warner. Her visit provided us with a vivid glimpse of the author who, in years to come, would achieve fame and wide recognition with *Lolly Willowes*. When it became possible to obtain the music so skilfully and painstakingly brought to life once again, the impact on many of us, both young and old, was immediate and exciting.

In his memoir and throughout his life Edmund Fellowes used the term 'amateur' as a token of innate modesty. As a result, many members of the Establishment (often organists in safe and cosy lofts from which the sound of diapason registration predominated) were inclined to raise gentlemanly eyebrows. Is he really an amateur, they asked, then by what authority . . .? A notable instance of this attitude was that of the Incorporated Society of Musicians, whose criterion for membership requires the status of professional musician, and thus declined to admit him for many years.

Shortly before this splendid man died, full of years, piety and honour, it was my privilege as Editor of *Making Music** to go to the Cloisters at Windsor Castle to thank him, on behalf of countless amateur musicians, for all that he had done for English music. While we were talking I became aware of his disappointment that the ISM had held out for so long against him. At that time the President was Henry Havergal, whom I instantly alerted and, as a result, Canon Edmund Fellowes was elected an Honorary Life Member. As I left the Cloisters, autumn leaves were drifting in a damp and chilly breeze: within a year came the news of his death. It was good to know that the last bastion had capitulated, though only just in time.

---

*A journal published by the Rural Music Schools Association during the period 1946 – 76.

CHAPTER 3

Household Music –
1. A Succession of Pianolas

A stay with relations in Surrey at a very early age was made memorable by the discovery of an angelus in the house. That formidable and aggressive precursor of the pianola consumed rolls and was worked by bellows – and spread across the hind quarters in a straight line was a formidable row of 65 wooden teeth. When these were placed over the keyboard of a sacrificial piano they proceeded, in the cause of music, to batter the life out of the unfortunate victim whilst masticating the rolls. In doing so, however, they revealed a great deal of new and exciting music. The encounter took place at too early an age for me to have retained any impression other than a glowing excitement and delight. It must have been the angelus that first thumped out for me a version of *Valse des Fleurs* from the *Casse Noisette Suite*. Once again, to my young and eager and as yet ingenuous senses, the sounds became as rich and rare as imagined music of the spheres.

The warm glow from the angelus was also illuminated from another source, then known as 'the new electric light'. This was provided by a busy little engine in an outhouse that droned the hours away. But to have a bedside light that could be turned on or off at will, was a rare treat for a small boy normally accustomed to taking a candle upstairs to a cold, dark bedroom, to be held under the gas mantle by an attendant adult. The gas would light with a 'plop' that frequently blew out the flame from the candle.

Since both sounds and railways are basic ingredients of this journey into music, an excitement during this visit was the discovery of the London, Brighton and South Coast Railway. Instead of emerald green engines, quietly and discreetly followed by coaches with upper panels of a unique and memorable pinkish light brown and dark brown below, here the dark umber introduced by Douglas Earle Marsh predominated. Gone were the days of William Stroudley's splendid 'improved engine green' which was, in fact, a glowing golden yellow-brown, set off by polished brass and copper for good measure. The sounds made by the Brighton were much more vociferous, the characteristic 'puff' had a deeper and more throaty sound than the gentle 'chaff' we knew so well. And the little tank engines that still operated the suburban lines were being worked to capacity: so that when stopping at stations their safety valves lifted to eject columns of steam skywards with an ear-splitting hiss. Much whistling added an urgency to the general bustle, here providing an alto to the South Western's treble. In terms of diatonic tonality, the difference might be compared with an aura of C sharp minor for the Brighton line, while the South Western suggested the more relaxed air of B flat major.

A year or two later we paid a visit to the Weald of Kent; to get there involved a journey on the South Eastern and Chatham. Again noise and bustle prevailed, as well as a multiplicity of tunnels. As we went on our journey, coal dust rained on the roof like hailstones: we were urged not to lean out of the window in three languages and also requested not to spit. After the bell-like sounds of many Dorset names, those in Kent had an altogether tougher and less resonant ring – Paddock Wood, Horsmonden, Knockholt, Dunton Green . . .

At the journey's end, deep in the Weald, we came to a small farmhouse where there was a pianola. This time it was a Steck, in which the digestive organs had been incorporated within the frame of a slightly extended upright piano, giving it a distinctly pregnant appearance. The days of assault and battery were coming to an end, but the keyboard action presented a rather dazed response, as though recovering from a local anaesthetic. There were still only 65 notes available for rolls, but the sounds emitted were of a much greater potential delicacy, according to the sensibility and manipulative skill of the performer. By this time I was able to produce enough pianistic powder and shot to make manual forays from time to time.

Our host evidently favoured light music, since the rolls bore titles such as *Mississippi Frolic, The Chicken Run, The Teddy Bear's Picnic* amongst other assorted fauna. There was one heavyweight in the collection – the second half of Beethoven's *Pastoral Symphony*. In this guise it had a distinctly sobering effect on youthful high spirits, but a considerable excitement was gener-ated by the mere fact of being able to hear and discover music in this remote valley. In those days silence could be a friendly presence, nor had the art of conversation been handed over to television personalities. The combined effect of angelus and Steck had the happy result of firing my parents with sufficient enthusiasm to acquire something similar – and if possible better. So, shortly after our return to Dorset, they and I paid a visit to Price's music shop in Bournemouth. There we found a Blüthner player-piano (the latest variant) with copious mechanization by Hüpfeld. This splendid hybrid possessed the ability to respond to

88 note rolls in addition to the familiar 65. There were copious controls, by which not only could either treble or bass be subdued, but the 'melodic line' could be 'brought out' by using a solo lever, the newer rolls being cut to make this possible. It was necessary to exercise care, as there was a tendency for solo notes to emerge with a 'puff' that suggested a small infant's response to being patted on the back after feeding. In retrospect it seems strange that my parents were able to acquire a new and wholly German product during the years of World War I. However, the Blüthner duly arrived: an event that involved parting with the Broadwood. After it had been taken in part exchange, my father became the chief performer; my mother never touched the piano again.

Since Price's music shop also sponsored a lending library for rolls, the chance to explore new music was eagerly pursued. We could choose up to twelve of them at a time: usually my father claimed the privilege, but there were blissful days when he was too busy and I would be put in as deputy.

From this moment composers began to have individual voices. The paternal fixation over Gilbert and Sullivan was sunk without trace, though sounds of the Savoy shared in the growing galaxy. As my own piano playing was by now well under way, the keyboard action of our splendid hybrid suffered less than in households where rolls held undisputed sway. Our first great excitement was the advent of so much Chopin that had formerly been beyond my mother's sensitive, though limited reach. For us, as in J. D. N. Rorke's *A Musical Pilgrim's Progress*, Chopin became 'the great detainer'. I also lost no time in learning to play as much of his music as I could. Attempts to succeed remain to this day both a delight – and a despair. Occasionally there has been the rare joy of coming within measurable distance of near-adequacy, without more than fractional damage to such fragile and delicately contrived textures. My father waded through the music in gumboots, though in doing so revealed more and yet more enchanting vistas for future exploration. His performances were well worth watching, since the responses invariably mimed the movements of a wayward virtuoso!

Chopin apart, there were many composers still in vogue in the days of do-it-yourself-at-home, though their music was by this time fighting a rearguard action against such innovations as our own new treasure. Pieces by Chaminade, Moszkowski, Benjamin Godard and others were still valid currency. Their sounds provided just the right admixture of moderate brilliance and ephemeral charm, much prized at the time: they were frequently assaulted by aspiring amateurs. Often they carried sub-titles such as 'Morceaux pour le Salon', thus qualifying for the epithet 'pretty' – a word much used by those women of the period whose natural habitat was an Edwardian drawing room.

As our enthusiasm for the pianola slowly waned, the gramophone began to emerge from an era of Caruso and scratch. So the time came when the player-piano was exchanged for a truly miraculous Blüthner grand, on which I proceeded to cut my musical teeth. And at almost the same moment my father appeared one evening with a gramophone and a pile of records. How he had caught yet another infectious enthusiasm requires another chapter. For my own part, another discophile was about to be hooked for life.

CHAPTER 4

Household Music –
2. Enter the Gramophone

One of my father's patients was a retired engineer, a splendid Welshman called John Lester. He had designed and made a cabinet gramophone of surpassing excellence, case and all, very much in advance of anything then generally available through commercial channels. On it the vintage records of the period glowed with an unwonted splendour. But the proud designer had little or no discrimination as far as music was concerned: like many technicians he was more interested in the quality of sound reproduction than in the music itself. This was well illustrated by an incident many years later, when he added a device for what became known as an automatic change for 78 records. A series of sides could then be heard more or less continuously, without intervention on the part of the listener. It was not until a considerable time later that the recording companies brought themselves to adopt the idea by providing suitable couplings. I had acquired several sets of complete works, one of which was used to demonstrate this home-produced triumph. Quite happily the proud inventor announced that we would be hearing sides 1,3,5 & 7 in that order; then, after a pause for adjustment, sides 2,4,6 & 8. When I mildly protested at the proposed disembowelment of a symphonic work, his astonishment and disappointment were all too evident. But he stirred my father into acquiring a modest Beltona 'table grand' by way of beginning the long ascent up the slopes of a discophile's Parnassus, thus becoming the sponsor of one of the major pleasures of my life.

Sifting the wheat from a great deal of recorded chaff (including the initial pile of records brought home by my father), our first acquisition of any real value lay in the field of English song. Paternal zeal stemmed from a particular interest in the career of Gervase Elwes. This was partly because relatives of the singer happened to be patients of my father, and also because of a genuine admiration for the particular qualities of voice and style revealed in his performances. There was a more subtle reason too. Both parents had a tremendous zest for the qualities that went to the making of what used to be called a gentleman: these the singer happened to possess in full measure, pressed down and running over.

Elwes was also an unforgettable exponent of English song. To it he brought precisely the right temperament and approach to the efforts then being made, by composers such as Ireland, Quilter, Vaughan Williams, Butterworth and others, to lift the art-form out of the sentimental quagmire into which it had been dragged by ballad-mongers. Despite the gallant efforts of Stanford and Parry, their solo songs had not even then made an impact comparable with that of their successors.

Another singer greatly favoured by my father was a tenor, Hubert Eisdell, whose records were eagerly acquired. His contributions tended to be of a more sentimental kind, but always presented with a welcome restraint when the words and music led him towards slush and bog! The composers already mentioned were still surrounded in popular esteem by others of a very different hue, among them Maud Valerie White, Lord Henry Somerset, Wilfred Sanderson, Hermann Löhr, Amy Woodford Finden, Liza Lehmann – and many more. Even to my youthful ears, those previously mentioned had an altogether different sound, instantly recognizable as belonging to a valid currency of communication, without the alloy of sentimentality.

Meanwhile my brother was making a collection of Regimental Marches, while I was feeling my way towards orchestral music, sorely tried by the monotonous rigidity and unrelenting precision emanating from the Band of H.M. Coldstream Guards blasting across our drawing room. At this time my father acquired two new recordings that ushered in a new dawn for me. Gervase Elwes and the London String Quartet made a recording of Vaughan Williams' song-cycle *On Wenlock Edge* – on five single-sided Columbia records with purple labels. The music evoked an immediate sense of recognition: here was something I had always known, only I hadn't known it (which is exactly how this composer described his own discovery of J. S. Bach). Housman's poems aroused an immediate urge to set out on my own to explore the surrounding countryside. Then the music had to be sifted through a surface hiss that characterized Columbia records in those early days, giving an impression that one was standing on the departure platform at Euston in the days of steam. Two entire verses of Bredon Hill had been removed without trace, yet this recording was a signpost that pointed towards the day when I came to know Ralph Vaughan Williams in later life.

The other revelation, surprisingly enough, was a performance of the *Henry VIII Dances* of Edward German, played by the Royal Albert Hall Orchestra with 'Mr.' Landon Ronald as conductor. (It was not until the advent of radio that the welcome extirpation of

'Mistery' and attendant variants was finally achieved.) While the *Henry VIII Dances* are hardly of the calibre out of which revelations can be expected, they are none the less light music of considerable charm, scored with consummate skill and artistry. But the quality that Landon Ronald achieved in this performance – a crowning touch that can transform music of any kind into something unexpectedly rich and rare – was an art later associated with Thomas Beecham. Nevertheless those old HMV black-label records that Landon Ronald made had a quality that has eluded most of his successors. Particularly memorable was his performance of the *Casse Noisette Suite* that, for me, effectively supplanted that elephantine travesty from the angelus of former years with the *Valse des Fleurs*. Hearing it again in a pale but authentic reflection of the composer's intentions, I remain grateful to this day for the quality of those vanished discs. Perhaps, beyond the world's end, there is an Elysian Field set apart for discophiles, where we shall be able to hear again some of the memorable music-making that, despite the inevitable mechanized shortcomings, yet contrived to shed so much light in the surrounding darkness.

It is surely both wise and desirable for the committed listener to have a stake, however small, in some form of active participation. By way of illustration, a friend and colleague of later days, Sydney Northcote, described his experiences before radio and records proliferated. He and his father explored the classical symphonies as piano duettists. There came a day when, approaching manhood, Sydney went for the first time to London. His father took him to the Queen's Hall to hear an orchestral concert, at which the fifth symphony of Beethoven was played. In the Trio section of the *Scherzo*, where cellos and basses encounter a swarm of notes, Sydney turned to his father and said 'There you are, Dad, that's the bit you never get right – and that's how it ought to sound!' Another young discophile went to his first concert to hear the *Eroica* Symphony. Towards the end of the third movement, he saw with astonishment the three horn-players shaking the accumulated spittle out of their instruments – and decided then and there to learn to play an instrument himself.

The third flash of enlightenment from the gramophone enabled me to reach 'take-off' point for this journey into music. A clerical friend had acquired the first recording of Elgar's *Enigma Variations*, made under the composer's direction (the version in which the penultimate twelve bars for full orchestra in *Nimrod* were mysteriously absent). Again I had the sense of instant recognition of something that had been around me always, though until then hidden and unperceived. The sounds on this occasion were spectacular, since the instrument was a forerunner of the large external horn variety that will always be associated with the name of E. M. Ginn, who first put this irresistible blandishment within our reach. By now radio was becoming tolerable for hearing music and proceeded to crown the *Enigma* experience with Honegger's *King David*, still at the time something new and exciting.

Ever since this threefold experience, the gramophone has played an indispensable part in my life, as commentator and consolidator of music heard away from it, as well as paving the way for fresh discoveries.

It had now become possible for these explorations to have, in addition to the first fine careless rapture, a sense of purpose as well as a means of self-identification and development. 'On Wenlock Edge the wood's in trouble' became associated in mind and imagination with a Housman-inspired walk during an autumn gale over Badbury Rings, when the leaves from the trees, on the crest of the hill-fort, were being swept like a flight of birds in clusters across the empty upland. First impressions of *Enigma* crystallized into a landscape with figures, against a background of September sunlight and fields of corn in sheaves, this last doubtless due in part to Elgar's orchestral colouring; but here, all around me, from farm, lane and field – and particularly in the woods – the very stuff of music lay in wait to be given the kiss of life by any composer in search of sleeping beauty. Poetry, the charm of words, friendship – and doubtless also in good time, love – all these ingredients were becoming interlinked and integrated into a glowing polyphony of youthful zest and growing richness.

CHAPTER 5

Music in the 1920s – 1

Now that it has become almost impossible to avoid the sound of music in one form or another, it is hard to believe that in the early 1920s we often had to go some distance to find it. There was time before and after the experience to indulge in the pleasure of anticipation and assimilation. With the coming of radio the whole pattern changed: new vistas opened, while a great deal of local activity was brought to a grinding halt.

To those who knew the spas and seaside towns of England when there was music to be found in them – not merely an annual festival or spasmodic tip-and-run visitations – these places have lost a great deal of their erstwhile charm. A special mystique grew up around the resident municipal orchestras, chiefly generated by their conductors, sometimes by the leaders. There was 'young' Basil Cameron at Hastings, Alick Maclean at Scarborough, Julian Clifford at Harrogate – and the incomparable Dan Godfrey at Bournemouth. Sir Granville Bantock once occupied the post of music director at the Tower in New Brighton and 'Dr.' Malcolm Sargent held sway at the Llandudno Pavilion.

For me the mecca was Bournemouth, where Sir Dan Godfrey presided at the old Winter Gardens, a unique edifice that seemed to have been evolved from a cross-fertilization between a glasshouse at Chatsworth and Marylebone Station. To it, at about the age of 12, I took myself one Saturday afternoon to hear an orchestral programme, in which the second half was given to a performance of *A London Symphony* by Vaughan Williams. As I had already been alerted to the composer by a recording of *On Wenlock Edge*, my expectations were running high; even so the effect of the symphony was overwhelming. It almost, though not quite, obliterated everything else that was played, though there is still a faint echo of an extended work for piano and orchestra by Arthur Somervell – it must have been the *Symphonic Variations*. At the time it did not seem to say anything in particular, but none the less said it very well! As I left the Winter Gardens to emerge, starry-eyed, into the autumn dusk, the sound of the symphony's slow movement lingered in the mind. The programme note quoted someone as saying that it recalled an autumn afternoon in a Bloomsbury square, where still the harness of dray horses jingled and street-vendors cried their wares.

Of the many other aspects of entertainment then to be found, two may well stand here as examples. During the immediate aftermath of World War I, much publicity was given to and by the St. Dunstan's Homes for sightless people. From them came organized groups of the more musically talented, to give concerts consisting of short and varied items. There was invariably a pianist, whose great moment would come when, after asking audiences to choose well known tunes, he would then proceed to improvise. This diversion must surely have been the dying fall of a proceeding that had flourished among pianists since the eighteenth century. The stronghold of extempore playing has ever been the organ loft. When Anton Bruckner visited England in 1871 and gave a recital on the 'new' organ at the Royal Albert Hall, one entire half of the programme consisted of improvisations – on Bach's *Fugue in E* (heard previously), on English melodies and 'original'. It is tantalizing to imagine Brucknerian treatment of *Rule Britannia, The British Grenadiers* and other well-known national tunes.

Alongside concerts of all kinds, there flourished an equally varied clan of characters calling themselves Entertainers. I vividly remember Alfred Capper, a specialist in thought-reading, who was appearing in Weymouth during a summer season in the early 1920s. He was billed to appear nightly for a week at one of the larger hotels on the Esplanade. When he made his entry it was all too clear that we, his audience, both shocked and startled him. So he began by telling us pointedly that, though accustomed to appearing before the crowned heads of Europe, he was prepared to 'make do' with titled personages. As for us – well, since he was here (God help him!) he supposed he had better try to bring a little sunshine into our drab lives. This he proceeded to do in no uncertain manner and in the most delightful way, picking out members of the audience, who were astonished to have their thoughts revealed. Shy young men, thinking of the names of their girl-friends, would hear the great man triumphantly announce them, to the utter confusion of the unsuspecting and usually cynical victim. Hidden pieces of jewelry and trinkets were described in detail, with a wealth of side-play and wit. A splendid man withal and a worthy representative of a vanished race. Hard as their lives must have been, the Entertainers none-the-less possessed the great advantage of being able to tour many places with the same basic material, a commodity that had to be tough enough to withstand the rigours of constant repetition.

For those of us who lived away from London, opportunities to hear live music were eagerly pursued in whatever neighbourhood we happened to be. During a summer holiday spent near

Tunbridge Wells, it was exciting to discover that Harry Joseph and his Orchestra occupied the bandstand on the Pantiles on fine mornings (retreating to the Pump Room if wet). A pleasant flow of light music, remarkably well played, gave a lift to the surroundings, as well as to everyone who happened to be in the vicinity. Among the players was a young trumpeter, then all too often confined to the cornet, who provided solos when required. He appeared in the programme as C. Pemmel, and as provincial papers are still fond of saying 'rendered' *Roses of Picardy* and *Poor Little Buttercup* and similar items with much panache and feeling. The orchestra as an entity concerned itself with pieces like *Admirals All* (Hubert Bath) and Coleridge Taylor's *Petite Suite de Concert*, then much in favour, particularly a part of it called *Demande et Response* – though memory hints that the eloquence of the Demande received a brush-off in the Response! Even so it seemed that the ghosts of former times came back to listen –

> "They sigh among the breezes and they sit
> Like bright-eyed birds along the roofs,
> And a friend in a whisper says to a friend 'It's time,
> High time we had good music in this place.' "*

Thirty years later C. Pemmel was to emerge once more into my orbit. In the interim Charlie, as he immediately became, had played his trumpet with conspicuous éclat in the London orchestral world and had become a 'fixer' of considerable eloquence and persuasion. When, for the Festival of Britain, I had provided the music for Kay Baxter's play *Your Trumpets, Angels*, commissioned for a six weeks' run in Southwark Cathedral, Charlie not only 'fixed' the brass and percussion players, but himself took part in many performances.

For them we also had an admirable flautist in Joan Harris, with string players from the Bromley Orchestral Society, shepherded by Marjorie Whyte of cherished memory. So many, not least among them I, remember with gratitude and deep affection all that she did for us. The unfailing skill and sensitive quality of the Bromley string-players provided a sure foundation for the music, in which hard-line professionals and dedicated amateurs seemed unusually relaxed and at ease. This untroubled, almost family feeling, was in large part due to the Provost of the Cathedral, Hugh Ashdown, whose kindness, practical encouragement and spiritual benediction made a special contribution to the occasion. Soon Southwark

---

Don Juan: a play by James Elroy Flecker

was to become a runway for him to a Bishopric in Newcastle. Some of the music has recently been sieved into a concert overture which has already received a first performance and is now in line for a second airing.

Returning to the 1920s, I was to find more music in Brighton. At the Pavilion on the Palace Pier, James Sale and his Orchestra were playing to steadily diminishing audiences – now decoyed by the onset of radio. There were still afternoon symphony concerts under the direction, not of James Sale, but his assistant Mons. E. Dupont. While the waves splashed below and the late autumn sun seemed about to fall into the sea somewhere between Spithead and the Isle of Wight, I heard my first Haydn symphony – No. 88 in G – played with delicacy and eloquence to a half empty hall. Yet another vista appeared for discovery and exploration.

It seems that Brighton was one of the cities that steadfastly refused to establish a resident orchestra. In his book *Music in Spas and Watering Places*, Kenneth Young has a pretty tale to relate of a councillor, reluctantly persuaded to attend an orchestral concert, who afterwards complained that his intelligence had been insulted by what he described as 'anaesthetical' notes! There were, however, exciting occasions at The Dome. There I heard Kreisler, with Charlton Keith as pianist, play the *Kreutzer Sonata*. If there is another violinist in the world who can produce so golden a sound, I have yet to hear him or her. Here also came Paderewski, whose playing had an almost ethereal quality, partly due to the rather thin-toned Erard on which he invariably performed. He still retained the habit of playing notes in one hand a fraction before the other – a not uncommon characteristic of many 19th-century exponents.

Backhaus in his heyday gave vital and splendidly masculine and straightforward accounts of Beethoven, Chopin and others. Joseph Hislop sang – and Dame Clara Butt boomed. She had a ditty in her bag called 'It's Quiet Down Here' that she sang in (what for her) was a whisper, though her consonants rang through the hall like pistol shots. For the last line of this misbegotten ditty 'God is very near' an unobtrusive figure had sidled into the organ-loft, turned on the wind, pulled out every stop and coupler – and let fly with the lot. As a supreme example of the worst possible taste, this bombardment stood in a class by itself.

Sometimes the London Symphony Orchestra appeared, at the behest of a local organist who evidently fancied himself in the role of conductor. The programmes consisted of the usual best-sellers; Willy Reed, as leader, pulled him safely through and generously allowed him most of the applause. There were also orchestral concerts at the Regent Cinema on Sunday afternoon, these became gala occasions when Basil Cameron appeared as guest conductor. It is sad that so fine a musician did not receive the same enthusiastic recognition in later life, mainly perhaps because of his variable and unpredictable temperament. To judge from a recording made of his reading of Sibelius' second symphony in the 1940s, the gramophone companies lost a rare opportunity to acquire a superb set of these works, as fine as any – and certainly better than most subsequent versions.

In Bournemouth Dan Godfrey continued, in his afternoon symphony concerts, to give both the standard repertoire and many new and interesting works. Concerts of chamber music were rare, even in London, so it was a great event when the National Gramophonic Society engaged the Spencer Dyke Quartet (with other players) to produce on disc the Debussy Quartet, Beethoven's *Harp*, the Schubert E flat Trio and Schoenberg's *Verklärte Nacht*. Life was becoming one long discovery of new-found treasure.

CHAPTER 6

Music in the 1920s – 2

Contemporary English music at the time was still a comparatively young and tender plant. It was not until the next decade that various influences, of which more in due course, were to give a much needed stimulus. In the 1920s the musical scene, as the majority of us knew it, was dominated by three potent and, at the same time, restrictive factors. These may be summarized as, firstly, a misty concept of sublimated Englishry, of which Parry's *Jerusalem* and Holst's *I Vow To Thee My Country* are typical. While these examples are admirable in themselves, the basic source from which they came gave rise to a strong bias towards a 'Brothers we are treading' approach, particularly in choral music.

There was also folk song, from which the salty tang of the original afflatus had been firmly and almost completely extracted, by order of the (then) Board of Education, so that the songs might be rendered 'suitable' for use in schools. Thirty years on, the publication of Cecil Sharp's notebooks by James Reeves, combined with Britten's admirable gesture with 'The Foggy Foggy Dew', at last restored the inherent vitality of these victims of Edwardian prudery. When, in later years, Vaughan Williams was asked to provide *Folk Songs for all Seasons* as a cantata for the National Federation of Women's Institutes, his comment was 'I wonder if the W.I.s know that almost every folk song is either about drink or love-making.'

The cult of the amateur flourished. The twenties were the high noon of competition festivals which, in rural areas, were more often than not sponsored by the local gentry, who saw to it that the distinction between amateur and professional was clearly defined. From it came a predictable side-effect that was bound to influence the trend of music-making. Parry once said to a pupil 'Write music that befits an Englishman and a democrat.' Since art is not concerned with frontiers in the matter of expression, such arbitrary considerations had the effect of putting a bearing rein on a potentially mettlesome steed.

In the study of music there was a strong accent on history. Musicology, as practised in other countries, was confined to the interest and enterprise of a few individuals, not yet recognized by the establishment as such. The great composers of the past rested securely on their pinnacles, regularly cleaned, often whitewashed. Their more human frailties were discreetly covered, lest their collective image be tarnished. To look more closely at the prevailing *zeitgeist*, some copies of *Music and Letters* of the period 1924–27 provide interesting commentary.

In 1924 Charles Villiers Stanford died. In earlier days Spy produced a characteristic representation of him with the wry comment 'He found Harmony in Ireland.' Here are tributes from an impressive array of former pupils – Walford Davies, Vaughan Williams, John Ireland, Frank Bridge, George Dyson, Herbert Howells, Nicholas Gatty, Ivor Gurney, Edgar Bainton, Leslie Heward, Sydney Nicholson, Henry Ley, James Friskin, Harold Samuel and S. Liddle. Time has done some winnowing here, but what a superb teacher he must have been – and what pupils he had!

Stanford – furiously denouncing Gladstone, writing pupils' reports 'Has had a fit of chromatics – hope he will soon grow healthy and diatonic.' Again – 'Your music comes from Hell, me bhoy, H-E-double-L.' There had been a proposal to build a chapel for the Royal College of Music: Stanford's comment is not only characteristic, but also – one cannot help feeling – apt. There would have to be, he said 'One Altar for the Roman Catholics, another for High Churchmen, a third for Low Churchmen, a shrine for the Buddhists, a bath for the Baptists – and within half-an-hour of the opening there would be bleeding noses all round!' Of *Tod und Verklärung* he remarked 'I wouldn't like to go out to the sound of a tam-tam: if it's to be Richard give me Wagner, or if Strauss let's have Johann.'

As evidence of the way in which tastes have changed, we find York Barnard writing of 'Superior persons of our own day who are so advanced that they no longer care to consider Mozart's music.' Bizet is rapped over the knuckles for opportunism, while Berlioz is by no means regarded with unqualified approval. It is claimed that there had not yet been a performance of *L'Enfance du Christ* in London. Here it must be said that Hamilton Harty and the Hallé Orchestra had already begun a crusade that was to restore Berlioz to his rightful inheritance in England.

Alexander Brent-Smith, writing of Chopin, praises the *F minor Ballade* (good of him one feels!) but finds the *Nocturne* in the same key 'a vulgar little creature.' Play the opening bars a little quicker, he says, and you find yourself singing what he calls 'Hampstead-Heathenish' words to it – 'Me and Sue were walking hand-in-hand.' Other writers indulge in this kind of personal prejudice commentary, gravely passed to the reader as expertise.

We have already encountered Canon Edmund Fellowes scouring the land for material with which to complete his edition of

Tudor Church Music. From his memoir it seemed as if the whole project stemmed from a casual remark at a tennis party in the Canon's early days, when rain stopped play. A great deal of activity in music, as in much else, grew from such wayside encounters. A similar instance had resulted in the rescue of folk songs, when Cecil Sharp, staying with his friend the Rector of Hambridge in Somerset, heard the gardener, John England, singing *The Seeds of Love* as he mowed the lawn.

Herbert Bedford writes about English songs and compares settings of Yeats' poem *The Cloths of Heaven*. These turn out to be by Thomas F. Dunhill, Landon Ronald, Rebecca Clarke, Frederic Austin and 'my own'.

We find Dr. Ernest Walker – and others – giving a good deal of speculative attention to the appoggiatura. The good Doctor floats happily along with such sentences as 'But nevertheless we may, I think, come to a definite conclusion that, unless the circumstances of the individual can give a lead otherwise, this interpretation, unorthodox though it is, should always be favoured.' Exactly what 'this' interpretation is, the reader finds it hard to discover.

Cherubini's alleged lack of imagination receives some caustic comment, though he is conceded to have been a good influence on Beethoven, whose forthcoming centenary is given a great deal of advance attention.

The music of Schoenberg, Berg and Webern was virtually unknown, except for some performances of early Schoenberg, such as the *Five Orchestral Pieces*, by Sir Henry Wood. Stanford's 'healthy and diatonic' was a heavily defended fortress against the inroads of chromaticism. Serial music had yet to be granted a visa for entry to these shores, being still an infant in the Schoenbergian clinic. But *Pierrot Lunaire* had been taken on tour by a gallant and enterprising group that gave successive performances in Rome, Paris and London. In the words of L. Fleury, who took part in the performances, 'The amazing thing that we played three times last November . . . that caused torrents of ink to flow and opened the floodgates of invective.' To the comment that 'you can play any notes you like and they would sound just as well' the writer gravely comments 'That is a complete mistake.' In Paris the restive audience hissed, in Rome it laughed, but in London, nay, South Kensington 'At the most daring places in the score I watched the audience out of the corner of my eye. They never blenched. They sat there, calm as a boxer who takes punishment with a smile.'

At the other end of the spectrum the silent cinema still relied on local performers to provide the accompanying music. There was a growing tendency to carve bits and pieces from the major works of the masters. These were often given with incorrect tempi and phrasing, thus causing alarm and despondency in the musical press.

Books of the period showed a strong bias towards generalities, skimming over vast fields of exploration very swiftly. Here are some titles from the review pages: 'The Philosophy of Music' (William Pole), 'Music and Mind' (Yorke Trotter), 'The Scope of Music' (Percy Buck), 'The New Music' (George Dyson), 'A Survey of Contemporary Music' (Cecil Gray) – and so on. Often the reviewers' style is grave and even portly, as here – 'Dr. Dyson's book is indeed one of the most notable masterpieces of our latter day scholarship: we can confidently brandish it in the face of our enemies at the gate when they speak to us in fairly loud voices as they still (after some centuries of habit) are occasionally inclined to do.'

Turning to the advertisement pages, the Oxford Press announces 'A Cheap Edition of *Tudor Church Music*.' Curwen's list includes a symphonic fantasy 1812 – by C. Hubert H. Parry. Elkin proudly flaunts a slogan 'Melody with Musicianship – Modernism with Moderation.' The window of the firm's premises in Kingly Street would reveal pride of place to Edward MacDowell and Cyril Scott. Chesters are championing Manuel de Falla (*El Retablo de Maese Pedro*) and giving a hefty shove to a book by Casella. It was called 'The Evolution of Music Throughout the History of the Perfect Cadence' and described as 'One of the most original and comprehensive theoretico-aesthetic books on music published for a long time.' So one might imagine! Among smaller advertisements we discover that 'Mr. Gordon Jacob gives lessons personally, or by correspondence, on all theoretical subjects.'

Among the piano manufacturers, those represented include Steinway, Broadwood, Moore and Moore, the latter issuing a cordial invitation to visit Albion House, New Oxford Street. It is left to Chappell to play the trump card: 'One can find a Chappell piano in the home of almost every great artist in Europe.'

The London Colleges reveal the RAM and RCM as having most of the Court Cards in their presiding VIPs. The Academy comes off best with His Majesty the King, Her Majesty the Queen, and Queen Alexandra as Patrons: as President, The Duke of Connaught and the Director, Sir Alexander Campbell Mackenzie. The College follows with the The King, The Prince of Wales and Sir Hugh Allen. The City of London Corporation and Sir Landon Ronald guide the destiny of the Guildhall School of Music and

Drama. In this galaxy Trinity College of Music has Lord Shaftesbury, Sir Frederic Bridge and C. W. Pearce as Director of Studies, while E. F. Horner is in charge of Examinations.

The B.B.C. at Savoy Hill was in process of championing Arnold Bax, causing uneasy reactions amongst the elderly and much pleasure in other quarters, despite the still uneasy digestive systems of many receiving sets. A considerable impact was made, however, by a suave and coaxing voice that came through crackling loud-speakers and asthmatic headphones 'Good evening. listeners all.' There then followed another widely popular talk by Sir Walford Davies, mostly illustrated by neatly-tailored snippets from the Beethoven piano sonatas. Through these talks, countless listeners acquired an abiding interest in, and love of music.

Among composers Elgar stood pre-eminent as a laureate, who had not only hymned the glory of our blood and state, but had also written some magnificent music. His position had many similarities to that of Kipling in literature. Occasionally he would appear in London, trying his valiant best not to look like a musician. Holst and Vaughan Williams, often happily together, were 'up and coming', the former having already had a considerable acclaim for *The Hymn of Jesus* as well as *The Planets*. Vaughan Williams had produced his *Pastoral Symphony* and the *Mass in G minor*: he was soon to conduct the Bach Choir in the first London performance of *Sancta Civitas*. *Hugh the Drover* had been received with delight by the folk song fraternity. At the same time it gave a welcome shot-in-the-arm to English opera in the days before that commodity became exportable.

Two dashing young composers, Constant Lambert and William Walton, with their respective *Rio Grande* and *Portsmouth Point*, aroused considerable expectations; what would they be up to next? Walton had already created a considerable stir among the Chelsea élite, with *Façade* first given under Sitwellian auspices, with Ernest Newman present to give an account in the Sunday Times, with particular emphasis on the music of 'Mr. W. T. Walton.' By way of contrast there was also a public performance at the Aeolian Hall that actually roused a section of an English audience to vociferous protest. Another young composer, Arthur Bliss, had written a *Colour Symphony*: here was someone else to be watched with interest.

Importations from abroad varied considerably. From America, dance music apart, little or nothing was heard except Gershwin. Manuel de Falla and Stravinsky had made a considerable impact through the visits of Diaghilev's Russian Ballet. Of Stravinsky it was said his more recent music showed a sad decline and that he was 'played out.' Heads were shaken, lips pursed: how wrong they were! From France, apart from Debussy and Ravel, there were intimations of Ibert and Milhaud that were overshadowed by some early Poulenc piano pieces (Honegger's *King David* has already been mentioned). Fauré was seldom heard or known, apart from one or two songs and smaller pieces. Richard Strauss in Germany was being succeeded by Hindemith, who also appeared at concerts in the role of viola soloist. Of Strauss the general impression was, that with the early tone poems and *Der Rosenkavalier* he had said his say, though the avant garde at the time hailed *Elektra* as a breakthrough. Again, subsequent works from his pen were thought to show a falling off from previous achievements. *Salome*, despite biblical associations, had been in trouble with the Lord Chamberlain, that erstwhile stern guardian of our moral welfare. Sir Thomas Beecham has left an intriguing account of the first attempts to mount this opera in London.*

Anything approaching adequate recognition of Delius was not achieved until the memorable festival of 1929. Similarly with Sibelius, the tide was to turn when Robert Kajanus came to conduct our orchestras in programmes devoted to his works in the following year. Though both composers had been represented by performances over a long period of time, it was these events that secured for both of them the general acclaim for which they had waited so long.

Bruckner and Mahler were both, symphonically speaking, fringe bodies, so that only isolated movements from their longer works were infiltrated into concert programmes. They were regarded as fields of exploration for specialist devotees. There was, however, quite a stir when Respighi produced *The Pines of Rome* – and included the gramophone as an integral part of the score to give the actual sound of a nightingale. Again lips were pursed, heads were shaken. 'This,' they said, 'could well be the thin end of a very long wedge.' How right they were!

---

*A Mingled Chime. An Autobiography. Hutchinson

CHAPTER 7

Doctor Gradus

My attempts to learn the violin, and subsequently the cello, foundered on the impossibility of getting near enough to the music to be able to read it. So, until the age of 17, when I was at last able to muster just enough vision to write some music on paper, the piano remained the sole motive power for the journey. With it I could get as close to the printed page as my nose would permit.

Piano teachers, within whose varied galaxy I have sporadically mingled, present a fascinating spectacle when viewed as a species. During five years I spent at a co-educational boarding school, they came and went with breathtaking rapidity. Initially there was Mrs. Allison, a superb performer, but more than a little impatient with her pupils; Mrs. Hewson, as Irish as they come, brimming with bosom and bonhomie, though bowled middle stump when requested to play 'Our National Anthem' at a school function to which she had forgotten to bring the prompt copy – how I longed to do it for her! Miss Shutler, who favoured the percussive school and is now, I trust, somewhere in Elysium with a prepared piano to dismember. A procession of others less memorable was completed, first by Violet Eardley, who combined charm, skill and severity in equal proportions: finally Tony Palmer Stone, full of youth, glamour and pianistic splendour, whose entry into our small pond caused a gigantic splash in several directions. I was fortunately spared the attentions of the headmaster who, though given the same baptismal names as Handel, belonged to the penny-on-the-wrist and ruler-slapping rabble – a race now virtually extinct.

Tony Palmer Stone perceived my ardent devotion to Chopin, proceeding at once to urge me on to breathtaking assaults on unsuspecting masterpieces in a manner undreamed of by his predecessors. He also perceived a certain youthful pride in my modest achievements; this he ruthlessly cut down, almost to the roots, far too drastically, as time has sadly proved. The result was a temporary afflatus that lacked any real foundation. The afflatus subsided, taking with it too great a loss of confidence for the flame to be completely revived.

It was consequently a sharp drop in temperature when, moving on to Down House at Rottingdean, I found the expert in occupation to be a visiting organist from Hove. This benign and friendly fellow sat comfortably by the side of his pupils, rolling and smoking endless cigarettes in a sort of trance, from which he would occasionally emerge to point out a wrong note, though offering no clue as to the right one, other than naming it.

Parental intervention resulted in a shift to the Brighton School of Music. In the early 1920s this unique and fascinating establishment stood half-way up North Street. One entered it by the side of a florist's shop, through a dark and dingy doorway into a stone-floored passage that led, up some steps, into the Athenaeum Hall. In the gallery stood a large three-manual organ with heavy tracker action. This leviathan made a continuous clatter, like someone in Brobdignag having trouble with dentures. On it I was soon to have some lessons from Dr. Alfred King, formerly organist of Brighton Parish Church and now a Director of the School. He had become ancient and venerable, dressed in a long black habit, with flowing beard and skull cap, also black. Two incidents from these encounters remain in the memory: one of them is recalled later in these pages*, the other occurred when I brought to a lesson *The Holy Boy* by John Ireland. This innocuous effusion, believe it or not, he found excruciatingly modern – 'How can you possibly enjoy such ghastly dissonances?' As an indication of the depths to which adolescence can sink, I was having a love-affair with the vox angelica (Yes, with tremulant!) though fortunately the virus quickly subsided. Soon I came to think that The Little Fellow (as Jeeves might have called Him) is a typical, though rather soft-boiled specimen of Chelsea High Anglican vintage, not really worthy of a composer who has written much fine music that has yet to receive the recognition it so richly deserves.

Outside the Hall, at a draughty spot in the passage where more steps led up to the office and teaching rooms, the guardian of the place presided. He was known to all as, simply, Mitchell. For long hours and a scant wage his only additional bonus, apart from occasional favours from staff and students for services rendered, was a bottle of port at Christmas.

Dr. King's Co-Director was Sydney Harper, an elderly, kindly man who lived in perpetual terror of a visitation from his wife. Under her basilisk stare and withering silences, her husband lost his habitual geniality and became as much like the proverbial cat on hot bricks as it is possible for a human being to simulate. As soon as the ominous presence withdrew, he resumed his role of administrator and bursar with evident relief. When, perpetually hungry, I

---

*Organists and the Clergy. Page 167

had spent my return bus fare on chocolate, he would quietly hand it to me without comment. On other occasions, when time allowed, I would walk the four miles back to Rottingdean over the downs.

The senior professor for piano had the impressive name of Herbert E. Lomax Earp, to whom I was allocated as pupil. This wise and kindly man was to prove a valuable friend for several years, though I have since wished that he had taken a far tougher line with me in those once-for-all formative years. But his teaching hours were overlong and, I suspect, ill-paid. We all knew him as Bertie, though in those far-off days it would have been unthinkable to address him as such. Also at the School was his cousin Emma Lomax, who not only taught theory and counter-point, but also presided over fortnightly students' concerts, at which I soon made regular appearances. At one of them I had reached a point in *La Cathédrale Engloutie* where a soft chord is held with the sustaining pedal. Then, unheralded, unannounced came a gargantuan sneeze, from which an echo roared its way through strings and soundboard. Never, before or since, has applause been so comforting!

Soon these modest contributions were to receive encouraging notice in the local press, to the astonishment of my fellow-travellers at Down House, for whom I patiently plodded through contemporary dance tunes and the inevitable Sullivan on the common room piano.

It was impossible not to respond at once to Emma's charm of manner and warm friendliness. Her discerning commentary and critical encouragement were unfailingly perceptive and construc-tive. She had been a pupil of Frederick Corder in the Royal Academy's Tenterden Street days. Emma Lomax had also known Ebenezer Prout, from whom she acquired the rather diverting set of words he attached to the fugue subjects of the 48 preludes and fugues of J. S. Bach.*

At the Brighton School of Music, the regular end-of-term concerts presented a gathering of an otherwise scattered clan. The Athenaeum Hall was duly prepared for the occasion, in order to minimise the overall state of subdued shabbiness, and so assumed an almost festive air. Here and now the School Orchestra assembled on the platform to be conducted, first by Dr. King, followed, with much more flair and verve, by Mynheer Van der Velde. String playing flourished, with Madame Menges to foster

*See Page 188

high standards in violin and viola, while Mynheer's special province was the cello, which he taught extremely well, to judge from results. The assembled orchestra consisted entirely of strings and percussion: wind and brass parts were simulated from the organ, which produced a rich warm tone that blended exceptionally well. Happily the overall sound provided an effective coverage for the resonant clatter from the organ manuals.

Dr. King invariably opened the proceedings with a Cherubini overture: he also brought the proceedings to an end with a festive march, often with an innocuously pleasant essay of his own – a presentable specimen of a breed from which later progeny, such as *Pomp and Circumstance, Orb and Sceptre* – and you may add the *Dam Busters* – were to be born. After these exertions the dear old man would take his bow and totter triumphantly back to his seat in the front row of the audience. Mynheer would opt for more virile fodder, from composers such as Auber, Nicolai or Flotow, which he produced with a flair and vitality that never failed to rouse his audience to enthusiastic applause. Occasionally there would be a movement from a concerto, though nothing in the way of chamber or music ensemble. It must, I think, have been lack of teaching accommodation that prevented the appearance of wind and brass. The rest of the programme consisted of solos from those of us considered worthy to show our paces.

During these years I had been eagerly awaiting the time when I might seek entry into the Royal College of Music, on which I had firmly set my sights. It therefore came as a shattering blow when the eye-specialist, in whose care my parents had placed me, absolutely forbade any such 'madcap scheme'. I know in my heart of hearts that he was wrong, but the business of growing and slowly overcoming a not inconsiderable handicap had left me too shattered and exhausted to fight. Now, fifty years on, a wave of sadness comes over me whenever I happen to be in the neighbourhood of Prince Consort Road.

The transcontinental express was on the move – and I had missed it. For me it would from now on have to be the slow train, calling at all stations. In the mind's ear I sometimes hear the rush and roar of the *rapide* that many of my contemporaries managed to catch. For them the ascent to Parnassus: for me the more gentle slopes of nearby hills were to prove hard enough to climb. From them I would look on a pleasant enough countryside, count my blessings and try to do as much as possible with an incomplete set of tools in my bag.

CHAPTER 8

'I too will something make'

One of the masters at Rottingdean, Inglis Allen, was connected with the literary world. He was a contributor to *Punch*, a writer of short stories who also infiltrated lyrics into contemporary revues and the lighter side of the theatrical life. Every year he produced a concert in this genre, in which the highlights were short one-act sketches written for the occasion. These were greatly enjoyed by both actors and audience. By way of contrast he added some lyrics for good measure, for which he persuaded me to supply the music. Since writing them out on paper was still beyond my abilities – in any case most of the hearty extroverts who were to sing them were unable to read notation – they had to be catchy enough to be assimilated by ear. Many of the splendid fellows concerned were already fairly knowledgeable about wine and women, though rather shaky on song. These occasions were the only opportunity to supply our own products for the home market. The collaboration had a sad ending. Unknown to me, Inglis Allen successfully placed one of the lyrics I had set with George Robey. It was called 'Thingummy Bob' and frequently sung by the great man – to someone else's setting. Since I had, with help from a friend, produced copies of my version, I took a poor view of this sleight-of-hand action. But it taught me a valuable lesson in the ways of this far from straightforward world, making me more than ever determined to muster sufficient sight to write down my own music. Gradually the process became less of a struggle, though never less than the equivalent of manual labour. But I could now go ahead, though in low gear, as a composer.

There came the inevitable moment for a change of piano teacher. On the advice of a friend, I went 'hat in hand' to Evlyn Howard Jones. At the back of his house in Eaton Terrace was a large music room, in which the great man received me with impressive kindliness. Howard Jones was known to be a friend of Delius, whose music, thanks to Beecham, was beginning to be widely known. This contact with the mysterious old egocentric at Grez-sur-Loing created an aura of glamorous dedication to the Nietzscheian cult of supermen beyond our shores. The affiliation was proclaimed with conscious pride, being not infrequently infiltrated into commentary during lessons. Among other pupils at the time was Edmund Rubbra, more sphinx-like than now, padding his way along the London streets in sandals, then

something of a rarity in male attire. A constant flock of adoring
young women hovered in the offing, the charms of one hitting me
hard, though I was too well aware of my shortcomings to tell her
so.

The motive that led me to this shrine had been a wish to prepare
for a diploma: but Howard Jones would have none of it. 'You're
going to be an Artist' he said 'And Artists don't waste time over
diplomas – they need every minute of their working day to
become better Artists.' During two or three years I learned a
great deal from Howard Jones, by which time it had become
evident that my firm intention to become a reasonably competent
working musician lay well below the prevailing snow-line, above
which Artists and Supermen worked out their splendid destinies.
In a letter written during this period, Howard Jones quoted some
advice given by Delius – 'In any art the whole process of
education depends on finding an Artist you can trust and by whom
you are convinced. Then pick his brains to the last ounce and
profit by his experience until you feel strong enough to go on your
own. If then a man cannot be an Artist he had better not try, for in
a multitude of counsellors there is confusion.'

These highflown intimations lacked sufficient economic and
realistic oxygen to be of much practical help. But if I had doubts,
there was also genuine admiration. Howard Jones in top form was
very good indeed. Particularly valuable were his wide-ranging
allusions to poetry, painting and the other arts as a means of
acquiring greater understanding in the sphere of interpretation.
At about this time he made a recording of some preludes and
fugues from the 48, in which his playing of the F sharp major pair
from Book I has remained in my memory as an all time 'high'.
There was an occasion when the two of us set out to walk from
Dorchester over the downs to Abbotsbury. On our way we met an
elderly countryman who might have stepped straight out of a page
in *The Dynasts*. 'This 'ere downland track where we be now' he
said 'were part of an old coach road to Weymouth. 'Twas along
un that King Jarge did come in summertime when 'e did visit thik
girt town. From 'is coach 'e could view that there clop o'trees
over yonder – young saplings they'm were in 'is day I 'spaac.' At
Abbotsbury we stayed at an inn where every window was
hermetically sealed. Howard Jones said he must have some fresh
air in his bedroom, about which he consulted the landlord. 'Ah
now, 'e don't open, nor 'ave done, not in all the five-an'twenty
years I bin 'ere. But do you push your bed up against that old
chiminey-piece: you'll find all the air you need – ah! and a bit
o'soot too I shouldn't wonder – 'e ain't bin swep' for years.' So the

Artist who so eloquently proclaimed the joys of simple country life (as it was in those far-off days) found the reality not greatly to his liking.

In recalling this incident I find it strangely revealing as being entirely characteristic of Howard Jones. His tendency to over-emphasize idealistic concepts inevitably resulted in disillusion when applied to stern reality. There was a strangely elusive element in his character: everything seemed so admirable – he was wise, kindly, discerning – a superb talker on many subjects. Yet some essential vitamin seemed to be lacking: perhaps the hard facts of life were unable to bring themselves to fall in with the preconceptions so generously offered to them.

Ultimately I was to find as much pianistic salvation as I could assimilate under the guiding hand of George Reeves. At the time of our meeting he had become well known as an accompanist of rare ability, who was already appearing with internationally famous singers and instrumentalists. It is impossible to exaggerate the debt I owe to his wisdom and skill as a teacher, his absolute sincerity, his deep and true musicianship. These qualities were combined with no illusions as to the often unsatisfactory conditions that all too frequently occur in a musician's life, to say nothing of jealousy, favouritism and intrigue. No one I have ever met has had a more abundant sense of humour, ranging from the Rabelaisian and fantastic to the gently sardonic. George also possessed an almost Socratic passion for the truth, as manifested in both character and performance. This last attribute gained him many firm friends, though it also alienated certain would-be aspirants for his commendation. Any attempts to present second-rate work garnished to appear as best would be instantly detected.

The precepts of George Reeves – who had himself come up in what is called 'the hard way' – have been my foundation and guide in playing and teaching the piano for fifty years. If such building on them as I have been able to achieve has remained on ground level, the reason is solely that other activities have left insufficient time and energy. Our friendship remained an unfailing source of delight for many years, interrupted by his sojourn in New York, and terminated by his untimely death. But his teaching took me as far as the Wigmore Hall for a recital of 'sound playing' as one of the London papers phrased it. I also made another appearance to accompany a group of newly published songs: this was to prove the direction to follow, although there would be a great deal of both playing and teaching the piano for many years to come.

CHAPTER 9

'And joy in the making'

An ability to churn out settings of patter songs with chorus for a school concert might, given time and luck, lead towards success as a tunesmith, but I had already determined to try and compose something less ephemeral. The difference is well illustrated by a shrewd comment made about an established composer who had just conducted a recently completed symphonic work of bulging proportions. 'That young man', said a feminine acquaintance 'can write a pretty enough song, but when it comes to *real* music it is quite another matter!'

The occasion was an orchestral concert in Bournemouth, the year somewhere around 1930. 'That young man' was Rutland Boughton, who had incidentally caused an additional flutter by appearing on the rostrum in plus fours. The work was his *Deirdre Symphony*. Apart from the usual lack of rehearsal time, we were all distracted by his copious and detailed programme notes, of the kind that urges the listener on no account to miss the entry of the oboe at the forty-third bar, this having some bearing on the literary background to the music.

Indeed we had all been both impressed and beguiled by *The Immortal Hour*, as well as by Boughton's setting of Thomas Hardy's *The Queen of Cornwall*. Doubtless the remark was made with the song 'How Beautiful they are' from the former in mind – as natty a piece of homegrown Gaelic mystique as ever took root and bloomed within our shores. There was a good deal of pentatonic as well as modal nostalgia in the air at the time, aided and abetted by some very successful arrangements of Hebridean songs of a haunting and nostalgic beauty.

By now I had established a firm diplomatic relationship with Dan Godfrey. Afternoon symphony concerts would be followed by tea with the great man. Also present would be Hamilton Law, who presided over the Bournemouth Conservatoire of Music and provided programme notes: also the lady who, in addition to the Boughton comment just quoted, manipulated the teapot and saw to it that we maintained a reasonably decorous conversation. Invariably the main topic would be the visiting soloist or composer. Dan's comment on the soloist would be something on these lines: 'He (or she) certainly gave us a run for our money – but why, in that semiquaver passage in the finale when he ought to have gone dee-a dee-a dee-a did he keep on with yuddy, yuddy, yuddy? Does he think we don't know the work?'

Dan Godfrey could be either remarkably tactful or extremely caustic. An example of the former occurred at a party given for a young pianist, who was obliged to show his paces on a brave but battered and exhausted veteran. Our hostess said 'I do hope, Sir Dan, that you like my dear old piano.' 'Madam' he replied, 'it is irreplaceable – quite irreplaceable!' Similarly his comment on a group of my own songs 'Very suitable they are – *very* suitable.' So much for tact: two instances of the caustic were, firstly, concerning a visiting composer of extreme and venerable respectability who, in earlier years, had evidently deviated from the paths of righteousness – 'You wouldn't think, to look at him now, that he'd once served six months in the second division, would you?' This was said in a resoundingly confidential tone to someone in a crowded artists' room. Attempted shhhh-ing by Lady Godfrey only partially reduced the volume. On another occasion he was recounting a conversation between himself and the widow of a composer who had recently died. Anxious, it seemed, not only to encourage more performances of her late husband's works, but also to keep her charms in operational condition, she rashly invited him to spend a weekend with her. One can readily picture the stern disapproval that must have registered in the great man's features as he said 'I don't imagine you would enjoy it at all, for such a doubtful privilege I should charge a very high fee!'

In the days when I was still hoping to become a concert pianist, I played the Schumann Concerto with Dan and his orchestra. This event was duly reported in the local press 'Local Doctor's Son: Plays Concerto At Winter Gardens!!' (Note the exclamation marks). Incidentally this particular programme makes interesting reading today.

Overture	*The Uninhabited Island*	Haydn
Suite	*Mother Goose*	Ravel
Song (by Gerald Kaye)	*A Wandering Minstrel I*	Sullivan
Symphony No 2 in D Op 36		Beethoven
Nelson Conyers (Art Impressionist) in *Cameos of Colour*		
	Interval	
Piano Concerto in A Minor		Schumann
Songs	*A Song Remembered*	Eric Coates
	Beloved, I Shall wait	Guy d'Hardelot
Royal Hunt and the Storm (The Trojans)		Berlioz

This marathon was described as a Light Symphony Concert. As to Cameos in Colour, I must leave the reader to guess their substance. My fee was two guineas.

As though that were not more than enough, the same orchestra had given a full programme of light music at 3 o'clock on that same afternoon, with Montague Birch as Deputy Conductor. What gluttons we seem to have been – and how much, for how little reward, did these gallant players contribute to our enjoyment, often to a half-empty hall. In the same programme, among the advertisements, one inserted by the Royal Exeter Hotel proclaims 'Splendid Orchestra under the direction of Mabel Stocks – 4 to 5.45 & 8 to 10 *every day*.' Can we wonder that the Musicians' Union has since become militant over the welfare of orchestral players?

I had found a valuable friend in Henry Lamb, the artist, then living in a Georgian house in one of the narrow streets near the Harbour in Poole. At this period he was deeply interested in the music of Bach (with Busoni overtones), Mozart and Beethoven. He had made some interesting piano transcriptions of Bach Choral Preludes and of movements from late Beethoven quartets. Periodically I would spend an evening at 10, Hill Street to play newly acquired additions to my growing repertoire. After playing, I was given a commentary that could often last for nearly an hour, ranging widely and giving as penetrating an insight on the philosophical and aesthetic content as Tovey from the musician's standpoint.

Henry Lamb's sojourn in Poole had been troubled by gangs of hooligans, who maintained a fierce rivalry in the locality. As a means of protection he sought out the leader of one of the gangs who, in exchange for having his portrait painted, guaranteed protection from rival groups. In those days thugs and vandals kept strictly to their own areas.

In answer to a letter, in which I had mentioned various pieces added to my stock-in-trade, Henry wrote 'I'm glad to hear of all the masterpieces laid low that have rashly stood in your all-conquering way. I wonder if, when we next meet, I shall be able to supply a little artificial respiration to the lifeless corpses!' In his stimulating company I also attended many concerts, again enriched by much enlightening commentary. This, however, was almost entirely confined to the period 1700–1850 – from Bach to Berlioz. It was a great disappointment to me that he showed no interest whatever in more recent music, with the honourable exception of Sibelius, whose seventh symphony he acclaimed with considerable enthusiasm.

To Henry Lamb I owe, not only a full and complete initiation into the splendours of late Beethoven, but particularly long and fully illustrated dissertations on the Sonatas Op 109, 110, 111 and the *Diabelli Variations*. As we talked and played I would be aware of paintings on the wall that revealed new vistas of imaginative exploration – paintings that are now part of the nation's heritage. Friends from this other sphere would appear from time to time. I recall an evening with Stanley Spencer in full verbal spate, shedding new light on many subjects, notably religious responses. The famous Resurrection painting had recently caused a flutter amongst the pious: studies for some of the ingredients had been made in the nearby village churchyard at Corfe Mullen.

Two other notable musicians were also living in Bournemouth; Gordon Bryan, a pianist and composer of considerable achievement, and Graham Peel. Shy and elusive, the latter lived in a house called Marden Ash in the Bath Road, long since demolished. Here he maintained a bachelor establishment of considerable luxury, remaining completely detached from the musical scene. Of more than a hundred songs, only *In Summertime on Bredon* and *The Early Morning* seem to have survived. Graham Peel took a poor view of the competitive aspect of the contemporary scene and devoted much time and care to the rehabilitation of prisoners. A typical example of his innate courtesy was shown when, as chairman of a committee formed for this work, a member proceeded at great length to expound a purely personal viewpoint. Becoming aware of boredom around him, he paused and said 'I hope, Mr. Chairman, I'm not being tedious?' Graham Peel raised himself from his seat and said very gently 'A little, perhaps – just a little!'

The B.B.C. had opened a local radio station in the Holdenhurst Road, to which I went for an audition as pianist. After I had played a couple of pieces, the official in charge said 'I suppose you couldn't possibly come back this evening and play two short groups for us? It seems that the artist we had engaged will not be coming.' So I happily obliged on this and other occasions.

Intensive pianistic aspirations were finally extinguished by the impact, in my eighteenth year, of poetry. An immediate and overwhelming impulse to compose songs – and anything else that could reasonably hope for a hearing, however amateur – took absolute priority. Happily this afflatus arrived just after the long struggle to muster enough eyesight to write my own music had been achieved. Through a chance encounter while I was staying at a friendly *pensione* in Florence friends provided an introduction to kindred spirits in London. Some settings of mine of poems by

Thomas Hardy were given an airing at the friendly and welcoming Oxford and Cambridge Musical Club, then happily situated in Bedford Square. The splendid fellows who belonged to it kept a hole in the wall, through which they sometimes permitted less educated folk to enter. In a quiet panelled room at the back of the house there were fortnightly evenings of music. My singer was A. N. G. (Anthony) Richards, who invariably, then as later, went straight to the heart of the matter. No composer could have wished for a more ideal interpreter. The Florentine contact also brought an invitation to attend the London première of Stravinsky's *Apollon Musagètes*. The date must have been August 1929, a fortnight or so before the death of Diaghilev in Venice. Hearing this radiant score, in which the key of C major is given a rich glow from sunlight emanating from E, was an unforgettable experience. Matched by the quality of dancing and production that this strange maestro had created, the effect was overwhelming.

In Dorset I began a lifelong friendship with Monk Gibbon, whose first two books of poems* had just been published in Winchester by Alister Matthews' Greyhound Press. Monk, still suffering from the aftermath of active service during World War I, had found a welcome sanctuary as a member of the teaching staff of the school in Swanage at which I had been a pupil. Though nurtured in the prevalent Celtic Twilight atmosphere of Dublin, here was a poet and author who looked steadfastly towards the full light of day. Ever mindful of his native Ireland, he has made his inheritance a runway to a wider horizon than many of his contemporaries.

Living nearby at Woolgarstone were two young singers, Norman Notley and David Brynley. Both became firm friends – and they also took my songs with them in their travelling bag, singing them in the same rare and responsive way as Anthony Richards. Also within the shadow of Corfe Castle, Hilda and Mary Spencer Watson lived at Dunshay, where a converted barn became a theatre for mime, formerly carried on in the clattering purlieus of Notting Hill Gate. Here Monk's poems and my songs frequently appeared in the programme, performed under ideal conditions and with the added dimension of imaginative mime. At one of these occasions a setting of Psalm 120 that I had recently made for voice and piano was to be accompanied on a harp. Since the chromatic changes were of a kind to produce a harpist's

The Tremulous String and *The Branch of Hawthorn Tree*

nightmare – also knowing only too well the hazy notions theatrical folk have of the mechanics of music-making – I awaited the results with anxiety. In due course a young woman appeared, looking as though she had just stepped from a Burne-Jones window. Seeking to make my peace with her after the performance, which she had miraculously contrived to bring off very well indeed, I was expecting a quiet, intense, more-in-sorrow-than-in-anger response. In the generally muted but glowing raptus her voice and manner came from an entirely different world. In a patois not unknown within the sound of Bow Bells, she tossed her lovely head and hanging hair as she remarked 'Yes, well it was a bit of a bloomin' rout march, I must say!'

Two doors away from my parents' home in the Straight Borough at Wimborne lived Ronald Gomer – organist, violinist and poet. Not only had he given me generous help in the business of writing music, but had encouraged me to write some for his church, St. Luke's, Winton, and even performed it. Alone of the denizens of the Borough, we shared many interests and enthusiasms, particularly a deep and abiding love for the countryside in which we were both born and bred.

When I was twenty-one, Hubert Foss at the Oxford University Press accepted a small unison song to a poem by Eleanor Farjeon – *Cradle Song for Christmas*. I was offered either £5 or a 5% royalty on a copy costing about fourpence. Perennially hard up, I chose the £5. In the following year Chesters accepted four solo songs, and my journey into music by the slow train had begun.

CHAPTER 10

Some Three Choirs Festival Memories (1925–27)

In 1925 when, at the age of seventeen, I had been prevented from fulfilling my long-held ambition to become a student at the Royal College of Music, it was a consolation to be invited to attend, not only the Gloucester Festival in that year, but the two following Meetings at Worcester and Hereford. The experience was a lifeline thrown by a friend of ever blessed memory, Constance Baker, who lived at Pilford, a Dorset hamlet. A suite of that name for elementary string orchestra still exists as a modest but sincere token to her memory.

To reach Gloucester involved a leisurely journey on the Somerset and Dorset railway, with long pauses at stations with more bell-like names – Spetisbury, Sturminster Newton, Shillingstone, Midsomer Norton among them. A brisk and exhilarating top-up to the journey, on what had just become the London, Midland & Scottish, brought me to Gloucester well into the afternoon. Walking with my bag towards the city I overtook two figures in deep conversation, evidently well content in each other's company. They proved to be Sir Edward Elgar and W. H. (Billy) Reed, memorable and greatly loved leader of the London Symphony Orchestra.

So good an omen was immediately followed by another – the sound of the Cathedral chimes playing the splendid C minor tune that Dr. Hayes had written for them in the late 18th-century. As Alice Meynell truly says 'The spirit of place calls out and peals in the Cathedral bells.' Since that moment, whenever Gloucester is mentioned, the sound of Dr. Hayes' chime comes to mind, like a signature tune. It so happened that the programme was to include a set of orchestral variations based on it, by Joseph Hathaway, a copy of which, arranged for piano, is still in my possession. There was a slight family connection here since Joe Hathaway had once held the post of organist at Tonbridge Parish Church. The regular congregation included several of my aunts, the youngest of whom seems to have been far from insensible to his skill and charm. I was to meet him myself, by a strange coincidence, twenty-two years later when a work of my own was being rehearsed for another Festival in Gloucester. This was *Five Psalms* for soprano, chorus and orchestra, the final form evolved from an original song-cycle, part of which had given the Pre-Raphaelite harpist at Dunshay her 'bloomin' rout march.' When I met Hathaway, he had but a few weeks to live. He was a kindly, gentle man who belonged to a generation when a succession of organ lofts was almost the only available ladder for dedicated 'all-round' musicians.

In 1925 Herbert Brewer was still in charge of the proceedings at Gloucester, though shortly to be followed by Herbert Sumsion. Brewer had succeeded C. Lee Williams just before the turn of the century. It was thus both fitting and moving that his predecessor, then very frail, should have made a brief appearance to conduct a setting of The Lord's Prayer. Though not particularly memorable, it provided a link with the Cathedral's past history. Everyone 'rose to their feet' in salutation.

Apart from the Cathedral, the pivotal point of the Festival centred on the presence of Elgar who, except to his special friends, revealed an aloof, unpredictable and moody aspect, elusive as the missing clue to his Enigma theme. For me his outstanding contribution was a performance of the A flat symphony. With Billy Reed as LSO leader, there was an immediate sense of communication that resulted in a reserved, yet deeply expressive interpretation of this glowing masterpiece. Between moments of heraldic splendour, the many quieter, veiled and deeply personal episodes became fused and integrated, as if those diverse elements in the composer's character had for once called a truce. Even now, more than fifty years on, the effect of the closing section in the slow movement is still vivid in my memory. It seemed as if the veil that shields 'another world than this' flickered for an instant – and almost lifted.

At Worcester in the following year, at a gathering in the house of Sir Ivor Atkins for a pre-lunch glass of sherry, I found myself standing next to Elgar. He was resplendent in morning coat and accompanying regalia, after a performance of one of his works. Any mention of music in his presence was known to be taboo, being certain to produce an outburst of Brahmsian rudery. Sure enough it erupted when a more than usually gushing lady approached him and said 'Oh Sir Edward – it was *so* lovely – your wonderful music I mean of course – I was completely transported – yes, transported – there is no other word for it.' The great man at once assumed an expression that suggested a Prussian general confronted by incompetent junior officers. He scowled as he remarked to the company at large, in a quite unnecessarily loud voice 'Yes, it was a pity the weather was so bad this morning; I was unable to bring my dogs with me.' The gushing lady, pink and abashed, retreated miserably.

At Gloucester there had also been Vaughan Williams, who conducted The Explorers movement from *A Sea Symphony*. From the moment of the opening phrase 'O vast rondure swimming in space' to the closing section 'For we are bound where mariner has not yet dared to' – out and away, beyond the rocky headlands of duty, penury, piety, convention and all the other inhibitions through which, in those days we were obliged to steer our way with so much care – it seemed as if the Cathedral, in which these splendid sounds echoed with such resonance, would at any moment cast off moorings and sail away towards those unknown regions with which the composer had been so preoccupied in his younger days.

It was at Worcester in the following year that I had to take my courage in both hands and make myself known to R.V.W. Armed with a photograph of him I made my way to College Green. There he was constantly to be seen, walking slowly and thoughtfully, the famous panama hat being about mid-way through a long and distinguished career. He duly signed the photograph – and thus began a friendship that was to be 'kept in repair' for thirty years. At Hereford, on a glowing September afternoon, there was a performance of *A Pastoral Symphony*, of such eloquence that it seemed as if the surrounding countryside had suddenly found a voice and become articulate. Writing of the performance, A. H. Fox Strangways claimed that the music belonged to all time. As an instance he cited the Benedictine monks in pre-Reformation days, going about their work in field and woodland, to whom he affirmed that this music would have been equally clear and eloquent. One other member of our party was equally stirred; the others, chattering gaily, found nothing unusual about it. Indeed this symphony either makes a very deep appeal, or none at all – there are no half measures.

Another composer present was Granville Bantock, walking the streets in a thick Harris tweed Norfolk jacket, his Gaelic afflatus then in full spate. This latest manifestation had followed gustily after similar dalliance with Chinese and Indian mystique. Since the prevailing wind was now blowing in gale force from the nor'west, it was fitting that we heard the *Hebridean Symphony*. Bantockian waves of sound broke with considerable splendour on the orchestral shore. Here is music that I would wish to hear again, in the hope that it would provide a more persuasive advocate for Bantock than the recently revived *Fifine at the Fair*. This agreeably unspectacular young woman, brought out of retirement by Beecham to be given another turn on the merry-go-round, seems now to reveal a somewhat faded charm, particularly in her preoccupation with dominant sevenths.

Holst's *Hymn of Jesus* made a deep impression, the tonal clashes still sounding new and exciting in the days before we became aware of Bartok's ability to squeeze the last ounce of tension from adjacent semitones.

There was an evening concert in the Shire Hall at Gloucester that got away to a spirited start with *The Wasps Overture*. Among the items that followed were Patrick Hadley's short and penetrating setting of Marty South's lament over the grave of Giles Winterbourne in Hardy's *The Woodlanders*. But it seemed, then as now, open to question whether those particular words leave anything unsaid that music can add. Billy Reed produced a sprightly suite called *The Lincoln Imp*, music of the lighter kind still being *persona grata* on these occasions.

The standard works were under the guiding hands of the three Cathedral organists. Sir Herbert Brewer invariably kept strictly to the prevailing speed limits, taking his corners with care and giving the prescribed signals. With Sir Ivor Atkins at the wheel, performances showed a tendency to vary, but contained some exciting moments – not all of them, it seemed, turning out quite as expected! Percy Hull, still comparatively youthful, favoured high speed driving, thus keeping both orchestral and choral passengers on the alert.

A galaxy of singers included Dorothy Silk, Elsie Suddaby, Agnes Nicholls, John Coates, Steuart Wilson among the more memorable. The first and last morning and afternoon sessions were traditionally given over to those two evergreen marathons *Elijah* and *Messiah*. The Elijah of the year was Horace Stevens, whose performance was a dramatic *tour de force*. Memory hints that he came from Australia – and adds for good measure that he was the only singer known to me who ever roamed the streets of a west country town in an immaculate bowler hat.

Many of the regular devotees were absent when *Elijah* and *Messiah* were being given. Their places were taken, in full measure, by the entire human contents of country rectories, complete and *en famille*. Every morning train to arrive at one of the three cities would disgorge whole phalanxes of them, each reverend dad bearing under his arm the proud device of a Novello octavo score. It was fairly safe to assume that many Mr. Quiverfuls would, on the following Sunday at Mattins, treat their village congregations to a ringside account of the proceedings, allied to a suitable text. One of them was known to begin with unfailing regularity 'During the last few days I have been privileged to hear . . .,' after which his congregation, knowing the rest, would subside into patient inertia. Imagination boggles at what might have emerged from many rural pulpits had the programme been changed.

These and the other Cathedral meetings were invariably framed by prayers, before and after the music. There was one elderly cleric in charge at Worcester who was invariably trapped into giving the Blessing during the well-known silent bar near the end of *Messiah*. We pictured him peacefully dozing, suddenly aware of silence, bored to distraction and eager for a cup of tea. His pious utterance was swept away in a burst of Handelian splendour. The second – and successful attempt – sounded a trifle tetchy in consequence!

Years later when *Elijah* was revived at a single session, duly trimmed round the edges, I was sitting just behind a well-known composer. At half-time he peered cautiously round, first one side, then the other – and crept towards the door. Thinking, rightly as it turned out, that he was making for a nearby hostelry I followed him. 'I have never managed to hear the work until this evening', he said 'but I had no idea it was anything like *that*!' His recovery over a pint of beer was rapid and effective.

Looking back over those three Festivals in the distant past, remembering the atmosphere of the West Country as it was, the infinite kindness shewn on all sides, brings the realization of great comfort and stimulus at a moment when it was badly needed. The treatment begun was to be continued by friends – and to some of them another chapter must be given.

CHAPTER 11

Dorset Landscape with Figures

A great deal of social life in an English country town during the 1920s was played out in a recognized system of moves that closely resembled a game of chess. From the opening move of making and receiving calls, life proceeded smoothly enough, provided the players knew the rules and kept to them. In retrospect it seems that there were not only inhibitions that hung like clouds, behind which the sunshine of spontaneity remained permanently obscured – but there were also taboos that had to be respected. A young man, for example, who appeared in a dinner jacket and rashly produced a coloured handkerchief was automatically 'a bit of a bounder' and socially *persona non grata*. To light a cigarette after dinner before everyone had finished the ritual of drinking port was another solecism. It seemed that God, not least among His many attributes, must inevitably assume the role of a fine old English country gentleman, Conservative to the last ditch! The seething crowds of the under-privileged were exemplified by Labour. On the day after the Labour party first assumed power, silence and gloom prevailed at the breakfast table and lingered like fog for several days, slowly and only reluctantly dispersing.

In such an atmosphere anyone actively engaged in the arts was regarded with mixed feelings. While on one hand there was genuine admiration for solid achievement, there was also anxiety about the behaviour and response of artists to the prevailing *modus vivendi*. These wayward men and women were liable to present a disturbing element in a settled and established order: they were inclined to be unaware and even careless of the correct moves on the board.

Into this milieu, on a visit to ultra-conventional friends, came Clare Leighton. Her hostess belonged to a school of thought to whom it was unthinkable to invite guests for luncheon without first putting on a hat in which to receive them. Clare felt, as she said, 'like a bombshell straining at the leash!' Happily she was unleashed in our direction. Then in her twenties, Clare exuded vitality and zest for life, as well as being extremely decorative and possessing an outgoing personality without a trace of simulation or pretence. The wood engravings with which her name will ever be associated were already receiving recognition and acclaim. She and I became – and have remained – firm friends, despite her later allegiance to America. There her fame has spread, not only through her painting, but also in some magnificent stained glass windows, notably the series designed for the Cathedral at Worcester, Massachusetts.

Soon after our initial meeting, Clare and her former friend Henry Noel Brailsford were to design and plan the house they built at Monks Risborough called 'Four Hedges'. An illustrated book that Clare has written about the venture remains a permanent and cherished token of the partnership. Among the many pleasures to be enjoyed there was the music that emanated from a large E.M.G. external horn gramophone. Sojourns at Four Hedges coincided with the era of Leopold Stokowski and the Philadelphia Orchestra, whose playing of the Brahms symphonies, filtered through fibre needles, gently diffused within those cavernous recesses, gave the music an almost unearthly glow. There were also the initial discs of Cortot, Thibaud and Casals, notably in a performance of the *Archduke Trio*. The recorded sound of the Lener Quartet was on the wane, while the rising star of Adolf Busch lay just below the horizon.

There would be music during breakfast, when the best days began with Bach. There was one disastrous occasion when nothing seemed to go right: we had rashly chosen the Schubert Quartet in G for our Morning Office. That heart-searching and deeply revealing piece, like the first drink, comes better at a later hour. To those who grew up to the sound of those old E.M.G. instruments, not all the manifold splendours of Hi-Fi reproduction can ever quite recapture the lost magic. So greatly prized were these gramophones that one could imagine their dedicated possessors pouring libations of linseed oil to them at the time of full moon! So much is surely owed by so many to their only begetter E. M. Ginn. His successors maintained that memorable shop in Grape Street (behind the Princes Theatre) that became not only a mecca but also an honorary club, where chance encounters could often lead to friendship.

Soon also after our first meeting, Clare and Noel came once more to Dorset, on this occasion to Egdon Heath, staying at Tadnoll Farm, where Tom Burdon and his wife contrived to make a livelihood from – it seemed – far from easy or particularly fertile land. The visit to Tadnoll had been brought about by a commission for Clare to provide a set of engravings for a special edition of *The Return of the Native*. A print of one of these hangs on the wall in front of me as I write. It is of Diggory Venn the reddleman, sitting outside his caravan, smoking a pipe and thinking long thoughts of Thomasin Yeobright. Evening light shines over the dark and swarthy heath that Hardy has so vividly described. The elemental and almost primeval beauty that once cast a spell over this stretch of country has vanished: perhaps beneath the subsequent accretions of afforestation and atomic power, the spirit of Egdon lies sleeping.

For the bonfire scene on Rainbarrow, Tom Burdon mustered a fine demonstration for Clare to illustrate. When she sent a print of it to him, his wife replied 'Father has seen himself in the photo – and he's that proud.'

The year was 1927, since the visitors had brought with them a portable gramophone with some new recordings that had appeared during the Beethoven centenary. Also the Brahms Violin Concerto, played by Kreisler, with the Berlin State Opera Orchestra and Leo Blech. It was the sound and shape of this particular work that seemed to merge with the light and shade – and the stillness – over the Heath. I, for one, could wish that it had been this performance, rather than the later and less happy Kreisler recording, that had been perpetuated.

Partly, though not invariably through association, certain pieces of music, a tune even, can have a strange power of attachment to the spirit of place. The Brahms Concerto and the Egdon of former times is a case in point. There are country lanes in Hampshire where Haydn's *London Symphony* invariably comes to mind: in Scotland the sound of Sibelius seems to emanate from the landscape and to be carried in the breezes that blow there with such unrelenting constancy.

It was a great sorrow to Clare that she was unable to meet Hardy during her stay at Tadnoll. His second wife, however, kept a close guard on him, keeping the door closed on all except a fortunate few. It was at this period that Holst came to Egdon. In addition to writing one of his most memorable scores, he was admitted within the portals of Max Gate.

Only a handful of my own settings of poems by Hardy have survived. *The Colour* later found a place in a cantata called *The Echoing Green*: the remainder became merged into *Six Country Songs*, set for soli, chorus and orchestra. They were written in response to a commission from the Kent County Music Committee, for performance at a summer school in Benenden many years later. Hearing them in a recent broadcast made me reasonably content with a modest token of deep and abiding gratitude for all that Hardy has given to the world.

Thomas Hardy, during his lifetime, was regarded by many sections of the Dorset populace with suspicion and even aversion. Possibly this originated from the general reaction to Tess and to Jude when these books first appeared. Had they been written forty years later, their reception might have been less troubled. But in Victorian, Protestant, Non-Conformist Dorset – and elsewhere – not only the pious, but the players on the social chessboard (mentioned earlier in this chapter) were unable to bring themselve to approve. Here were revealed aspects of life from which they protected themselves by keeping mental telescopes firmly held to the blind eye.

On the day after Hardy died I was conscious of a deep and irreparable sense of loss. In Wimborne – where he had once lived – I met an acquaintance to whom I sadly mentioned the news. 'Who?' she asked: then 'Oh I know who you mean – wrote books and that, didn't he?' Later, when *The Echoing Green* was being performed in Dorchester, the combined choirs had just sung *The Colour* with – it seemed – moving effect. This poem 'half remembered from an old Wessex folk-rhyme' is an echo of a singing game in which various colours are offered – and rejected. Here it finishes with the acceptance of black –

> "Black is for mourning –
> And black will do."

At this point someone within earshot whispered to her neighbour 'Just the sort of deplorable sentiment that tiresome little man would think up.' An attempt was made to have a plaque placed on the house where Hardy had lived in Wimborne during the 'eighties and where he had written *Two on a Tower* amongst other works. The idea was supported by members of the local Council, some of whom had been unaware of the association. But the owner of the house steadfastly refused to have any such questionable past episode brought to light! Perhaps rock bottom was reached by the man who remarked 'Hardy a good writer did you say? Why, the feller couldn't even describe a gentleman!'

In the stimulating company of Thomas Tunnard Moore, who possessed an open AC two-seater car that he drove with virtuoso precision, we explored many of the Dorset hills – Bulbarrow, Hod, Hambledon, High Stoy, Badbury Rings, Creech Barrow and others. Some of them, such as Golden Cap, Pilsdon and Lewesdon, lay too far westward then, though in recent years their call to return has been insistent. Those forays also included churches, inns and people.

One day Tunnard and I found our way to the home of Theodore Powys. We had both been delighted to discover *Mr. Weston's Good Wine* and felt impelled to seek out the author of so invigorating and original a book. So we made our way to Bethcar, a redbrick house that stood at the top of East Chaldon village, sideways on to the road and facing the downs. Between the five-bar gate and the door of the house there was little, if any, recognizable path, strangely characteristic of a man as reserved and shy as the owner. Again the chessboard players were not interested in a writer who could begin a novel such as *Mr. Tasker's Gods* with a description of *servants undressing*! Few, if any other writers, have so vividly reflected so many aspects of country folk, in the times before the tentacles of mechanized progress brought so many benefits and so much discontent. In all the books of T. F. Powys there is surely nothing more eloquently descriptive of this vanished world than *the Fable of Mr. Pym and the Holy Crumb*.

Theodore Powys in his speech, as in his prose, communicated in perfectly formed sentences of simplicity and clarity. Reserved and shy as he was, it seemed that he carried his own particular angle of vision with infinite care and even tenderness.

At Stourpaine we encountered the Rector, Herbert Cooke. In his study there lurked, beneath palm crosses and other religious bits and pieces, large photographs of railway engines of Brighton vintage, proudly attended by bewhiskered and top-hatted characters. It transpired that our host, in younger days, had been a locomotive inspector under no less a chief than William Stroudley. My instant recognition of the name delighted him: palm crosses and the rest came showering down from the walls to reveal a series of Stroudley tank engines, each with a name proudly emblazoned on the side. Immediately the talk turned to boiler pressure, gradients and the wayward exploits of drivers. The letter in which the great engineer confirmed Herbert Cooke's appointment contains this sentence: 'With regard to your hours of duty I put you on your honour as a gentleman to come and go as you know you ought to do in your position, so it is of no use to make stated hours.'

From those days one of Herbert Cooke's daughters has remained a lifelong friend. Some years after the family had left Stourpaine, she returned to visit various friends. Among them was an old and bedridden lady who, in her talk, recalled a memory of the former rector that reveals the old style country parson in a very endearing light. 'Once when I wer' took bad, Mr. Cooke 'e did go all the way into Blandford to buy I some grapes: ah – and did sit by me bedside while I did eat 'em – an' 'eld out his 'and so that I mid spit out the pips into 'en.'

By way of coda to these glimpses of a vanished world, let us finish at Corfe Mullen. Here, at Mill Farm, lived George Hibberd, most welcoming of hosts. Here, alone and with friends, there would be walks in Henbury Woods during the winter months: in summer there was bathing in the Rolling Bay. This was a moss-covered waterfall with salmon leaps at one side, a deep pool below the foaming water that led to a shallow stretch of river overhung by a magnificent willow. At midsummer George would see to it that the hay was cut round the edge of the meadow that led to this enchanted spot, losing no time to urge us to come and picnic in the hayfield that flanked the weir. Opposite Mill Farm stood 'The Cock and Wheatsheaf': there, in Mrs. Adams' cosy bar Parlour, a tankard of Groves' XXXX Strong Old Ale in hand, George would be 'in the chair' and undisputed Master of Ceremonies.

An incident that has an association with this admirable hostelry concerns a carter, Hayter by name, who still bedecked his team of horses with a full set of bells. Every year he came to Corfe Mullen to help a farmer relation carry his hay. To do so involved bringing his wagon over the railway by an occupational crossing. One evening in the 'Cock and Wheatsheaf' he was in a thoughtful and contented mood. 'I be glad to be going home to-morrow' he said, more than once. The next day would see the crop safely carried and stacked. He knew by heart the times of all the scheduled trains on the Somerset and Dorset line. But on the next morning, when he was leading his loaded wagon up the short slope to the crossing, a fast excursion train suddenly appeared, bearing down towards him. He was just clear of the line, but the head-wind from the train caught a piece of chain on the harness of the leading horse that hit him on the temple. He was killed instantly: the horses and wagon were unharmed. So he did indeed go home that day – may he rest in peace.

At Corfe Mullen now, Henbury Woods have virtually vanished in the cause of progress; the spoliation of the Rolling Bay was gradual – and in the end total. First came a pumping station to draw water from the valley for Poole and Bournemouth: the river-level fell dramatically; the foaming moss-covered weir became first a trickle, then virtually ceased to flow. Pylons marched across the Elysian meadows, to be followed in due course by the Catchment Board, that sworn enemy of natural beauty. Having replaced the old moss-covered weir with stone and concrete, the Board's officials levelled the banks and felled the splendid willow to the ground. After which they passed on for the next kill.

I have already mentioned the Dorset hills: perhaps after all it is the rivers that exert an even stronger tug at the heart. Among them the Pydel, Frome and Stour. For me, first and always, the Stour. Another Dorset man, RHB, my friend of former years, wrote a poem about this enchanted river. I set it to music in *The Echoing Green*.

> "There, all the day, the quiet waters keep
> Their courses between banks of lucent green,
> Moving as though they travelled in their sleep
> Towards some haven dreamed of but unseen.
>
> There, in the shade of reed or willow-herb,
> The lazy trout may cool his dappled flanks:
> The cattle browse in indolence superb,
> Knee-deep in buttercups along the banks.
>
> There one may come on beauty unawares
> That broods above the shallows of the stream,
> Or in the kingfisher, as swift he fares,
> Behold the very substance of a dream.
>
> Forget-me-nots beneath the willow bough
> Reflect all day the pale blue of the sky,
> Even as my thoughts reflect their likeness now –
> There I was born, and there I fain would die."

CHAPTER 12

'That can sing both high and low'

Best of all the presents for my twenty-first birthday was a puppy. He was a black and white cocker spaniel: since I was already held in thrall by Boswell's *Life of Johnson*, he was naturally called Hervey ('Sir, if you call a dog Hervey, I shall love him'). The litter, of which he was one, had been decanted into the world during a period in which King George V had been seriously ill. Daily bulletins, giving news of the royal invalid's progress, were signed by the King's Doctors. Their names were impressive: Lord Dawson of Penn, Sir Humphrey Rollestone, Sir Farquar Buzzard among them. One of these names was initially attached to each whelp, Hervey's namesake having been Sir Farquar Buzzard. Many years later I was to meet that distinguished physician when he had become Regius Professor of Medicine at Oxford. It was pleasant to be able to tell him that a dog of exceptional sagacity and resource had once borne his name.

Before setting out for the walk with which this chapter is mainly concerned, I must record two incidents concerning Hervey, when he and I were in London. Once, to win a five shilling bet, I walked him from Southampton Row to King's Cross keeping to heel and without a lead. On another occasion, during a walk in Kensington Gardens, he suddenly streaked away from me to pass the time of day with a fellow spaniel, who proved to be his brother Lord Dawson of Penn, subsequently called Beau. Hervey took a poor view of London, though our brief sojourns there were greatly helped by both of us being able to spend our nights at the Oxford and Cambridge Musical Club. A small garden at the back of the house provided Hervey with an essential amenity, in which the occasional bone kindly donated by the Steward, Mr. Laws would be discreetly laid to rest among bushes that flanked a diminutive lawn.

From the parental home our walks varied between watching and photographing trains, investigating local pubs to discover, not only the quality of their beer, but also the general 'feel' and response of the landlord and his satellites, not forgetting the shove ha'penny board, as and where one could be found. Another quarry would be churches and, if possible, their resident incumbent.

Since the early abortive attempts of my parents to provide a spiritual runway, through regular attendance at Services in Wimborne Minster, my responses to Anglican blandishments had taken a turn for the better. At the school where all those music teachers came and went, the ritual was, if any thing, even less promising. But at Rottingdean, where Lewis Verey was Rector, there were sermons of real illumination, relating Holy Writ to the vast, glowing and as yet undiscovered fields of literature, poetry and philosophy – of a quality that most of the clergy encountered since might well seek to emulate. To this experience must be added a protracted sojourn with a greatly loved clerical uncle, Hugh le Fleming, to whose Vicarage in the Isle of Wight a varied assortment of brother parsons came and went. They provided a fascinating study – and gave me a deep and abiding interest in the vagaries of Anglican clergy. Since my uncle was a bachelor, there was much talk of 'shop' during meals, unhampered by the presence of wives and families. It was fascinating to overhear the comments of these fellows over the different ways in which they interpreted Standing Orders. Some, climbing up the slippery ladder toward the altitude from which they could be addressed by their flocks as Father This or That: others, feet firmly on terra firma, remained, to borrow an Army phrase, confirmed Bible punchers.

The rival claims of High and Low Church loyalties had received a vigorous stir by the appearance of the 1928 Prayer Book. Rejection of it by Parliament was taken by some as a triumph for the righteous, by others as a deep disappointment and a grievous setback. So the fascinating Ding-Dong continues – merrily on High, somewhat defensively on Low. As Sir Shane Leslie once wrote 'The ideal of the English Church has been to provide a resident gentleman for each parish in the kingdom, and there have been worse ideals.'

Come now for a country walk to view the Church Militant in a remote corner of Dorset as the nineteen-twenties are almost at an end. As Hervey and I set out and 'from Wimborne take our road' northwards over Walford Bridge, he will be keeping closely to heel. When cutting across open country we invariably find a basic courtesy in the people we encounter at work on the land: even farmers and landowners return our greeting with civility, and often friendliness. On these occasions Hervey would walk demurely by my side, looking as though he would not dream of leaving me. But when we are safely out of sight, away from the crops or the woods where pheasants are reared for the annual autumnal slaughter, I would say 'Scoo-loo' and away he would go.

In due course we arrive at the village of Hinton Martell. Here we find *Father* Baverstock happily proclaiming and practising the ritual of Anglo-Catholicism. Proceeding northwards once more we climb the hill to Chalbury, where *Mr.* Lines would be discovered tuned to a very different Liturgical **A**. No frills here, basic ingredients only – plain wholesome stuff, a trifle simple perhaps, even under-cooked for some palates. Following the road down the further side of the hill we come to Horton, past the picturesque but sadly decaying folly, from the summit of which anxious watchers once scanned the southward view for signs of a Napoleonic invasion.

At Horton Mr. De Bary is a thoughtful and studious pastor, whose sermons contained more food for thought than some of his less complex parishioners were able to assimilate. Mr. De Bary has spent much time in literary endeavour, though, it seemed, without much reward or recognition. His wife, Anna Bunston De Bary, is a poet whose work has appeared in several anthologies, her best known piece being the touchingly sincere *Under A Wiltshire Apple Tree*. These two made a charming, kindly, though somewhat wistful pair. They and their way of life, in company with many others, disappeared in the vortex of World War II.

Finally we come to Woodlands, where we find Father Knapp keeping in ritualistic step with his opposite number at Hinton Martell. We find him a bit 'put about' at the moment, for he has discovered that Mr. De Bary has been holding an occasional evening Communion Service. As the Catholic traffic-light for this enterprise is still at red, Father Knapp is both disturbed and displeased. The fact that some of his brethren regard his practices with very mixed feelings is neither here nor there.

Nonetheless he is a high-powered and militant priest. An incident that illustrates his character was an occasion when a parish outing to Weymouth was fixed on a day that dawned with heavy rain pouring from leaden skies. As soon as the bedraggled and depressed party had assembled, they were hastily shepherded into church for Mass. At the very moment the Sanctus bell sounded, the sun appeared through the clouds to usher in a perfect summer day. Not a man to be trifled with!

The interior of Woodlands Vicarage glows with the warmth of friendship. As well as Amy Knapp, the Vicar's wife, there is Ethel Lucas, her sister, brimful of charm and accomplishment. As if by magic an omelette appears for the weary walker, whilst a crunching noise in the vicinity indicates that Hervey's need for sustenance has also been recognized.

Each year at Woodlands there would be a parish pantomime, libretto by 'the reverend' and an occasional tune of mine when traditional sources failed to accommodate Father Knapp's rather wayward and straying metre. A strophic song would begin with admirable verve and clarity, but by the third verse, cross-currents of other influences such as Gerard Manley Hopkins, would demand tailor-made rather than off-the-peg setting.

Among the Woodlands folk was a shepherd, William Miles, who still retained memories of folk songs from his youth in Cranborne Chase. The genuine article had become inextricably mixed with ditties of a more recent age and of very inferior quality. One in particular about a girl called Nelly Ray was sung with such gusto that we expected plaster to fall from the ceiling. Among the genuine remnants were some hitherto uncollected verses to The Dark-Eyed Sailor and a rustic ditty with the refrain 'Shepherd O shepherd will you come home!' Despite offers of gargantuan meals, the invitation is refused until the final blandishment, 'Clean sheets and a pretty girl' at which the singer leaps from his seat and makes an ecstatic exit – to the plaudits of all present. It is doubtful whether either Mr. Lines or Mr. De Bary would permit a ditty of this nature to be performed at a parish function, but at Woodlands it raises an encore every year.

To end our walk, Hervey and I would set out for another two miles to Verwood station, from which we would catch the evening train that pursued a leisurely course from Salisbury – and so to home and bed.

Near Woodlands there stood a tree among fields and over a ditch, where the Duke of Monmouth had been captured in an abortive attempt to usurp the English Crown. From the shelter of the ditch he had been taken to a nearby farmstead known as Holt Lodge: thence to Ringwood and finally to a tragic end in London.

To end this chapter of High and Low, I add a tribute to two other 'resident gentlemen' in their parishes. At Corfe Mullen Canon Edrupp was one of those rare Anglican clergymen who had the happy knack of remaining half way up the ladder. It is surely in this position that the majority of people most appreciate their pastor – a position all too few of them seem inclined to adopt. Now, stepping down several rungs, we come to Kingston Lacey where it is a pleasure to know Mr. Benison. Here there blows a strong north-westerly spiritual gale in vigorous Protestant fashion. No nonsense here either: the voice from this pulpit will make our position absolutely clear. 'Mysticism' proclaims Mr. Benison 'and witchcraft – and *all* other forms of sorcery' are castigated before being swept away into one large untidy, discarded heap. Other and similar pronouncements were motivated by a burning sincerity that earned a deep respect, whatever contrary views might be held. None the less it seemed unduly harsh treatment for the mystics!

Now that country livings have been formed into clusters, it is no longer possible for those once comparatively leisured fellows to thrive on the delightful pastime of deriving stimulus from disagreeing with their immediate neighbours' contrary views and practices. Nor to write those many delightful books on anything and everything from botany to fighting ships. Or the time to pen those carefully documented histories of remote villages, where world events scarcely disturbed their meditations. In such places year in, year out, the church bells pealed or tolled for the eternal verities to be affirmed on every Sunday, down through the gently flowing years, decades and centuries. Or so it seemed in the days when Hervey and I once roamed an as yet unmechanized countryside. For us the world was full of the sounds and scents of early summer: when, at dusk, the sound of nightingales filled the woods as the rising moon 'lifted with slow majesty till it swung clear of the horizon and rode off, free of moorings' into the open sky.

CHAPTER 13

R.V.W.

After I had written to Vaughan Williams to tell him about William Miles and his folk songs, I paid my first visit to 13 Cheyne Walk, a house that looked out over the river Thames by Chelsea Reach. Here the composer and his first wife, Adeline, lived for many years. Autumn dusk was closing in, with an after-sunset glow still reflected in the river. The time of day – and of the year – was uncannily identical to the moment when, a few years earlier, I had emerged from the Winter Gardens at Bournemouth, after Dan Godfrey's performance of *A London Symphony* that had so greatly excited me at the age of thirteen.

It was Mrs. Vaughan Williams who opened the door, greeting me with the words 'Come up – and join us for tea.' My first impression of her was clear and vivid, despite the deepening twilight. There was something pre-Raphaelite in her appearance that, together with a sense of serenity, made me instantly at ease in her company. Already there were signs of a cruel arthritic onslaught that for so many years ruthlessly attacked her. Even then she walked with a stick: her voice was soft, her speech slow and very clear.

I followed her up a flight of stairs to the first floor where, in a candle-lit room, tea, consisting of toast and jam, was proceeding in a leisurely, discursive tempo. R.V.W. was being gently and firmly questioned about some letters he was supposed to have posted. 'Just look in your overcoat pocket, Ralph, and see if by any lucky chance they are still there.' The great man shambled slowly over to a chair on which an enormous overcoat had been thrown. There was a pause – and a huge hand emerged from one of the pockets with a cluster of letters. 'My dear, I *am* so sorry – I must have forgotten them.'

Shortly after this encounter R.V.W. and Maud Karpeles came to Woodlands to hear William Miles. Once again the unfortunate Nelly Ray was proudly introduced before the singer, after a good deal of searching in the mind for 'they old 'uns', was persuaded to sing the songs we all waited to hear. Thus a few oddments were added to the archives of the E.F.D.S.

Subsequently there were more visits to Cheyne Walk, later to Dorking, with scores in hand, on which R.V.W. generously gave me much advice and help. At Cheyne Walk the greeting would be 'My husband is in his top room – go up.' There I would find

R.V.W. sitting, wreathed in pipe-smoke, looking out over the river. Pages of manuscript would be scattered over floor and furniture. After each session I would emerge in a moderately chastened, though reasonably encouraged state of mind. In later years my wife and I would visit The White Gates at Dorking. Then advice was blended with friendly talk. On one occasion when Hervey was with us, the resident cat was outraged by his presence. 'He is usually very amenable,' said Mrs. V. W., 'and fortunately accepts music as part of his normal life. But there was one occasion when he ran screaming from the room: I am afraid it was during a performance on the wireless of my husband's *London Symphony!*'

When war came R.V.W. undertook A.R.P. duties, during which he became a drill instructor to Civil Defence volunteers on Sunday mornings. He also took to planting vegetables, taking us proudly to see the results of his labours. Half the garden had been planted by a skilled helping hand: the rest he had undertaken on his own account. It was both touching and delightful to see how, over half the ground, straight rows of young vegetables marched over the area in military precision. Midway the ranks were broken and scattered, though still flourishing. So must Falstaff's scarecrow army have marched into Gloucestershire!

One of the major delights of the immediate post-war period was the revival of the Three Choirs Festival at Hereford in 1946. At Gloucester in the following year my *Five Psalms* received a first performance. They had now emerged in the full regalia of soprano solo, chorus and orchestra. Despite a withering criticism in *The Times* after the first performance, the work has made many friends, both in these islands and overseas. A partial explanation for this onslaught was given by the critic concerned to a mutual friend. When entering the Cathedral he confided that he was suffering from a 'bellyfull' of music and was in no mood to suffer any more. So it was particularly cheering to have warm praise from R.V.W., who cited for special commendation a place in the score where strings and harp are joined by a flute that doubles the first violins an octave higher. 'I shall crib that,' he said. But the belligerent notice killed the chance of a second performance in London when the work was launched. Perhaps in the future the Psalms may receive the performance for which they have waited so long. Even so R.V.W. included them at the Leith Hill Festival, one of many occasions when they have received a warm reception.

A chance encounter in Dublin revealed a truly characteristic incident. Vaughan Williams had paid a visit to Trinity College in that city and was being driven back to the airport for his return flight. 'Have we,' he asked the driver, 'time to go to Herbert Street to stop for a moment at a house there?' The driver assented; the car duly drew up. R.V.W. slowly got out, walked up some steps to the door. He then stood for a moment, took off his hat, bowed slowly and gravely, turned and came back to the car. As he did so he said to the driver 'I expect you think I'm quite mad: but, you see, Charles Villiers Stanford was born in that house.'

Another incident came to light when I visited Thomas Wood, author and composer, at Bures in Suffolk. In a book kept to record special occasions, two entries attracted particular notice. Shortly after the end of World War II, the Royal Philharmonic Society, of which Thomas Wood had been Honorary Secretary, gave a dinner in honour of the presence of Richard Strauss in London. Strauss was then full of years and honours, with but a short time to live. The dinner had been a welcome gesture of abiding international peace in the world of music and musicians, despite the strife and chaos between nations in time of war. Before the end of the evening Wood had asked Strauss to commemorate so historic an encounter by writing something in his book. 'Vot shall I write?' Strauss had asked: in reply came a discreetly soft intimation of the opening phrase, heard softly on first and second violins, of *Till Eulenspiegel*. It was duly inscribed and signed. Passing on to Vaughan Williams, Wood made a similar request. Immediately came the 'leaping' theme in *Also Sprach Zarathustra*, associated throughout the music with 'the enquiring spirit of Man in the presence of Nature' (in the apt phrase of Norman Del Mar). Underneath the phrase was written 'Leider nicht von R. Vaughan Williams'. Seventy years earlier Brahms had used these same words on a similar occasion when he had written the opening phrase of *The Blue Danube Waltz* as a token of deep admiration for the music of Johann Strauss II.

I had first encountered Thomas Wood long ago, in boyhood days when he had been the young and high-powered Director of Music at Tonbridge School. It is sad that the later resounding success he achieved as world sponsor of *Waltzing Matilda* should have obscured other achievements. These include, not only a considerable amount of effective and enjoyable choral music, but also two outstanding books – *Cobbers*, written in praise of Australia and *True Thomas*, an autobiography of exceptional interest.

By now I had become Assistant Director to Mary Ibberson for the Rural Music Schools Association. As a result of V.W.'s long-standing interest in the welfare of amateur music-makers, the

Rural Music Schools had already, in early days, chosen for their first combined concert in London, the cantata *In Windsor Forest*. The moment had now come when we were planning a twenty-first birthday celebration for the RMS movement. Since the day when two boys living in a Hertfordshire village had asked Mary Ibberson if they could have violin lessons, there were now Schools in nine counties, working in association with education authorities. So our celebration would have to be planned on a large enough scale to include representatives of thousands of students and their teachers, including virtual beginners as well as experienced professional players and singers. We took several very deep breaths – and booked the Albert Hall for the morning and afternoon of November the 18th, 1950.

For the occasion we would need a new work to be specially written. Since the basic industry of Rural Music Schools was – and is – string teaching, both in class and individually, we naturally thought in terms of a Concerto Grosso, for which special parts would be included. There would have to be a *concertino* in which some of our teachers could display their skill, as well as a large *tutti* for the rank and file of students. In addition, we also required extra ad lib parts, so that some beginners might be added to the ranks of those taking part. As we considered various contemporary composers, we were unanimous that Vaughan Williams must be our first choice. But would he do it?

One afternoon I went down to Dorking to discuss the project with R.V.W. He was at once not only interested, but delighted at the thought of writing tunes to be played on open strings as part of the plan. 'The only thing is', he said, 'I am very busy indeed just now writing music for films, but let me think about it.' The story of R.V.W. and his film music has been told elsewhere, but a characteristic reflection about it came out during our talk. In previous films, such as *Coastal Command* and *49th Parallel*, the music had of necessity been both rousing and spectacular for these manifestations of courage and adventure. 'It was a long time' he said 'before they would give me any love music to do.' Recently the chance had come to provide just that very commodity for the film, based on Sheila Kaye-Smith's novel, *The Loves of Joanna Godden*. At last R.V.W. had been given his chance to provide something more deeply expressive and at the same time pastoral in character, evocative of the lonely stretches of Romney Marsh.

A few weeks later a card arrived by post at our London office. 'Your Concerto is finished – come and vet it.'

As soon as our string specialists began to study the score, they found that the simplified parts presented problems that were going to prove incompatible with contemporary methods. The composer had evidently based his approach on the way in which he had himself been taught in early years. At a preparatory school near Brighton* he had been given violin lessons by a Mr. Quirke, that culminated in a performance of Raff's *Cavatina* at a school concert. Seventy years later, at an informal occasion during a Three Choirs Festival, he had been moved to seize a violin and to give a repeat performance, double-stopping and all.

Since the composer's boyhood, considerable changes had taken place in teaching methods. So another journey to Dorking was made, this time in company with Gertrude Collins, to explain our predicament. We needed to obtain R.V.W.'s consent to adapt the parts to present needs. We need not have worried – we returned with the composer's consent to modify the beginners' parts so that those using only first position might be kept from having to shift to half-position. 'You take my music away with you' R.V.W. said to Gertrude 'and write it for me: I am sure you will make it sound much better.' But we kept the composer's own direction 'For those who prefer to play on open strings only!'

Through the co-operation and kindly assistance given by Alan Frank and the music department of the Oxford University Press, scores and parts became available in ample time for rehearsal. Another visit to Dorking was needed to add both the overall time of performance as well as the durations of each of the five movements. On this occasion Arthur Trew was with us: with him, as with Dr. Johnson's friend Edwards, cheerfulness invariably 'broke through' at some point or other, even in deeply serious discussions. It certainly enlivened the mimed performance of the Concerto that took place, for which I would have given much to have had a cine-camera and tape recorder.

R.V.W. with the score on a table in front of him, conducted an imaginary orchestra, singing whichever part happened to catch his eye. Arthur, proud of his acumen in reckoning seconds, chanted ABCDEF 1, ABCDEF 2 while I kept tally. Our task was made more complex by interspersed remarks from the composer such as 'O bother, I meant that to be repeated, but better go on now . . .' I think, on balance, the result was pretty near the mark.

The first performance duly took place in the Royal Albert Hall, with Sir Adrian Boult firmly in control. We had placed the Concertino group on the platform, while the entire Arena was filled with players for the other parts, including some open string

---

*St. Aubyn's, Rottingdean.

specialists! Just as Sir Adrian raised his baton to begin, the Arena lights fused. While they were being repaired, Sir Steuart Wilson emerged from the shadows to make the bidding speech that had been timed to take place elsewhere in the programme. Soon the lights came on – and the sounds of the opening *Intrada* filled the Hall. Of it Frank Howes, then *The Times* Music Critic, wrote 'The composer sets all the bells ringing, with that particular alchemy of which he alone possesses the key.' Also in the *Daily Graphic* the next morning was a picture of a lady from Hampshire, up from the country, complete with shopping bag as well as a violin. Under it was the caption 'Coming, Sir Adrian.'

In the audience was Queen Elizabeth (later to become the Queen Mother) and our President Lord Harewood. R.V.W. was presented with a silver tuning fork that had been specially made by the Goldsmiths Company.

During the 1950s I had several brief meetings with R.V.W. Many of us remember two occasions, one at a Three Choirs Festival, the other at a Philharmonic concert in London when his ninth symphony was first performed. Both audiences rose to their feet when this greatly beloved man appeared. It was heartening to see, during those last years, how much happiness and youthful zest his marriage to Ursula had given him.

In his speech at the Albert Hall, Steuart Wilson quoted some words of Bunyan that could hardly have been more apt. 'Music in the House, music in the heart, music in Heaven for joy that we were there.' For her memoir, Mary Ibberson has taken the last six words: but for all of us who were fortunate enough to have known R.V.W., they will serve admirably as a valediction for a composer 'whose music runs in the veins of England.'

CHAPTER 14

S.H.N.

Towards the end of the 1920s Sir (then Dr.) Sydney Nicholson relinquished his duties as organist of Westminster Abbey to establish a School of English Church Music. In later years this enterprising venture has become widely known and respected as the Royal School of Church Music at Addington Palace, near Croydon.

As a first step S.H.N. acquired a large house at Chislehurst, known in early days as the College of Saint Nicholas. The house provided accommodation for staff and choristers, as well as for offices, library and chapel, the last duly consecrated and be-organed. A stable block was skilfully converted into a hostel for students, mainly aspiring organisti, who would practise their prowess in accompanying services as well as providing the voices needed to complete an *a cappella* choir.

A basic income was to be derived by affiliation fees from cathedral and parish church choirs, not only in these islands, but also from Commonwealth countries. These were as yet mainstays of the British Empire, on and over which it was thought that the sun would never set. To inaugurate the scheme S.H.N. undertook a series of tours, during which he would lecture: there would also be demonstrations as and when suitable singers were to be found. In due course he set his sights on Wimborne Minster.

Since my father, as well as being one of the Minster Governors, was also a member of the choir, he invited S.H.N. to stay with us during the two or three days allotted for the immediate neighbourhood. The presiding organist, an admirable musician though, like many of his kind and generation a rugged isolationist, removed himself from the dangers of contamination! Despite this hazard, the visit was a resounding success, so that S.H.N. was able to add several affiliations to his travelling bag.

A happy sojourn ensued, since S.H.N. wisely left himself sufficient time to enjoy some relaxation. He showed a spontaneous and appreciative interest in the music I was writing and persuaded me to come as a student to Chiselhurst for the ensuing summer term. While there I would take my part in the choir, attend lectures, practise the piano and be given practical help in composing by S.H.N.

Sung services in the Church of England were still flourishing. In those three months we worked our way through both good and indifferent fodder for worship, singing much fine music and a fair amount of pious aspiration – or so it seemed to a 'fringe body' such as I was – and still remain.

So, in May 1930, Hervey and I set out for the College of Saint Nicholas, he as accepted Junior Chorister with a badge attached to his collar.

One of our regular duties was to provide a choir for the Sunday morning Eucharist at St. Sepulchre's, Holborn, where our chaplain, G. H. Salter, was the vicar.

In our composing sessions S.H.N. provided a complete contrast to R.V.W. Unlike Vaughan Williams, who naturally approached problems from a strongly individual standpoint, Sydney Nicholson possessed the ability to mirror any given style of music, since he clearly lacked a characteristic idiom of his own. He would give rapid and brilliant demonstrations – 'This is how Holst, or Palestrina, or Haydn would have gone to work on this tune of yours.' He took me to hear his eight-part setting of the Communion Service at a ceremonial Eucharist in All Saints Church, Margaret Street. Apart from the fun and games inseparable from such above-the-snow-line altitudes of Anglican ritual, the impression that remains of the music is one of impeccable and even brilliant writing, though any hint of burgeoning individuality was invariably swept aside by intimations of other men's music. It was as though a succession of familiar friends had dropped in for a chat and, while present, tended to monopolize the conversation.

In retrospect it seems sad that S.H.N. gave so little of his time and skill to an aspect of music in which he so greatly excelled. As a demonstrator of 'How they might have done it' he was brilliant: so exceptional an ability for applying and explaining different styles and techniques made him an ideal mentor. As might be expected, S.H.N. possessed a flair for extemporization. Any reservations that some of us might have held over his abilities as a composer or choir-trainer were charmed away in a few brief moments before Services; his voluntaries, by way of run-up to the Liturgical wicket, were unfailingly both apposite and masterly.

During the Chislehurst sojourn I also continued an interesting and varied part-time assignment of reviewing records for what was then the Columbia Graphophone* Company. Records, either prior to publication, or previously issued overseas, would arrive

---

*Spelt thus because the word gramophone was the copyright property of His Master's Voice.

periodically. Several people such as I would write commentaries as to whether we felt them to be suitable for the home market. By far the most impressive arrivals at this time were test pressings of Sibelius symphonies 1 and 2. These performances, with a British orchestra conducted by Robert Kajanus, were sponsored by the Finnish government. Since most of us at the time knew little of the composer beyond *Finlandia, Valse Triste* and a curiously uncharacteristic but ubiquitous *Romance in D flat*, the impact was immediate and lasting. By way of contrast, an all-time low was plumbed in a recording from Holland of an organist inciting his Mighty Wurlitzer to decant *When You Come To The End Of A Perfect Day* on to unsuspecting wax. As fodder to chivvy the more idealistic of my fellow-travellers, it never failed to elicit a blasphemous response!

These pleasant explorations, for which I was allocated the latest (Piano-Reflex) Columbia instrument, not only revealed much that was new and exciting, but also provided some invaluable pin-money. The scheme, which lasted for several years, was operated by Herbert Ridout, Columbia's Advertising Manager, a shrewd and kindly man who played no small part in the evolution of the recording industry at a crucial stage of growth. Both at the Head Office in Clerkenwell Road and the studios in Petty France, Westminster, there was a friendly and welcoming atmosphere.

An overwhelming experience at the time was Toscanini's visit to the Queens Hall with the New York Philharmonic Orchestra. For the first concert I was able to obtain a seat on the platform immediately behind the percussion. The first half of the programme consisted of a performance of the *Eroica Symphony* such as I have never heard equalled, let alone surpassed. There was an immense breadth and spaciousness in Toscanini's interpretation at that period. After the interval came Brahms' *Variations on a Theme by Haydn* and a truly majestic account of the overture to *Die Meistersinger*. Towards the end I was obliged to lean back in my chair to make way for the manipulator of the largest cymbals imaginable, so that the player could execute the two notable clashes without inflicting actual bodily damage on a member of the audience! On my return to the College it was surprising to find the organisti entirely oblivious as to so significant an occasion.

Another event, involving the home team this time, was the first massed gathering of our affiliated choirs in the Royal Albert Hall. There we combined to give a gargantuan demonstration Evensong. Our little choir led the entire company in procession from the back of the Hall to the Platform. As we entered, singing the first verse of 'Through The Night Of Doubt And Sorrow' to Martin Shaw's tune 'Marching', S.H.N. stood on the distant platform, in full Doctorate regalia, frantically waving his arms to try and extract more sound from us. The Hall was dimly lit, except for the platform, as befitting a temporary odour of sanctity. It seemed that our long, slow journey through the arena was indeed a twilight of doubt, if not a night of sorrow! However, by the time we reached the third verse, sufficient reinforcements had emerged from the shadows to calm the conductor's panic and to convey to him that the Dawn Chorus had begun.

S.H.N. took life fairly easily whenever he could: choir-practices of a new and complex motet or anthem consisted of one, perhaps two run-throughs. After which we would be told 'Yes, all right, boys, do the best you can with it when we come to the Service.' When some of us were taken on a visit to give a demonstration away from the College, we would return in the evening by train. S.H.N. always generous, would give us dinner in the restaurant car. There was a charming ritual in the matter of drink: when a waiter emerged, proffering sherry by way of prelude – 'Sherry, gentlemen?' 'No thank you, Waiter.' As soon as this human St. Bernard had passed on to the next table, our host would scratch his head, a sure sign that an idea was about to be launched. Then he would say 'Well, you know, it's been a busy day, a very busy day indeed; I think perhaps for once, just for once; – Hi Waiter, we'll all take sherry please.' A similar performance would be given over a drink with our food, sometimes even for brandy with coffee!

It is pleasant to recall many informal discussions when the great man, swinging one of his short though purposeful legs over the arm of a chair, digging the stem of his pipe into his grizzled hair, would show himself over and over again to be a rare conversationalist and beguiling raconteur.

Among visitors to the College, some of whom would give lectures, were Geoffrey and Martin Shaw, holding each other in touching loyalty and affection. Charles Hylton-Stewart, then at Rochester; Harvey Grace, living nearby, would join us for Sunday Evensong. During the week he edited *The Musical Times* as and when he could tear himself away from cricket at Lords! Kindly ecclesiastics of all grades from Bishops to Deacons, would drift in and out, sometimes pregnant with sermons, at others just for the pleasure of watching the laity at work or to fraternize with all and sundry.

As students we tended to divide ourselves into two groups – either for the Establishment or in Opposition. For the Establishment Gerald Knight, already the anointed Heir Apparent, was chief spokesman. Soft-voiced, as befitting a Cornishman, he would gently chide us when he felt we needed to become a little more decorous in our general bearing. Leslie Green, as Secretary, kept a watchful, tolerant and sometimes amused eye on us, without ever being drawn into a discussion. Godfrey Hewitt, then emerging from his native Yorkshire for the first time, went his way in an exemplary manner: subsequently to achieve notable distinction in Ottawa. Harry Barnes, when not singing tenor parts or busy in administrating our affairs, would appear in the garden preceded by an outsize cigar, behind which he would contemplate life with a quizzical, friendly gaze. Invariably cheerfulness would break through any heated discussion in which we would try in vain to inveigle him.

The undoubted leader of the Opposition was Frank Baker, then assistant secretary, later to win considerable acclaim as the writer who created Miss Hargreaves, most memorable of many characters. At the College he was zealously aided and abetted by his friend John Raynor, subsequently the composer of many songs, still too little known, but which bid fair to win posthumous fame for their begetter. John was one of the musicians whose responses lie very close to the terrain of words, since he was also a poet. It was Frank who brought to light a description John had written about his childhood, that was later to be published under the title of 'Westminster Childhood'. Both of them proclaimed a wider interest in life than most of the other students; both were apt, as I was, to look further afield and to be less amenable to petty restrictions and conventions, less dedicated exclusively to the prevailing total addiction to the mystique of the organ loft.

Also, surprisingly in this company and as fleetingly as myself, was Robin Richmond, with sights firmly set on Mighty Wurlitzers and John Compton organs that still held cinema audiences in thrall. It seemed that some members of the Establishment found his presence unsettling, but to the Opposition he was a considerable asset. When returning from an occasional evening visit to a nearby pub, Robin would walk gravely up to a lamp-post, stop, take off his hat and say 'Good night, old chap; nice to have met you – thanks for the light.' Quick on the cue, Hervey would proceed to leave his card on it.

Within the Chislehurst perimeter there were various colourful characters who seemed to occupy squatters' rights on the hinterland that, a year or two later, became Petts Wood. These varied individuals turned up regularly at certain pubs for their evening libations, welcoming any addition to their company with eager zest. For them the prospect of a new audience made an excuse to give repeat performances of very tall stories. These added zest to our evening jaunts, made a welcome change from prolonged doses of Walmesley, Croft, Harwood and other purveyors of blameless euphony, but seemed to give short measure in vitamin content. When funds permitted, we would stand drinks to the narrators.

The College grounds were tended by two custodians, Messrs. Meakins and Baker. They were true countrymen of a kind now increasingly rare; in courtesy, forbearance and in what used to be called good manners they excelled, while at the same time maintaining a sturdy independence. Like Harry Barnes, they looked on life with a quizzical eye, but their responses were at the same time sardonic, yet tolerant. They were staunch believers in traditional country remedies and the use of herbs for ailments. Of these memory recalls only an unshakeable faith in the efficacy of June rain. During that month they would catch and bottle as much as they could for use in the coming winter.

The garden was said to be haunted, as indeed it was, since it provided an experience – for others as well as myself – of a strange and sinister visitation. Before giving an account of a totally unexpected and strangely dramatic experience, I must emphasize that, in a visit paid to the place nearly forty years later, it seemed beyond doubt that the shadow that had formerly given so strange and sinister an aspect had been completely exorcized and dispersed – there was no trace of it at all. Let the reader who shuns contact with the supernatural, or who regards such matters as moonshine, turn now to the following chapter.

A few weeks before making my entry as a student at Chislehurst, S.H.N. had asked me to come and see both him and the College. We were to discuss arrangements and I was to receive a briefing in what would be expected of me while there. It was a glowing afternoon in early spring: the expected 'little talk' took place as we strolled round the garden. We had left the terrace and made our way down a grass path towards a tennis court that had been cut out of steeply-sloping terrain. The court was thus surrounded on three sides by a steep bank on which rhododendron bushes had been planted. The fourth side was flanked by a path that ran downhill towards a gate, with a fork that led up through some trees towards the house. Near the tennis court we paused beside a large and splendid beech tree. As we talked I felt a light touch on my arm. I heard myself say 'Yes, what do you want?' S.H.N. gave me what country people sometimes call 'an old-fashioned look' and said 'Perhaps we'd better move on.' That incident I forgot – until later. Strangely it was an intimation of what was to follow, after my return as a student. On a Saturday evening in May, soon after the College term had begun, I was returning from London alone. There were three stations near the College; I had chosen one from which there was a short cut back through the garden. As I came in through the gate the light was fading. Coming up the path, down which S.H.N. and I had strolled in the opposite direction a few weeks earlier, the beech tree stood to the left of it, while on the right the rhododendron bushes on the bank, now in full bloom, showed clearly in the dusk. A pavilion, painted white, was also visible. Standing on the tennis court I saw a man, in full evening dress, with a pistol pressed against his forehead, his hand on the trigger. Involuntary I called out 'Look out what you're doing with that thing.' When I looked again, the figure had vanished. As I walked into the College there was – or seemed to be – a woman in the shadow of some bushes outside the main entrance, in a state of considerable distress. She touched my arm and said 'Don't let him get you – *please* don't let him get you!' I gave myself a shake – and, believe it or not, dismissed the incident from my mind. It seemed that I was imagining such things.

On the following Saturday I was again returning from London at about the same time, in company with three or four other students. As the train slowed for the station at which I had previously alighted, I prepared to leave the carriage. 'Come on' I said 'Let's go back by the shortest way.' Nobody moved: 'No' they said 'We're going back by the road.' As no further comment was forthcoming, we duly returned by another route. Later, in response to questioning, one of them said to me 'Look – we never use the garden way after dark. The story goes that a previous owner of the place did a murder here – some woman or other – and then went into the garden and shot himself. So I should keep to the road at night if I were you.' Then of course I remembered – all too vividly – my own experience of the previous week.

During my three months sojourn it seemed that, as the shadow of evening lengthened over the garden, we became aware of an emanation, indeed a presence of something sinister and malignant. As the rhododendrons faded the influence appeared to diminish in potency, though several of us were constantly aware of it. So that our return visit forty years later was made the more pleasant by the discovery that a cloud had been effectively dispersed.

Shortly after I had left the College, the beech tree was felled. Nobody knew why – it was a fine tree and in prime condition. S.H.N. would impatiently brush aside any questions asked about it. There is, however, an age-old link between certain trees that are said to become the habitation of unquiet spirits. Ariel had been imprisoned in an oak until released by Prospero. Meanwhile, by way of valediction, S.H.N. had given me a cautionary talk, in which he urged me to keep what he called my 'morbid imagination' within reasonable bounds. At the same time he admitted that there were said to be 'strange happenings' around the place. 'I've looked for them' he said 'but never found a trace of anything strange or unusual.' In my own experience, there have been several strange encounters of a similar nature, though none as dramatic or as vivid, so that I am thankful to have kept clear of such things for the greater part of life. One world at a time should be enough – if not too much – for most of us. So let me end this chapter with a prayer for these, and all other troubled and restless spirits, May they find peace and rest from their exile, for assuredly it is not only the living who need our intercessions.

CHAPTER 15

Songs of Summer

Immediately after the end of term at Chislehurst, the College was filled with visitors. Men and women of all ages came to sing under the inspired direction of Sir Edward Bairstow, the presiding maestro at York Minster. One or two of us stayed on to share in an unforgettable experience.

Bairstow had a rare gift for taking a modest and unassuming anthem or motet; he would then immediately recapture the inspiration of the composer when writing it. I remember with particular delight our singing of *How Goodly Are Thy Tents, O Jacob* by that staunch Anglican, The Rev. Sir F. Gore Ouseley. We were given a short account of how the composer, seeing for the first time the plain of Lombardy in bright sunshine while travelling over the St. Gotthard Pass, had been moved to recall a particular passage from the Book of Numbers – 'As the valleys are they spread forth, as gardens by the river's side . . . and as cedar trees beside the waters.' The spirit that had moved Ouseley all those years ago was truly with us then. Towards the end of the summer school the stimulus had reached boiling point. As a much needed antidote I took myself one evening to London where, from the departure platforms of Euston and King's Cross, I happily watched the night expresses begin their northward journeys. This experience, assisted by bread, cheese and beer at a nearby hostelry, contrived to restore as much stability as I could muster at the time. But what a stir there would be to-day if Royal Scots and Claughtons reappeared at Euston, while Gresley Pacifics and Ivatt Atlantics once again made Cubitt's rounded roof ring with the triumphant hiss of steam.

On the following day Harry Barnes and I set out for Dorset, in a car we had contrived to borrow from a mysterious member of the theatrical profession. It was an open four-seater Phoenix that had obviously led an eventful and somewhat raffish life. Provided we gave it almost as much oil as petrol, it behaved in an exemplary and uncannily responsive manner.

By way of valediction Frank Baker had given me a poem, by Dean Hutton of Winchester, that had just appeared in *The Church Times*. Frank had been a chorister at Winchester, where he remembered the Dean with esteem and affection. The poem – 'In A Sleepless Night' – is the meditation of a dying man, listening to a singing bird at first light. The coming of day is a symbol of future release and fulfilment. The setting was to become the first of the four songs that were to constitute a modest bid for a hearing in the market place.

During our stay in Wessex we spent several days exploring the Isle of Purbeck. Apart from a spreading rash of what was known as 'ribbon development' along the lower road between Corfe Castle and Swanage, Purbeck was still an idyllic land, with valleys filled with little fields and skilfully tended hedges. The downs, open and welcoming with only an occasional fence, had not been criss-crossed by barbed wire and cultivation. Larks sang above them, as yet unaccompanied by the drone of tractors with their attendant exhaust fumes. We could walk from Corfe westward along the ridge of the downs, past Creech Barrow and on to Arish Mell Gap. There, in the hollow, lay Monastery Farm, where a gargantuan tea could be had at half-a-crown a head. At the *Greyhound* in Corfe, there was never any problem about providing bacon and eggs for those unable to afford a full lunch or dinner.

Other memories of Purbeck abound in the mind. Shared sessions of poetry and music in the company of Monk Gibbon: sojourns with Norman Notley and David Brynley in their cottage at Little Woolgarstone. Two voices wonderfully blended singing duets by Purcell and others in peaceful 'hearthside ease'. Once when there I awoke to a perfect summer morning at daybreak and 'stole out unbeknown' to watch the sun rise from the top of the down above Rempstone Woods. Poole Harbour lay spread across the middle distance, grey-blue in the half light, surrounded by heathland over which the heather was just coming into bloom. Eastward lay the Solent; over it, just above the western tip of the Isle of Wight, the sun rose. The first beam showed the Needles in pure white. The whole scene became a vivid realization of Monteverdi's glowing madrigal *Ecco Mormorar L'Onde*. In the earlier phase, before this spectacular moment, the air had seemed full of intimations such as Delius so eloquently proclaimed in *A Song Before Sunrise*.

Down on the heath below, not far from the harbour edge, lay Fitzworth Farm. There, every summer could be found in residence Cuthbert Kelly, founder and onlie begetter of the English Singers. To them came the privilege of bringing the rewards of Edmund Fellowes' English Madrigal School to rebirth and acclamation. Visitors to Fitzworth would be met at the donkey gate hard by the Studland road in a veteran car. Cuthbert's manipulation of the heathland track to the farm was performed in a manner worthy of Hereward the Wake. Happy and carefree days would begin after breakfast with a Morning Office that consisted of playing Haydn symphonies in an arrangement for two pianos and eight hands. When other singers were also present the sound of voices would mingle with the song of larks in the sky.

Among these voices none fell more gratefully on the ear than that of Nellie, our hostess, Cuthbert's beautiful and kindly wife, who would accompany herself on a lute. Violet Carson, her sister, later to achieve resounding fame as a denizen of Coronation Street, would delight us with her own special brand of charm. Songs such as 'These Foolish Things' and 'The Way You Look To-night' were flowing on their happy way through our days. Except for Frederick Loewe's superlative tunes for *My Fair Lady*, that particular brand of alchemy seems to have left no other progeny. Among the singers who came and went during those summer days were Dorothy Silk, Joyce Sutton, Steuart Wilson and Eric Greene.

On one occasion when the English Singers needed a replacement on the tenor line, Cuthbert told us that he had found and engaged a young and quite unknown singer. 'The name is Pears' he said, 'Peter Pears – and I think he may well surprise us all before very long.' Those who knew Cuthbert Kelly remember his particular insight into problems of interpretation. 'Always *wait* upon the music' he would say 'and find out what it wants to do with *you* – never what you think you ought to be doing with it.' In the evenings Cuthbert would read aloud, almost invariably with an essay of Max Beerbohm included. Of these we would demand repetitions, in particular 'William and Mary' and 'A Clergyman'. (O Dreams, O Destinations . . .)

The holiday with Harry finished with a visit to the Cotswolds. Returning to the point where our ways diverged, we stopped at an inn at Cricklade for a morning libation. In a very few moments Harry had produced his violin: we were invited into a room where there was a piano and proceeded to play the César Franck violin sonata to the most appreciative audience imaginable. Our hostess – memory suggests that the family name was Maunders – generated an enthusiasm which, with the aid of exceptionally well-kept ambrosia, sent us out into the sunlight street in a state of bliss. The Phoenix seemed to know what was afoot – it was evidently an old hand at taking charge! So, though in considerably greater degree, had the carters, returning from Wimborne market, processed up the Straight Borough with horses, their ears pricked, in complete control!

An unexpected invitation to join some friends in Galloway awaited my return. In my pocket were the poems of Mary Webb, whose work was having a posthumous boom after Stanley

Baldwin had praised it in a radio talk. Alone and happily exploring Glentrool I came upon a poem called *The Hills of Heaven*. When, in the following year, my setting of this was first sung at the Wigmore Hall with Edward Forsyth as singer, two people of particular significance were in the audience. One was Mary Webb's husband, Mr. H. B. L. Webb who, in a subsequent letter, wrote 'Your setting would have delighted Mary's heart.' Also present, to our great delight, was John Coates. Though singing less than formerly, he nevertheless took the song to his heart and sang it. In a moment of youthful zeal I sent him a photograph of myself, a gesture he reciprocated. His comment was characteristic – 'I shall let the photo's admonishing look quizz at me while I negotiate The Hills of Heaven!'

Rupert Shephard and I had kept in touch since our early school days together. Once more back in Wimborne, he came to share the end of this particularly carefree holiday. Rupert had just emerged from the Slade School and was on the threshold of his painting career. In exchange for a sample of his skill, I made a setting of a poem of W. B. Yeats – *To An Isle In The Water* – for which he seemed to be needing a tune, since lines of the poem kept emerging in a meditative way as he worked. Like everyone else who had attempted to set any poems by Yeats to music, I encountered the invariable stonewall lack of response to a request for permission to do so. Fortunately Monk Gibbon was at hand to intercede, which he did with only partial success, though, it seemed, just sufficient to enable the song to be heard. In his book about Yeats, Monk claimed that I had taken 'french leave!'*

For this poem there was already a formidable rival in the field, since Rebecca Clarke had already made and published a setting. She took a disapproving attitude to what she considered an encroachment on occupied territory. After a conciliatory lunch generously provided by our mutual friend May Mukle, we called a truce. It was shortly after this encounter that May had the happy thought of founding the MM (Mainly Musicians) Club in Argyll Street. There, for many years, musicians of my generation happily forgathered.

It was said that Yeats had been encouraged to set his face against the encroachment of music after an occasion when he had received an invitation to attend a massed choral event. The programme was to include a setting of *The Lake Isle Of Innisfree* for

---

*The Masterpiece and the Man: Yeats as I knew him Monk Gibbon, Hart Davis 1959

innumerable voices in consort. Since the poem clearly expresses the passionate plea of one man for solitude, the poet must have felt that musicians and music-makers were an unduly cloth-headed race. Even Peter Warlock, or in this case his *alter ego* Philip Heseltine, encountered similar resistance in his attempt to launch *The Curlew*, that strangely haunted, powerful and sorrow-laden song-cycle.

The fourth song was an arrangement of *Sheep Shearing*, a Dorset folk song that had come to me through an arrangement for male voice chorus by E. J. Moeran. It was sung on a record by John Goss and the Cathedral Male Voice Quartet. This beautiful song had been collected at Wootton Fitzpaine. These singers had taken to Richard Terry's recently published arrangements of sea shanties with skill and zest. Bracing sea breezes had given a welcome lift to the folk song industry, then showing signs of wilting. Tunes such as *Billy Boy, Shenandoah, Haul Away, Joe* and others had retained more of the original vitamins than many other reclamations that had undergone virtual castration in the interests of school and drawing room consumption.

While Rupert sketched and painted in the environs of Wimborne, I was busily watching and photographing trains. During a discreet trespass on railway property I encountered Peter Trodd. We at once made contact and I was invited to pay a visit to his signal box. The box controlled a junction where a spur of the Somerset and Dorset line joined the old South Western route between Southampton and Dorchester. It stood high on an embankment, hard by a truly baronial arch that carried the line over a one-time carriage drive to Canford Manor, then in process of becoming a public school. There was a fine view over the Stour valley, enough rail traffic to keep one's interest gently simmering, with intervals for the occasional cup of tea. In later years Peter became a guard: several homeward journeys were made extra pleasant by sojourns of talking en route.

He was a true friend and loyal railwayman, but there was an occasion when the latter quality was put to a severe test. In earlier days as a signalman, Peter had been working near Basingstoke. Returning from duty one night he noticed, and reported, an earthslip on an embankment that carried the main line. In due course he was summoned to Waterloo to receive a reward for an action that must have averted a serious accident. The Chairman solemnly handed him a cheque for £5! Peter looked at it, blinked and said 'I think there's been some mistake here; this had better go to the Orphanage.' In such company the sound of 'slowly stepping trains' pursuing their leisurely way through a summer landscape made a truly Dvorakian coda to a youthful holiday now half a century ago.

During the intervening years Rupert Shephard has established himself as an artist of high quality and integrity. Meanwhile my own journey by the slow train has brought many compensations.

CHAPTER 16

A London Overture

With a Wigmore Hall recital only a year ahead, the time had come for intensive piano practice. I had arranged to spend several months in London, sharing a flat with George Reeves, my friend and teacher, and Edward Forsyth. Edward, after a meteoric rise to reasonable affluence, gained by applying Scottish acumen on the Stock Exchange, had decided to investigate the possibilities of a career in opera and song. He was lucky enough to have some coaching from Raimond Von Zur Mühlen, a celebrated singer who had known Brahms. Now he lived at Wiston Old Rectory in Sussex, to which place of pilgrimage came singers from far and near. From these sessions Edward would return full of elation and with profound admiration for the ageing Meister. From this exalted quarter, in due course, came a benediction on my songs. Many of Mühlen's Rabelaisian comments have passed into legend, as when a young soprano from Lancashire came to be coached in an operatic role, which she proceeded to sing throughout from tonic sol-fa. Mühlen's astonishment found vent in his remark – 'Do you know, she sang the whole role from pigeon-shit!' On the other hand, as others have testified, his unflagging quest for the highest possible quality of beauty of tone in voice production has been an inspiration to countless singers.

Fortunately our flat in Cornwall Gardens was at the top of the building, so that a good deal of the sound emitted in tripartite music-making floated skyward. The denizens immediately below seemed to take their share of the backwash with kindly forbearance.

Intensive practising was interspersed with invaluable, though often ruthless, coaching from George. To him came a constant stream of recitalists and pupils. His skill both as accompanist and teacher is a cherished memory to almost everyone with whom he came in contact. As a teacher he was infinitely patient and wise, invariably demanding the best – and usually getting it. Some would emerge from a session elated, others chastened and wistful. On one occasion a rehearsal with a temperamental young cellist came to an abrupt and premature end. After she had made a dramatic exit, George appeared, looking very sad. 'Look' he said 'at this lump on my forehead; she threw something at me – I think it was a box!'

During our meals together he would describe these encounters

with illuminating commentary, quick to praise as well as
'unmasking' attempts on the part of some to appear other than in
their true musical entities. There was a famous soprano who
seemed to have an endless supply of pornographic literature.
Notable examples would be left between visits for our entertainment, and often sheer amusement. On one occasion we had
mislaid a copy of *The Life and Loves* of Frank Harris, then only
available from Paris *sans* imprint. As we had a splendid young
woman of sturdy independence and unquestionable virtue to look
after our material needs, we naturally felt some responsibility for
her moral welfare, particularly as she had come from an
orphanage. When we anxiously asked her if by any chance she had
seen the book lying around, she said 'Oh that – you needn't have
worried – I read it at my last place!' This was surprising in that she
had been passed on to us from the household of a composer, whose
modest output of educational music is remarkable for its sustained
dullness.

Of many concerts during those months, three must suffice for
recall. Whenever possible we would go to the Wigmore Hall
when, as on many occasions, George was accompanying – 'At the
piano' was the current phrase. During a cello recital given by
Maurice Eisenberg, the programme included a Sonata (No 1) by
Jean Huré. Just as in Proust's great novel, a phrase in a violin
sonata by Vinteuil so greatly caught the imagination of Swann, so
here were several phrases of lyrical eloquence that immediately
'had me by the heart.' Huré, who is said to have been born of
Breton parentage, composed this piece in 1906. Anyone who has
ever played the piano part will not need to be told that the
composer was also an organist. Never, except perhaps in Busoni
transcriptions, has the player more urgently needed three hands –
or a pedal board. Since George possessed a flair as an interpreter of
French music, Huré could have had no better advocate. We shall
never know whether Vinteuil's phrase derived from Fauré or
from Franck, or that it may perhaps have been an amalgam of
both composers that produced a cross-fertilization in Marcel's
mind.

There was a recital by Rachmaninov: on the platform he
appeared withdrawn and aloof. He would give an occasional
glance at the audience, as though we were a necessary and
inescapable reality that had to be endured and reluctantly
placated. So might Orpheus have appeared at the gates of Hades!
From the very first note a spell was cast. Here was *legato* playing of
rare and surpassing smoothness, a *legato* that pervaded every shade
of dynamic from velvet *pianissimi* to climaxes shot with gold and

silver tone. Nothing was unduly emphasized – there was no need for underlining or italics.

Occasionally there would be encounters with the eminent. After Szigeti had given a glowing performance of the Brahms *Violin Concerto* at Queens Hall, George and I visited the great man in the Artists' room. During a recent tour he and George seemed greatly to have appreciated each other. We duly praised Szigeti for his performance, telling him how well he had played. After a moment of thought, he cordially agreed with us. 'You are right' he said 'You are quite right. To-night I play well, yes, my best, I think, my very best.' By way of follow-up he added 'Next week I go to America' (here a gentle nudge) '*Fifth* time I go to America. It is sad, but I must leave my wife and little child in Paris while I go.' Here we made sympathetic noises; but he smiled, shrugged his shoulders and held out his hands in a gesture of despair as he added 'But, you see, it is *my* fault – it is after all simply my *own* fault that I must go.' So we bade him farewell, bon voyage – and came softly away.

Szigeti was one of the earliest among performing musicians to champion the cause of Bartok's music, then scarcely known in England, apart from some smaller pieces for violin and piano. He was thus truly prophetic when he said 'You see, you in England are not yet ready for Bartok – he is much too advanced for you. But you will come to recognize and acclaim him as one of the greatest — if not the very greatest – composer of this century.' Twenty years later, when the six string quartets were first performed here as a cycle, we realized how right he had been.

The London orchestras were in a state of flux. The B.B.C. had recently sponsored a greatly enlarged symphony orchestra that, under the guidance of Sir Adrian Boult (he was still 'Dr.' then) was to set a new standard in performance. The old order, in which the deputy system proliferated, was on the wane, soon to disappear to all intents and purposes. Sir Thomas Beecham, losing no time in once again mustering new forces, brought the London Philharmonic Orchestra into being. The LSO, ubiquitous then as now, had no regular conductor, but maintained a gallant and competitive place in the triumvirate. From Manchester there came the Hallé Orchestra in a series of concerts directed by that splendid Irishman Sir Hamilton Harty. A strong sense of unity, as well as vital and exciting playing, made these occasions particularly memorable. In the music of Berlioz and Sibelius, Harty and the Hallé excelled. The Establishment had already surrendered to the claims of Sibelius, but were still apt to look askance at Berlioz. After Harty had revealed in full measure the splendours created by that engaging Frenchman, the diehards capitulated. Twenty years on, others were to perform a similar service for Bruckner and Mahler.

With Bruckner it was a case of gradual infiltration: but many who were young in the thirties owe their introduction to Mahler through a recording of *Das Lied von der Erde*, conducted by Bruno Walter and recorded (in a limited edition!) during a concert performance in Vienna. Again, a few years later, it was the gramophone that provided a similar act of benediction for Monteverdi, then virtually unknown in these islands and even 'played down', notably by Parry, as a composer of little importance or interest.

As winter gave place to spring, the call of the countryside was compelling. It was answered by an occasional day spent on Box Hill and the surrounding terrain. Sometimes the small friendly dog from the flat below would accompany me; his delight in the discovery of a completely new world was both touching and rewarding. After we returned he would subside into a coma all through the following day. It was ever the roads out of London that beckoned me, even though the time spent there was both happy and stimulating. There was still a sense of pride about the place, unlike the belittered squalor that pervades its streets today.

Friends whose company was particularly welcome included Rupert Shephard. He had recently emerged from the Slade and was painting, then as now, assiduously and with increasing confidence. From a characteristic lair in Fitzroy Square – invariably referred to by him as 'my place' – he would materialize as though from outer space to join in whatever frolic might be in view.

Christopher Wilson, urbane and always immaculate in appearance, would discourse with grave enthusiasm on the music of Brahms and of Johann Strauss. He was later to make a successful career in BOAC. We had first known each other on the Isle of Wight, his home and the scene of protracted sojourns on my part. From Ryde we had often walked out over Dame Anthony's Common to Firestone Woods and Mersley Down, tiring the sun with our talk and sending him down the evening sky. We also paid visits to Totland Bay where, in retirement, lived Richard Harris, who had been in charge of music at Cranleigh during Christopher's school days there. He now lived in a diminutive house, in which the sitting room was at least half filled by a magnificent Bösendorfer grand piano. His time was spent in almost equal division by playing it, smoking his pipe and in rounds of golf. Somewhere, squeezed between the walls, there must have been a

housekeeper to provide the magnificent tea he invariably proffered. Before and after it I would play recently acquired pieces in
exchange for gruff, though always constructive commentary.
Once a year he would visit friends in Berkshire where he would
encounter the two charming, if high-powered sisters Adela
Fachiri and Jelli D'Aranyi. They also will be appearing in this
narrative at a later stage. Aspects of Richard Harris' personality –
the bearded visage, the deep muffled voice that seemed to rise
from unprecedented depths, as well as his strong addiction to golf,
vividly recall Vladimir Brusiloff in one of Wodehouse's *Oldest
Member* stories.

Daniel Kelly became a friend and companion whose company
was specially welcome, notably in moments of depression. He
would come with me for an evening meal at Alexis in Lisle Street
when funds permitted. He was also a delightful companion for a
day's walking, often on Sunday and usually in Epping Forest
(before the thugs moved in). Quiet, kindly and wise, Daniel was
also, unlike Mr. Mulliner, a very good listener. His subsequent
achievement as an accompanist derived in large measure from
help and encouragement generously given by George.

Frank Baker, whom we last encountered administering the affairs
of the organisti at Chislehurst, became involved in a head-on
collision with those extremely conventional characters. A clash of
personalities led to an explosion: when the smoke had cleared and
the dust settled, Frank spent much time with us, to our delight. He
was still undecided as to whether to concentrate on composing or
writing, but wisely chose the latter course. Few people, encountered before or since, have proved as stimulating or original as the
future creator of Miss Hargreaves. Soon there came an offer for
him to play the organ at the church of St. Just in Penwith, together
with a cottage in which to live and to write in peace. Already the
Duchy had claimed his allegiance during a holiday spent there. In
a book that belongs to a later period – *The Call of Cornwall* – he has
given an eloquent account of a life-long allegiance to that western
land of legendary potency.

Thomas Tunnard Moore would appear sporadically, cheering
the three of us with his individual brand of wit and humour, as
well as inciting us to early morning bathes in the Serpentine. For
him also, the future was uncertain; many of us had been ill-
equipped to earn a living, mainly due to parental good intentions,
based on their own past experience and no longer valid for us.
Instead they insisted on unsuitable preparation for our particular
needs. 'We have to do what we think is best' they said: appeals fell
on deaf ears.

A notable *revenant* from Canada who appeared at this time was Jim Campbell McInnes. Older people recalled past glories when he and Gervase Elwes had sung together in performances of *Gerontius*. These had taken place in the days when entrenched Protestant interests had found Newman's poem too heady and Romish for their liking. Stanford, while admiring the music, had complained that the work 'stinks of incense,' while others, remarkable for lack of courtesy, grudged the Mother of God her prominence. Staunch advocates of Elgar and Newman had done much to quieten the uneasy prejudice of those to whom any point of view other than their own was anathema. At midsummer a party was given for Jim McInnes by Mary Fletcher, firm and true friend to many musicians. His singing still retained a quality of rare felicity that gave immense pleasure to all who heard him during his visit to England.

During that evening party in Notting Hill Gate it became clear that Mary Fletcher and I were to become friends. In the future there were to be many sojourns at her cottage in the Vale of Pewsey, under the lea of Martinsell. In these surroundings my wife-to-be and I did much of our courting. Also present was a young pianist from New Zealand, Vera Moore, whose playing, particularly of Couperin, was exceptionally sensitive and eloquent. So another friendship was formed, and continued during many country walks. During them Vera would discourse on many aspects of the arts; to her I owe an introduction to the poetry of T. S. Eliot, whose *Ash Wednesday* had just appeared, causing a considerable flutter in the literary dovecote. It provided an essential runway for the take-off of the *Four Quartets*, as they appeared, one by one.

So the time came to return to Dorset where, after duly giving a Wigmore Hall recital and another in Bournemouth, I set about building a teaching connection round the parental roof-tree. In this also Vera was to play a vital part, by introducing me to friends of hers who were to change the course of my life.

CHAPTER 17

Da Capo

Forming a teaching connection proved to be a slow and uphill undertaking. The first two pupils to arrive were both elderly. One of them, a redoubtable and ham-fisted lady, played the organ at a nearby village church. She habitually chose the hymns, excelling herself one Easter morning when, at an early Celebration, she and the choir led off gaily with 'The Day Thou Gavest, Lord, Is Ended!' The next pupil, a man, claimed to be in close touch with the Spirit World. He had been told by his chums in the spheres that I was the boy-o to whom he should reveal some songs. I was to give these a bit of a wash and brush up for possible unleashment on the home market. The words were by contemporary poets, the music allegedly despatched from Elysium in package deals by composers no longer in this world. These fellows were said to be anxious to decant their afterthoughts to anyone willing or able to take delivery of them. Transmission and reception on this occasion must have been even more primitive than usual under the circumstances, though honest and starry-eyed intentions were evident enough as a basis.

Other and younger pupils gradually appeared, including a cluster at a small and congenial girls' school in Southbourne. The Headmistress, Louise Wotton, soon became a true friend. After the day's teaching there would be tea with her, often in company with a nearby doctor, Tom Scott by name. His wife was an avid bridge-player, whose cronies filled the house during these orgies. On such occasions, which seemed continuous, she despatched her thankful husband down the road, so as to be clear of the fray. The result was our gain, since this kindly, wise and warm-hearted man was a delightful companion. After tea I would play to them: Hervey, still happily with me, would lie quietly all day while teaching was in progress. He always knew when sessions were about to end; then he would come to life and proceed to exert his considerable charm on all present. Unlike far too many other people's dogs, he knew his place in the pattern of life.

One of the mistresses at King's Cliffe School, Lilias Howden, had written a play called *Tweon-Ea*, The Land Between Waters. The plot was based on the legendary story of the building of Christchurch Priory, that stands beside the meeting of the rivers Stour and Avon, not far from the school. The legend tells of the first attempts to build the church on higher ground near Hurn, a few miles inland. From there the stones were miraculously moved by night down to the place where the Priory was eventually built. While this was in progress a mysterious, unknown workman appeared, dressed as a monk, at a moment when the workmen were lifting a heavy beam into position. It proved to be too short in length, but he urged them to try once more, when it slotted perfectly into position. The play also deals with the impact of the new Faith on the *dramatis personae*, many of whom cling firmly to the old pagan way of life, while others are caught up and held in the revelation of something new and strange. I was able to provide some incidental music: later the script came into my possession. It could provide the basis for an opera that I am unlikely to be able to complete. Perhaps another composer will be able to set a seal on the undertaking.

In the early 1930s there was still a demand for piano transcriptions. Thanks to Christopher Wilson, I had succumbed to the blandishments of Johann Strauss the Younger. This led to a search for a reasonably authentic piano realization of the waltzes, starting with *The Blue Danube*. Examples proffered by the Charing Cross Road fraternity may still be found as fodder for tap room pianos. Extending the search along Great Marlborough Street, I found various effusions known as paraphrases, designed to show off the perpetrators' keyboard dexterity, though showing little, if any fidelity to the unfortunate masterpiece subjected to assault and battery. These biological freaks seemed mostly to be of either Polish or Hungarian origin. So I set about producing the kind of pianistic approach I needed: it was immediately published and appreciated.

Ethel Bartlett and Rae Robertson had created a vogue for two-piano music that still made considerable use of transcriptions. For this medium I contributed an arrangement of *The Blue Danube*, together with *Tales from the Vienna Woods*. Both still survive from the period, together with some Bach, notably the *St. Anne Prelude and Fugue* for organ. This came into being after unsuccessful attempts to master the Busoni version for piano solo. In earlier days my arrangement was played by Cyril Smith and Phyllis Sellick, to whom it is dedicated. Such makeshifts have now become anachronisms, except for domestic consumption, thanks largely to the wholesale and welcome purgation in the breeding and cross-fertilization of the King of Instruments. No longer do the so-called glories of the English Diapason hang like a misty, soggy cloud over his utterances.

One morning Vera Moore, staying with friends in the New Forest, telephoned, inviting me to come and meet them that very day. So, after taking the push-and-pull train that ambled gently to Ringwood, I was met at the station by a boy of about 18 years of age. 'The name' he said 'is Crosthwaite-Eyre – and I'm Oliver.'

We drove over the top of the forest on a golden August afternoon with the heather in full bloom. At Stoneycross we turned to cross Ocknell Plain and, passing Long Cross Pond, drifted down through Bramshaw Wood. Vera's friends lived at Penn, in a house that stands between forest and common-land. Here was a veritable place of dreams: gabled, green-shuttered and ever-welcoming, in a landscape that might have been taken from a favourite painting – water-colour in summer, oil-textured in winter.

Here we found Dio, Oliver's mother, and Vera playing violin and piano sonatas. Over tea a plan was made for me to pay weekly visits, when Dio and I were to explore the possibilities of a violin and piano ensemble: in addition I was to teach Oliver's young sister Monica. This beginning was soon to lead to more work in the Forest perimeter and, later, to forming a music club there.

Meanwhile the prospect of taking on a very young and sensitive beginner led me to seek expert advice as to recently evolved ways and means of instruction. Among leading practitioners were teachers who had been students at the Incorporated London Academy of Music. The Principal, Dr. Yorke Trotter, had done some valuable pioneering in relating the teaching of an instrument to general musicianship. An enquiry revealed the name of a recently-trained satellite, Phyllis Tanner, who was upholding the Trotterian torch in Bournemouth. Readers of Anthony Powell's saga *A Dance to the Music of Time* may recall how the narrator, Nick Jenkins, meets a girl whom he instantly recognizes as the woman he is to marry. Thus it was to be for me when this encounter duly took place.

Helpful consultations led to combined weekly attendance at Dan Godfrey's afternoon symphony concerts. After them we would adjourn to Stewart's Restaurant for tea and muffins. A friendly and sympathetic waitress presided over our courtship with tact and solicitude. Some two years later, happening to be in Bournemouth, I returned to the familiar table for a meal. The same waitress greeted me and proceeded to enquire after 'the charming young lady who used to come here with you.' I told her the charming young lady had married, thereby eliciting sympathy and commiseration until I added 'But it's all right, you know – she married me!'

Dan Godfrey stood on the touch-line during these crucial negotiations. 'How are you getting on with that girl of yours?' he

Hervey — a set piece.

At the piano when young.

The author — from the portrait by Rupert Shephard.

The West Borough, Wimborne c. 1890 – from a painting by M. Turner

The last set of horse bells in regular use: Rowlands, Wimborne in 1925.

above *The slow train at Pewsey, with Hervey, 1933.* below *A sad farewell to steam, Dinton, 1949.*

This slow train, in the painting by the author's late brother, H. M. le Fleming, depicts a Somerset and Dorset Joint Railway 'local' in the year 1912. The artist, then ten years old, cajoled his father into taking a photograph of it from which, many years later, the painting was made.

The engine is no. 15A, a 2-4-0 originally built in 1864, on what must have been almost its last journey. The train is climbing the gradient out of Wimborne through Merley, en route for Blandford, Templecombe and Bath. It called in leisurely fashion at all stations.

top *From our window at Bramshaw.*
bottom *cider making in the New Forest 1935.*

top *The cottage at Fisherton de la Mere*. bottom *The School of English Choral Music, Chislehurst 1930. The holiday course at which this was taken included Sir Edward Bairstow (centre) and S.H.N. (in gown, centre back)*.

Ralph Vaughan Williams. The autograph that began a friendship.

Sir Dan Godfrey.

Benjamin Britten and Peter Pears at the first London performance of Britten's Saint
Nicholas, Southwark Cathedral, 1949 *and, below, Alfred Deller, Dr Reginald Jacques,
Maurice Bevan and the author.* (photos: J. L. Allwork)

above *Sir Sydney Nicholson*
left *Mary Ibberson.*

George Reeves.

John Coates
after the original drawing by H James Gunn

John Coates.

Evening on Egdon Heath – Diggory Venn the reddleman (from The Return of the Native, *by Thomas Hardy) – wood engraving, Clare Leighton.*

would ask. 'Let's see now, what is her name – is it Mabel or Ethel?' I led him away gently from such fancies – 'Phyllis, of course it is. Phyllis is me only joy' he quoted, adding 'Well, I hope she will be – nice girl that!' When our wedding was imminent he said 'I'd like to give you both a little present – how about a photo of meself?'

Among an increasing number of contacts made in the New Forest was Olive Boult, sister of the eminent conductor, then living with their father at Landford. She persuaded me to write a cantata for equal voices, suitable both for the young as well as for the many village choirs containing only women's voices. There was a dearth of suitable music of this calibre, particularly in the matter of presentable words. In choosing music for my singing classes I had found the general quality of this essential ingredient to be abysmal – 'Two little dickie-birds sitting on a tree' is an example that comes to mind. The upshot of this incentive resulted in *The Echoing Green*, that was to have the distinction of a first performance at the Mary Datchelor School in Camberwell, under the direction of that gallant and splendid musician Mary Donnington.

As a basis for the cantata I chose some of the *Songs of Innocence* by William Blake. To these I added some eminently settable examples from a sequence of unpublished poems. These had been written by a friend from school days who, behind the initials R.H.B. conceals the identity of a man whose reticence was only exceeded by his charm, wisdom and kindliness. The sequence, written in the form of homage to A. E. Housman and *A Shropshire Lad*, is entitled *A Dorset Dolt*. Interspersed between these two sources are settings of single poems by Hardy, Monk Gibbon and others.

Although *The Echoing Green* contains an altogether superfluous quantity of shepherds and sheep (reflecting a youthful zest for what has been well called rustic vacuity) the Green still echoes from time to time, despite bouts of near-hibernation on the publishers' shelves.

From letters received from R.H.B. during the *Dorset Dolt* afflatus, a quotation from one of them must find a place here. He had just been given the custody of a piano that had been a wedding present to his mother. When inspected by an expert, it was found to contain a thriving community of moth and other denizens. 'Picture the hoardings,' R.H.B. wrote, 'Come to the Broadwood near Blandford for Good Food, Restful Surroundings and Convivial Society. Miles of Virgin Felt still await the Proboscis of the Visitor. Thunderstorms practically unknown: no Bach or Beethoven will disturb our Guests – only Nursery Rhymes and Chopin (with soft pedal) at intervals. One of the longest Established and Select Resorts in this Historic County!'

The first year of semi-independence was celebrated by a holiday in the Mendip Hills, spent at a farm that stood on the site of an ancient fortified encampment near the Fosse Way. Here I was joined by Rupert Shephard and, for part of the time, by Phyllis and three young nieces. Rupert painted while I mulled over projected compositions. In the evenings he and I would sometimes go to the pub by Chilcompton Station, a place of cherished memories to former devotees of the Somerset and Dorset Railway. The line at this point lay near the summit of the gruelling ascent out of Bath, so that the performance of many varied types of locomotives at the head of trains making the gradient was, to say the least, spectacular.

The public bar fraternity made us welcome and permitted us to join in their discourse. The sound of those soft west country voices lingers still in the memory. There was William Vye, who drank rough cider out of a pink mug. His theory as to the cause of thunder ran thus: 'When the atmosphere do go up from groun' and the higher air do drop from sky, the two do meet, see, up in they clouds. R! Then they do crash together – an' lightnin's too be struck arf.' There was also Ted Emery, an astute and fiery amateur politician, the extent of whose nightly afflatus could be gauged from the number of times he referred to 'the affairs.' When this became over-frequent, and less clearly articulated, it was wise to agree with him. Our visits gave a vivid glimpse of the dying fall in a way of life that was then fast on the wane.

On my way home from one of these sessions, a way that lay across fields, I came on a little she-goat, caught in some thick brambles on the side of a steep slope. Her tether was at full length: after I had released her I sat down on the ground for a moment, when at once she crept on to my lap and thrust her little nose against my chin. On the following day I went to the farm to tell the owner how I had found her. 'You can 'ave she' he said 'for five shillin'.' So I 'ad she, and brought her back to the farm where we were staying. There she grazed happily, soon acquiring the habit of following me on my wanderings. In those days of acute agricultural depression, there were acres of unused grassland where one could walk without doing harm. When the time came to leave, I brought Nancy, as she had become, to the station, where she weighed 16lbs on the scales. During the journey in the guards' van she had evidently exerted her feminine charm on the guard, who showed some reluctance in handing her over to me again! After a short and happy sojourn in a New Forest home she strayed one day, only to find both yew and lupin to her taste. So her brief story ends with a funeral procession consisting of Oliver, Phyllis and myself, to Penn Wood where, by the light of the moon, we dug a grave and tenderly laid her in it.

Soon the Crosthwaite-Eyres took over the family estate and moved to Warrens, a large eighteenth-century house that, amongst many other activities, was to become the future setting for a music club. There was also a cottage in the village becoming vacant, in which Phyllis and I would be able to begin our married life together.

CHAPTER 18

'Drei Intermezzi'

I

Soon after Frank Baker had responded to the call of Cornwall, a succession of friends paid visits to his cottage, built of stone, at Boscean. It stood at the head of the Kenidzhak valley that falls gently towards the sea, close to Cape Cornwall. Relics of mining recalled former activity in what had become a deserted and wild stretch of country.

As the train bringing me there was threading its way towards Penzance, I went to the restaurant car in search of tea. Opposite me was a large and friendly clergyman. The old Great Western used to keep a special brand of chocolate biscuit, in tins with a vividly coloured picture of the Cornish Riviera racing round the four sides. Their arrival at our table set the seal on diplomatic relations with my clerical companion, whom I had correctly placed as favouring the Higher altitudes of the Anglican fraternity. Earlier during the journey I had been reading about the admirable schemes being undertaken in Somers Town to improve the notably bad housing conditions there, instigated by Father Jellicoe and a fellow priest. When I mentioned this to my newfound friend he smiled and said 'Oh well – that's me you know!'

During the visit to Boscean our days were filled by talking, books, music, friends, pubs – and long walks, with Hervey in close attendance. In a typically April mixture of sun, wind and shower we explored the coastline. It was one of these walks that was to make the visit particularly memorable.

Early one evening we went down the valley towards the sea, over which the westering sun, soon to set, was shining with spectacular splendour. Away below the horizon lay Newfoundland. Beneath the sea around us there is said to lie the lost land of Lyonesse. As the waves washed against the rocky shore, it seemed as if they carried the echo of tolling bells, ringing the Angelus from the towers of those many fair churches that stood in that legendary land, once part of Atlantis, the lost continent. At night when the west wind from the sea roared up the valley, the hooves of galloping horses could be heard, thudding up towards us at Boscean and onward towards the town of St. Just in Penwith.

As we reached the shore Frank decided to bathe in a rock-pool while I sat on the cliff above. Grassy slopes here were interspersed by clusters of rock, battered and scarred by wind and sea. One of these formations, as I looked, began to assume the shape of a watch-tower or chapel with a door, through which there emerged the figure of a monk. In his right hand he held a quill with a long white feather, the hand raised, as though in greeting. At that moment Frank called out that the water was ice-cold and that he was coming to join me. When I looked again, the rocks had resumed their normal appearance.

On the following morning there was a letter for Frank from a member of the local archaeological society, enclosing an account of the monks who, in former days, had manned the beacons round the Cornish coast, mentioning one that was maintained at the place where we had sat. Forty years later, when I next visited the scene, it was interesting to discover that the ruins of a chapel had been found – and revealed for all to see.

II

At the school where I taught in Southbourne there had been a piano pupil whose name was Elizabeth. She had shown a more than usual addiction to the Tales of Beatrix Potter. So I provided her with six easy pieces, each one suggested by either a character or an incident in the Tales. For good measure I added six duets. Knowing only too well the implications of the Copyright Act, I wrote to the celebrated authoress' publishers, confessing that one foot had been placed on guarded territory and requesting that the other might be given permission to follow it. A courteous, though stern, reply intimated that I had indeed been trespassing on private property. Further, it added, the writer would be glad if I would provide a written confession as to the enormity of my offence. When I called on the custodians of the Tales, a similar theme dominated the proceedings. 'You must realize, Young Man,' I was told, 'that the word Peter, if and when used in conjunction with the word Rabbit, constitutes an infringement of copyright carrying very heavy damages.' Chastened, but undeterred, I crept down a dark and narrow staircase into the sunlit street.

It had so happened that the Crosthwaite-Eyres had recently made a gift of land, on the edge of the New Forest, to the National Trust. The Secretary, Sam Hamer, paid a visit to them shortly after my encounter with the Potter Protectorate. He seemed amused by my account of the proceedings and said, 'Oh, we'll soon fix that for you.' He had known Beatrix Potter for many years, through her wonderful generosity to the Trust. Though then about to retire, he had been with the National Trust for many years. When he was first appointed it had been a very modest undertaking; during his tenure of office the growth had been rapid, in no small part due to so capable, kindly and wise an administrator.

Soon the three of us – Uncle Sam (as he had now become), Phyllis and I were bidden to go to Sawry, there to stay as the guests of Beatrix Potter. I was to play the pieces and (with Phyllis) the duets. Even so, the omens were not as yet propitious: 'What is all this about a young man and his musical rabbits?' The lights had at least changed from red to yellow: after our visit they remained at green.

On arrival at Windermere we were met by our hostess' 'Noah's Ark' – an elderly Wolseley landaulette whose driver, also elderly, had spent his early years as a coachman. Both equipage and driver had been acquired at a sale, thus giving a new lease of life to both. Certainly the car was driven in true equestrian fashion, the gears being changed on hills only as a last resort, after much leaning forward in the seat and frequent use of those cl'k cl'k noises that horses are supposed to understand had failed to achieve any effect on the car. We were given a warm welcome at Castle Cottage by Beatrix Potter and her husband William Heelis – a quiet, kindly man, Clerk to the Justices at Ambleside. Before supper we walked to Hill-Top, then kept as a retreat for our hostess. Here the now-familiar treasures were in process of assembly. It was a delight to walk up the staircase in the wake of Mr. Tod and to look through a window at the lane where the three puddle-ducks, Mr. Drake, Jemima and Rebecca, had taken their memorable walk.

Beatrix Potter was wearing an old grey jumper and skirt, topped by an even older wide-brimmed felt hat. In rough weather she would sometimes throw a bit of sacking across her shoulders. Walking a lane one day she met a tramp who greeted her with the words 'Poorish weather for the likes of us, Ma'am' to which she replied 'It is that!' Little can the tramp have guessed how much land had been acquired by her, or of her great generosity to countless people in need of a helping hand. During our visit we went with her in the Ark to visit various tenant farmers, on all of whom she kept a sharp and shrewd eye. 'Too many weeds in that crop there – I fancy he tries to take out of the land more than he cares to put into it' and other similar comments would be made during these tours of overseeing. As an instance of exceptional care and thought we were told how, after acquiring the land surrounding Esthwaite Water, she had evicted the coarse fish then in residence, replacing them with trout and adding, for good measure, a thousand water-lily plants on the surface of the lake.

After breakfast we were summoned to an upstairs room, in which was a piano – a slightly raffish upright, doubtless bought at a sale, though in good heart and reasonably responsive. On this obliging instrument we played the pieces and duets I had written. They were acclaimed, some were encored, in particular a duet that finishes with a hint of the 'soporific' effect of lettuce on the Flopsy Bunnies. Later some of these pieces were to be made into a suite for wind quintet, renamed *Homage to Beatrix Potter*.

When, shortly after the initial performance at Sawry, I played some other music I had written, the characteristic comment was 'Well, young man, why you want to waste your time over Peter Rabbit when you can write music like *that* I'm sure I don't know!!' During our stay repeat performances were demanded on several occasions: when William Heelis was within call, he was sternly summoned to attend.

One evening two girls from the village whose names (aptly enough for the locality) were Amanda Thistlethwaite and May Postlethwaite, came to recall tunes that had accompanied the singing games of their childhood. Our host and hostess had an abiding interest in anything traditional, direct and clear. The tunes were typical of other folk rhymes that have survived; they were delightfully presented.

After our visit Beatrix Potter made some line drawings for the first printing of the Peter Rabbit Music Books. They were published jointly by her sponsors and the firm where my four songs and some piano transcriptions had been placed. Incidentally, the two publishers had not known of the existence of each other until the moment of communication arrived. In recent years the gulf that separates the world of books from that of music has narrowed considerably. At that time one of the sponsors said to me 'Now, this firm you mention, are they er . . .?' I said yes, they were. The other, turning the pages of a telephone directory, turned and said 'By the way, how do these people spell their name?' The result of this cautious twinning was, of course, that the venture faltered through shared lack of responsibility.

As well as the drawings Beatrix Potter also wrote a brief introduction for me. Neither it nor the illustrations were included in subsequent reprinting, owing, they said, first to rising costs, then to wartime economy. The introduction recalls a faint echo from the vanished past, but how grateful I was – and have remained – for it:

'The rippling melody of this pretty music calls back many little friends. Again the Puddleducks pass, pit pat paddle pat, while kittens, squirrels, rabbits frisk and gambol.

Tiddly widdly widdly! Mrs. Tittlemouse with a mop follows the big dirty footprints of Mr. Jackson. And Lucy sips her tea, while dear Mrs. Tiggy-Winkle heats her smoothing iron.

Good luck to the merry company of Christopher le Fleming's tuneful numbers and to those lucky little people who will play them some day.'

Beatrix Potter

This second Intermezzo ends with a coincidence. Just as it had been an Elizabeth at Southbourne, so it was to be another Elizabeth – in Hampstead – who received the first copy of the music. This was 'the musical little daughter' of Sam Hamer's friend and doctor Lindsey Batten. Long after Sam Hamer had left this troubled world, she and I were to meet at Dartington Hall in Devon: she as a music student, while I was looking for future teachers in Rural Music Schools. In gratitude to Sam Hamer I provided music for his period light opera *Penelope Anne*.

III

The scene opened in a train, drawn by one of Sir Nigel Gresley's new L.N.E.R. Pacific-type engines, speeding northward from King's Cross on a grey afternoon, at the time when autumn gives place to winter. Vera Moore, David Brynley and I were on our way to Alnwick, where we were to give a concert on the following day. Vera was to play piano solos; David was to sing several groups of songs, including some of my settings, and I was to accompany him throughout the concert.

As we talked during the journey, one of the other passengers in the compartment leant forward and said 'Excuse me, but did I hear you mention . . . ?' We said 'Yes indeed you did.' He turned out to be someone of whom I had often heard through a mutual friend, though up to now had never met. We were to be the guests of Helen Sutherland, generous patron of the arts, at Rock Hall. As well as being near Alnwick, Rock was also close to Fallodon, where Lord Grey lived, surrounded by his cherished birds.

Though the concert was to take place on a Saturday, we were invited to stay over the week-end. On Sunday Lord Grey came to lunch at Rock: afterwards Vera played the *Waldstein Sonata*, then in the final stages of preparation for a London recital. After she had played it, Lord Grey told us how, after he had made a fateful and oft-quoted speech early in August 1914, he had promised to attend a late evening party. It was the speech in which he had said 'The lights are going out all over Europe; we shall not see them lit again in our lifetime.' Much against his will, feeling weary and sick at heart, he kept his promise. At the party there had been a pianist who had played this same Sonata. At a moment in the first movement a sudden illumination had come to him. If, he thought, Beethoven could write music such as this, then, ultimately everything, *everything* must come right.

Our guest had been given a special dispensation to smoke his pipe in the drawing room. His sight had so greatly failed that, in lighting it, he had been unable to locate the point of contact for a lighted match. But on the following day, when we all went over to Fallodon, he entered the room in which we were sitting; after greeting us he walked to the mantelpiece, took up his pipe, filled and lit it without a trace of hesitation. Such a trifling incident remains in the memory as a vivid instance of the effect that unfamiliar surroundings can have on those with limited vision.

The Fallodon birds proved to be, in the main, a varied and colourful assortment of water-fowl. On our way to see them, there was an incident with two robins. When a special favourite had alighted on our host's outheld hand to receive a proffered snack, another robin attempted a touchdown a split second later. Too late for the snack, it perched on a finger, neatly nicked a couple of feathers from the tail of the successful rival, tossed them groundward, refused a second tit-bit and flew away in a very marked manner.

During lunch we talked of writers and poets. Our host remarked that English composers seemed to be unaware of the lyrical side of Thomas Love Peacock's verse. In particular he praised the novel *Maid Marian*, in which one of the characters, Brother Michael is apt to break into song, as here, recalling his youth:

> "Little I recked of matin bell,
> But drowned its toll with my clanging horn;
> And the only beads I loved to tell
> Were the beads of dew on the spangled thorn."

This also was quoted –

> "For the slender beech and the sapling oak,
> That grow by the shadowy rill,
> You may cut down both at a single stroke,
> You may cut down which you will.

But this you must know, for as long as they grow,
Whatever change may be,
You can never teach either oak or beech
To be aught but a greenwood tree."

The reference here is to the love of Robin Hood and Maid Marian
for each other. By way of pendant, Lord Grey remarked 'One has
to achieve real maturity before acquiring a true appreciation of
Brussels sprouts!'

So persuasive an introduction to Peacock led to a choral work
that I called *The Singing Friar*. It was unlucky enough to be
scheduled for a first performance in London during October 1939,
during the silence of the period known as the phoney war. But it
was heard for the first time on South African radio, followed by a
B.B.C. broadcast from Bedford during those fateful years.
Despite some sporadic and scattered hearings, it has never as yet
recovered from the initial setback.

During supper on our last evening at Rock, a strange happening
caused a slight diversion. Four of us, Helen Sutherland, Vera,
David and I were midway through our meal, in a dining room
where the window was set in a deep bay recess. On one side of it
stood a highback chair that had been conspicuously unoccupied
during our sojourn. Glancing casually in the direction of the
window, I was suddenly aware that someone was sitting on the
solitary chair. It was a girl, tall and dressed in grey with a long
skirt and lace collar. Her hair was parted in the middle, and
gathered in coils on each side of her head. As I looked she got up,
walked across the recess and disappeared into the panelled wall
opposite. Vera, her back to the window, naturally saw nothing;
Helen, facing it, also saw nothing. David, opposite me, was
staring with astonishment at the place where our visitant had
vanished. He and I were gently called to order. After the others
had left the room, David said, 'So you saw her too – wasn't she
lovely?'

The later reaction of our hostess is hard to define; while being,
we suspected, rather pleased that the house, said to be haunted,
had lived up its reputation, she was a little peeved at having been
unable to share the experience with us.

On the following morning we began the return journey
southward, leaving Northumberland in bright December sunshine. Both land and sea were bathed in a quality of brightness that
is a special characteristic of the Eastern counties. This quality can
also be found in the Netherlands: it has been often caught and held
in the work of many Dutch painters.

CHAPTER 19

Forest Murmurs

Towards the north-east perimeter of the New Forest lies Bramshaw village, scattered and extending along four roads that meet at Stocks Cross. There stood the blacksmith's forge, from which the sound of Mr. Cooper's anvil rang across the fields on still summer mornings, blending in Handelian fashion with two antiphonal chaffinches in the trees beyond our garden fence. The cottage stood by the side of a farm-holding, the yard of which provided the only access to it. Our windows looked out on the forest; wild deer would emerge in hot dry weather, while ponies in groups held daily meetings. Pigs and cattle would also assemble by the yard gate. This was to be our home for three years, living happily enough without many amenities now taken for granted as essential.

During our first summer various friends and acquaintances, most of them still geared in greater or lesser degree to feudal living, would come out to the cottage. Elderly and tending towards the genteel, they professed to scorn tea as a meal. They would then proceed to put away large slices of bread, cut at the table, with farm butter and locally-produced honey. Replete and happy, they would amble out to their cars, hoping for an invitation to return, astonished to discover how civilized and comfortable such a dwelling could be. There was a good deal of coy twittering amongst the women as they tacked purposefully up the garden path before leaving.

We had arrived in May, when

> ". . . glad green leaves like wings,
> Delicate-filmed as new-spun silk"

had replaced and transformed the varied shades of brown that predominated through the autumn and winter months. When the moon shone during our first few evenings, the voice of a solitary nightingale came over the orchard below us. The sound, blending with the scent of wallflowers beneath the windows, echoed in the surrounding stillness, recalling Keats' 'magic casements.' A few days later some boys with sticks went for an evening walk; after they had entered the forest we never heard the song again.

As spring gave way to summer, the climate in our valley or 'bottom' became oppressive. The smell of pig hung in the windless air while flies proliferated. Then we would take our Austin 12 two-seater (bought for £12) and go, by the edge of Nomansland, through Heaven's Gate (where the forest ends) to the open Wiltshire downs, where larks soared in a treeless sky and the air was strong and clear. In September the winds of equinox began to stir; from then until the middle of May the forest climate was pleasant enough. The end of summer was heralded by the arrival, in our neighbour Tom Biddlecombe's yard, of a hand cider-press, with a tall, bearded custodian as high priest of the ceremony. When the ritual was about to end, Nipper, the farm dog, would be despatched into the barn to kill and retrieve a rat: after all the apples had been poured into the press, the sacrificial victim would follow, head first, thus adding the final relish to the brew.

Then would come the time of Pannage when, by ancient right, from Michaelmas to St. Cecilia's Day, pigs would be turned out on the forest to feed on beech-mast. Much gathering of wood for winter-fuel would follow, while smoke rising from bonfires would signal the funeral pyres of summer's bounty. After the leaves had spread a light brown carpet, the holly berries would appear in bright red clusters against the dark green leaves. They shone like polished silver in the sunlight of a December morning as the night frost began to thaw. After Christmas, signs of the turn of the year would appear very early – catkin, palm and snowdrops; soon a delicate flush over the willows would herald the approach of another spring. In early March we would begin to tackle the garden again, with the mower cleaned and oiled for the first cut of the year. Sounds that had been muffled by winter would ring clear once more: the postman whistling outside the window and milk churns from the yard hoisted on to the daily lorry with renewed zest and vigour.

Our neighbours were kindly; Tom Biddlecombe and family being next and nearest to us. Then there was Jack Hatch, whose wife kept a little shop and whose rhubarb jam was a revelation. They had a fine cluster of boys, strangely alike both in appearance and name, three of them being called respectively Kenny, Denny and Lenny. The family's quota of pigs grazed on the open land beyond the farmyard gate. Round the corner, in what was known as the Merry Orchard, lived Ted Cordry, whose dahlias made a rare showing, each one known by name and treated as favourite children. Ted was a bachelor and a kindly eccentric. Once a week he would take a bucket of water to the top of his stairs, pour it down so that the ensuing flood ran out of the open front door. Then, with a piece of rag firmly held under one foot, wipe each stair with it – the job done for another week.' He was said to have a keen eye for courting couples in the forest. His neighbour, Mrs.

Fry, warned us newly-weds to be careful when we were out walking. ' 'Tis in the thickets 'e do peer!' she said darkly. She and her husband, who looked on life with a somewhat sardonic eye, made us welcome and never failed to answer a call for help. Then there was Lizzie Winter, who had come from Hoxton and married a quiet and reserved husband in the village, always referred to as ' 'im'. She would sometimes come round to give us 'a bit of a clean-up' and bring bunches of flowers such as

"Sweet-William with his homely cottage-smell,
  And stocks in fragrant bloom."

Bramshaw Church stood on a knoll at the far end of the village. The vicar, George Noël, was a kindly fellow, though trained to do his wife's bidding and to keep her fully informed as to the welfare of his flock, in particular their problems and misdemeanours! When taking the Services he had an endearing habit of addressing the Almighty as one might speak to an elderly, deaf and rather forgetful country squire, who had to be frequently reminded of His obligations. On occasions when one of the faithful had been thought to err from the path of righteousness, his sermon on the following Sunday would swing round to the point in question when, by oblique reference, the offender's foible would be held aloft as a warning to the rest of us. The faithful, peacefully dozing in their pews, would stir a little, thinking 'Hullo – here it comes' and then subside into the prevailing coma.

Like many men of small stature, George Noël was strongly attracted to the music of Wagner. One day he said to me 'When I feel really depressed, I go into my study, shut the door and set up my little portable gramophone. Then I put on a record of the Entry of the Gods into Valhalla: after hearing it I feel fit for anything – and again my happy normal self.'

Soon Frank Baker came to Bramshaw, where he was with us for a year before returning to Cornwall once more – this time to St. Hilary, where his friend Bernard Walke needed an organist. In that capacity he persuaded the little organ in the West Gallery of Bramshaw Church to find a completely new voice under the alchemy of his approach to it. Wind-power was provided by William Henbest 'at the bellows.' When, after the Service, Frank's concluding voluntaries called for extra assistance, a Breughel-like head would emerge from the shadows 'D'you want some more wind, Sir? I can give 'e plenty more if so be you need it.' William also 'gave us a hand' in the garden. After he had lit a bonfire near the end of a straight brick-edged path, he would take his lunch-break in our little summer-house, from which he could watch the rising smoke. 'I like to think' he said ' 'tis a train taking me on a long journey, away from the coming winter months and where 'tis only sunshine, with sometimes a drop of warm rain to bring on the flowers and the vegetables.' Throughout his days William remained a kindly, friendly, child-like character. For some time now he must surely have taken his journey to those Elysian fields and gardens he imagined when sitting in a cold summer house on autumn days of long ago.

Frank also wrote and produced a Nativity Play during his forest sojourn. Recent experience at St. Hilary, where Bernard Walke's plays, produced by Filson Young, had been broadcast by the B.B.C., encouraged him to see if the Faith could be given a new lease of life in our village. After the play, however, which was memorable and wholly successful, everyone settled down again, replete with the glow of achievement, back to peaceful normality. A few months later Frank's first novel *The Twisted Tree* was published. As with Jude in earlier days, the pious were given a good shake-up! In such conservative and backward-looking circles, *The Twisted Tree* also was too far ahead of the local zeitgeist to be readily assimilated. By present standards it would seem to remain simply a very good novel that, as a paperback, would reach a wide and appreciative public.

At this time a Rural Music School had been set up in Hampshire. Following on Mary Ibberson's initial years of pioneering in Hertfordshire, a combined concert, given by players and singers from scattered villages, had been given at Hitchin Town Hall. It had been conducted by Adrian Boult and received an encouraging notice in *The Times*. His account so encouraged two readers, Sir Harry and Lady Stephen, who lived near Fordingbridge, that plans for a similar venture were set in motion for Hampshire. There were two candidates for the post of Director – Cicely Card and I. Wisely the choice fell on Cicely, under whose guiding hands the school grew, flourished and became integrated with the county's Education Authority. Our first combined concert took place at Breamore, when Mary Ibberson came to give a blessing.

Such a stimulus was both welcome and timely, since the rapidly growing influence of radio had been tending to exert a somewhat similar effect on amateur music-making as lettuce on the Flopsy Bunnies! Choral and instrumental groups, as well as individuals, were encouraged to new endeavours, while teachers found new scope for their work. Mary Ibberson's visit to Breamore was to prove a harbinger of things to come in my own case. Beginning with one weekly visit to conduct a village choir, it was to lead in a few years to my becoming Director of a similar school in

Wiltshire, and subsequently Mary's assistant in what had by then become the Rural Music Schools Association.

In early Hampshire days there was a concert at Romsey that had included a performance of my cantata *The Echoing Green*. Amongst those who attended was an extremely impressive wife of a Cathedral dignitary at Winchester. 'You must' she said to me 'have come a very long way to give us such pleasure to-day.' The temptation was too great to resist – 'No, no' I said 'my home is only a few miles from here.' At which she turned away abruptly and was later heard to say to a friend 'Such a disappointment, my dear; it seems he is only a local man!'

Meanwhile the Crosthwaite-Eyres were beginning to give some music parties, soon to become the Warrens Music Club. For several years we were able to arrange four subscription concerts each year, spread through the winter months. Members would arrive for tea, the programme finish by 6.30 (or soon after) so that everyone could return home for the evening and the artists comfortably decanted into the London train at Southampton. This arrangement has so many advantages, particularly in country districts, that it is surprising so few similar groups appear to have adopted it.

The 18th-century drawing room and annexe at Warrens made an ideal setting for chamber music. The Weiss Quartet from Vienna played on several occasions, giving memorable performances, notably the Schubert Quintet, with Valentine Orde as second cellist. Antonia Butler and I played the Brahms F major cello sonata with a combined abundance of youthful zest that I, for one, would give a year of my life to recapture. Dio Crosthwaite-Eyre, besides being the mainspring of these activities, took her part in performances. She had studied with Johann Kruse, who had been Joachim's second violin in the famous quartet. Some memories of their performances were later to be given me by his widow, Frau Professor Kruse, in an encounter to be described in due course.

Among pianists, pride of place must be given to Julius Isserlis. This most lovable and innocent of men had twice been the victim of political upheavals. He had been obliged to leave Russia at the beginning of a promising career. He then settled in Vienna, where he soon acquired an international reputation. After a narrow escape from the Nazi jack-boot he had arrived in England, together with his wife and son. By now fully middle-aged, Julius was obliged to begin again for the third time. Unluckily this coincided with a moment when the Incorporated Society of Musicians, justly concerned for their members' welfare in the face of increasing (and formidable) competition from the influx of arrivals from Europe, were making it unduly hard for them to become established. Through a chance encounter we were able to give Julius his first engagement in phase three. As an instance of the hazards to be faced, we were told shortly afterwards that he had been booked to play a concerto with the orchestra at Bournemouth. During both rehearsal and performance the conductor had proved singularly unhelpful: nevertheless Julius had done his best to overcome the situation, his characteristic comment being 'Really, for three guineas it was too much!'

Among singers, pride of place must be given to John Coates. Though by now elderly, the qualities that had made him a master of song and a wholly delightful and lovable man were still fully evident. Playing for him was a privilege, as were also several visits to rehearse at his home in Northwood. Here, in an imitation olde worlde house known as The Coterie, built by a retired sea-captain, he would discourse on many subjects, including invaluable commentary on the songs I had been writing. The garden provided an unusual quantity of summer houses-cum-sheds, in which were stored trunks containing a collection of operatic regalia worn in earlier days.

Another tenor with whom I worked with immense pleasure was John McKenna. Brimful of Irish charm and wit, he would sing like an angel when in form. Our happiest and most rewarding occasion was a complete performance of *Die Winterreise* together at Warrens. After a concert John would pour out a stream of anecdotes and stories that would have made him a fortune as an entertainer. At heart he was a sad and lonely man, whose death was a great loss to music. There was a distinct affinity in his character with much that we know of Schubert.

During these three years two of our sons, Michael and Daniel, were born. The little cottage was becoming totally inadequate; we had also been claiming the generosity of friends and patron quite long enough. At the crucial moment an unexpected legacy opened a new vista of possibilities. We had become more and more drawn towards Salisbury and the valleys that converge on it. Through an exceptionally kind and fatherly house agent, we found two thatched cottages at Fisherton de la Mere in the Wylye Valley. One had been restored and modernized: the other, separated by part of the garden, was no longer used as a dwelling. But it offered ideal scope for converting into a music room. Here we lived for the next seven years, two of them through the uneasy period of appeasement, while the cloud of war came inexorably nearer. The lights over Europe went out for the second time.

CHAPTER 20

'Cool Sequester'd Vale'

Fisherton de la Mere, with church, mill and village green, clustered comfortably round a lane, shaped like a letter U that hung suspended from the main road between Salisbury and Warminster. A footpath wound across the valley to Bapton and Stockton: a right of way across fields led to the village of Wylye. Halfway along it was a stile by a plank across a dike, known as Old Woman's Hatch, a distinct hazard for revellers returning from either *The Bell* or *The Swan*. One such had recently been encountered late one night, pushing an empty wheelbarrow; he was determined that it should be made to jump the stile unaided. Possibly some atavistic memory of recalcitrant horse or donkey had been revived by an extended potation: but the wheelbarrow received the flogging of a lifetime for refusing the jump! One would give much for a tape-recording of the accompanying commentary.

Between our cottages and the river lay two water-meadows called Little Hayes and Paradise. The river, on which we would have given much to have a boat, was strictly reserved for trout fishing. On the crest of the opposite downs were large areas of woodland – Great Ridge and Groveley. Beyond them lay another valley through which the river Nadder flowed gently through Dinton and Teffont. There it seemed that spring came several days before it reached us, though the end of summer lingered by way of compensation. It was a sure sign of rain when the sound of trains on the Southern main line came over the uplands. At Wylye the Great Western maintained a station with a staff of three admirable railwaymen, who loyally upheld the tradition built up over the years by 'the grand old Company.' Trains passing through the valley with unfailing punctuality marked the passage of time through the day. Beginning with the 7.53 up and the 8.02 down in the morning, the night train that left Salisbury at 1.50 still runs through a poem by Siegfried Sassoon, who lived at Heytesbury, a few miles further up the valley.

Northward, beyond the main road, the undulating green expanse of Salisbury Plain stretched onward and outward like an inland sea. A farm track led up to it through Cuckoo Penn – and on to Chitterne (St. Mary & All Saints). Continuing northward, by way of Breakheart Bottom, came

"Imber on the down,
Five miles from any town."

A few days before much of this beautiful expanse of isolated country was permanently requisitioned for military usage, a friend and I walked through it on a glowing September day. As we came down towards Imber we passed a field of flax that shone light blue in the sun. A magnificent tithe barn had just been newly thatched. Our destination that day was Westbury, by way of Bratton Camp, on the slope of which the White Horse (shorn of former potent masculinity to remain a gelding) provides a landmark for travellers to the west country.

It is said that Bratton Camp is the site where King Alfred had led the men of Wessex to a victory that had finally driven Danish invaders out of their land. These unwelcome marauders were said to be particularly memorable for the number of redheads they mustered. Edith Olivier remembered how, up to the early years of our century, children in nearby villages whose hair tended towards this colour were habitually called Daners – an instance of race-memory 'burrowing like a mole' beneath the skull.

Fisherton de la Mere, when we settled there, was virtually a feudal hamlet, in sharp contrast to Wylye, which had acquired independence by partition from the Pembroke Estate. We had three 'big houses', the denizens of which moved in their own social orbit. In addition to our cottage, two other dwellings had been adapted to reasonably civilized standards, one of them owned by a retired doctor; in the other lived an architect, George Imrie, of cherished memory. The miller was old Mr. Carpenter, whose household consisted of his daughter Alice and two middle-aged bachelor sons Bill and Arth, invariably alluded to by their father as 'they byes.' The rest were tied or rented cottages, most of them sadly in need of repair, maintenance and improvement. Between the dwellers in them and the big house triumvirate, there was a clearly defined social gulf fixed. We, in the middle, moved happily to left or right of centre.

At Wylye there was an innate suspicion of strangers among the older people. Here also were signs of expediency such as corrugated iron roofing as a disfiguring substitute for thatch. One lady, throughout our seven years, returned our 'good morning' with a silent basilisk stare. After we had left she was heard to remark ''Tis always the same; when good people comes they'm the first to go!' Another instance was revealed when a friend went to deliver a message to someone who lived in a semi-detached cottage, standing isolated nearly a mile distant from another building. The caller, receiving no response, approached the occupant of the other cottage, who was working in his garden. 'Would you,' he asked, 'be good enough to give a message to Mr. So-and-so when he comes back?' The neighbour paused, straightened his back, spat contemptuously and said 'We 'aven't spoke for fifteen year.'

In due course our more socially-minded acquaintances 'called'. One of them seemed concerned to discover that we were what she called 'musical' – giving the word an emphasis that implied a chronic and incurable disability. 'I am not, of course, myself at all musical' she said 'but we have some relations' (implying that they were somewhat distant specimens) 'and indeed a few of our friends who are *quite* interested in music.' Here we did our best to evince symptoms of normality: however, when the talk turned to gardens and gardening, the threatening cloud lifted, so that we were invited 'to take a dish of tea' – presumably when returning 'the call.'

Such people had few, if any, scruples about the welfare of their tenants if they happened to want one of their cottages. Though by this time it had become obligatory to offer alternative accommodation, however distant and unsuitable, a tenant need still be given only fourteen days to remove himself and family. A case of this kind arose at Fisherton where a widow and her daughter, after living quietly for 30 years, were subjected to this treatment. The alternative proffered was distant, isolated and, in the circumstances, impossible. When they were taken to court we had arranged for a solicitor to defend them, to the astonishment of the outraged landlord, a kindly enough man in other ways. The tenants won their case, but we were *persona non grata* in certain quarters for several weeks afterwards!

Being 'musical' had a lighter side: after a gruelling day writing music, I was doing some gardening when Arth, from the mill, came walking along the lane. He paused, gave me a quizzing look and said 'Ah – doing some work for a change I see!'

An example of what is known in Quaker circles as 'a leading' had recently taken place. Before leaving the New Forest we had greeted the incoming tenants of our cottage there. They were three elderly sisters who, on retirement, had returned to their native village. They duly appeared, dressed in black; one had been in service to Princess Helena. The tallest, self-appointed spokesman for the trio, was powerfully addicted to trying her hand at counterpoint exercises – from a book, she said, published by 'Au-Jenner.' 'Can you,' she sternly asked me, 'do strict work in six parts?' 'Not really,' I said, 'Can you?' 'I keep on trying,' was the reply. 'I suppose it is because I strongly dislike being beaten!'

A few days before this encounter Vaughan Williams had administered a firm and friendly shove towards further contrapuntal drill. So I went to my friend John Milne, then in charge of music at the Bishop Wordsworth School at Salisbury, when helpful and enjoyable evening sessions followed, topped up by a jug of beer from an adjacent pub. One two-part exercise, a setting of a poem by Stephen Hawes *O Mortal Folk* later acquired an accompaniment and, when published, was sung by many school choirs. For it the original publisher, on the plea of wartime stringency, offered me £3, surely an all-time record of parsimony among a fraternity who notably prefer receiving money to parting with it, even to those who provide them with an essential commodity. Our sessions abruptly ceased at the outbreak of war: then John lost no time in joining the Navy for the duration, enormously exhilarated by the birth of his second son Hamish, now a pianist of considerable distinction.

Encouraged by these sessions, a great deal of music got written. First came a song cycle to words by Walter de la Mare called *Earth and Air*. Playing it over one day to Bruce Richmond, I was delighted when he praised the songs, saying that he would write to the poet and tell him about them. The result was an invitation to tea on a summer Sunday to meet the great man and to let him hear what had been happening to his words. We had with us a young soprano, Wyn Lambe, when we went to Taplow, where the de la Mares were living. Memory recalls the charm of Hill House and feeling at first somewhat shy. There was a gilt cherub hanging from the ceiling in the Hall: being tall it seemed as though the top of my head tickled its shining navel!

At tea Mrs. de la Mare was anxious about the scones we were offered, as it seemed the cook had prematurely abandoned them – 'I shouldn't touch them!' she said. A window in the dining room looked on to a lawn, in the middle of which stood an old and gnarled tree. 'If you look at the fork in the trunk of that tree' said our host 'You will see a lifelike image of a witch on her broomstick.' So we looked – and indeed the figure was vividly suggested.

After tea we adjourned to a room where there was a diminutive piano. Also present that day was an American professor from a University in the Middle West. Memory suggests that his name was Elderberry Paine. Before we unleashed the songs the professor insisted on announcing a performance of 'Oith and Air.' Afterwards the songs were given a warm blessing.

Already at that time a former interest in English song had

been replaced by a growing awareness of the splendours to be found in the Lied. So, apart from sporadic performances, these songs remained unpublished until adapted, many years later, as a sequence for choral singing, in response to a request from a county Federation of Women's Institutes. But since hearing them sung in the original form by Wilfred Brown at a London recital, I believe they could well revert to the original form.

That meeting with Walter de la Mare led to many more, as well as to a setting of six epitaphs and a memorial inscription from his book *Ding Dong Dell*. The cycle was called *A Quiet Company*, and also gained approval. Later on I used to go to tea with the poet during his Twickenham days. It is strangely moving to recall how he used to lament the passing of the longest day of the year – and that he should have died on the day after it.

The two pianos in our music room opened up new vistas of exploration. We started a choral society, most of the members walking up through the black-out from Wylye. As expected, our progress was slow, our aims modest enough. At one stage we could only muster a single tenor, who usually escorted one of the altos to the weekly practice. One evening she arrived early, alone and out of breath. When we asked her what had happened she said 'E's on 'is way; to-night 'e offered me a bar o'chocolate. When a man offers chocolate to a woman there's no mistakin' 'is meaning – so I come on quick!'

During the war our music room became a focal point for groups of soldiers who, shepherded by Captain Charles Strafford, spent some happy evenings with us. As well as visiting musicians, the gallant Captain often performed with much enjoyment. Benches and mugs of cocoa would also appear as appendages provided by the Army Education Corps. Particularly memorable was an evening when, under these auspices, Geraldine and Mary Peppin came to play to us. The undoubted highlight of the evening was Arthur Benjamin's *Jamaican Rumba*, which proved a potent wartime tonic. After their visit the piece became known to us as Captain Strafford's Fancy.

In Salisbury the premises belonging to Toc H became a Services Club, largely through the inspiration and initiative of Eric Grant. Music played a prominent part; among many who came to play or speak were Sir Adrian Boult, Maurice Cole, Sydney Northcote, to name but three. We were all decoyed by Eric's persuasive charm of manner. There was even a visit from the Toc H founder the Rev. 'Tubby' Clayton, full of years and honour, young in heart to tell us of plans to do more good to yet more people. I gave many talks and some piano recitals. In times of stress, certain music can acquire an almost uncanny power to give solace and courage. It so happened that, in the evening of D Day, I was able to introduce and play the first ever recording (by Barbirolli) of Vaughan Williams' fifth symphony. Unmistakable intimations of certain, though distant peace made a profound impression. On the same day my transcription of Bach's *St. Anne Prelude and Fugue* had been heard at the National Gallery, in one of those memorable concerts instigated and carried through by Myra Hess, of blessed memory.

Meanwhile a Rural Music School had been formed in Wiltshire. For some years it had been operating on a financial shoestring. Again the venture had stemmed from the initiative and determination of one or two individuals. Here the name of Patience Plater comes to mind, a lady of boundless energy and an iron will. In the initial stages there had been one solitary peripatetic string teacher who, alone and unaided, had laid the foundation for future activity for a growing school, in which I was to have a responsible position in the near future. It seems fitting here and now to pay a belated tribute to the work of Dorothea Dalrymple, to whom the steady growth of music-making in Wiltshire owes an incalculable debt.

Such pioneering needs fairly frequent injections of stimulus from expert and professional performers if recognizably decent standards are to be achieved. For us in Wiltshire, as for so many elsewhere, Sybil Eaton will long be remembered with affection and admiration. The combination of brilliant and eloquent playing, allied to charm of manner, provided the essential vitamins needed to encourage the often difficult task of getting small isolated instrumental groups 'off the ground.' Sybil would offer two or three days and, in exchange for transport and hospitality, play to school and village audiences. There were also recitals in some of the larger houses: once at Wilton when we were playing the *Kreutzer Sonata*, the last movement, despite our rehearsed tempo, took flight on the violin at a speed that clearly foreshadowed the age of jet-propulsion! Up to that moment I had thought that Adolf Busch, then in full flight, held the speed record, but we were well ahead on this occasion. Afterwards I said as much to Sybil; she replied 'He certainly doesn't play it faster than we did to-day.' 'No,' I said, a trifle ruefully.

Among our own composers it seemed that the music of Vaughan Williams invariably brought solace during those troubled years. Sybil's playing of *The Lark Ascending* never failed to evoke a deep and grateful response, both to the composer and his dedicated advocate. Otherwise it was, then as now, the great composers of the past who continued to affirm the ultimate merging of dissonance into an ordered pattern of fulfilment, such as Lord Grey had once found in the *Waldstein Sonata*.

These occasions also had their lighter side. At a village concert in Hampshire, Albert Sammons had been the distinguished guest performer. According to local custom, the Lady of the Manor, heavily betweeded and behatted, swept in at the last possible moment to take her seat in the front row of the audience. After hastily seizing a programme and rummaging noisily in her bag for spectacles – everyone was waiting to begin – she then, glancing at the programme, remarked 'Ah! Beethoven – I always feel *safe* with Beethoven.' A soft but distinct voice from the row behind was heard to murmur 'Lucky old Beethoven!' In a room behind the platform that was doing duty as a refuge for the performers, there was the usual assortment of flotsam. Prominent among this hastily stacked collection was a baby's cradle. When Albert Sammons commented on this to the somewhat formidable lady she said 'I can't think who on earth can have put it there.' At which the great man gave her what is sometimes described as 'a knowing look' as he said 'P'rhaps they're a bit premature, your ladyship!' 'Tsch! Mr. Sammons' she said – and swept out of the room.

Throughout these years the Wiltshire Competition Festival carried on, despite many obstacles and difficulties. Among the adjudicators none was more welcome than Reginald Jacques, who never failed to say exactly the right thing in the right way to every competitor. He shared with Thomas Wood a unique quality, described in the latter's entry in *Who's Who* under the heading of hobbies and recreations, 'making friends and keeping them.' That the Festival survived so triumphantly was in large measure due, once again to an individual dedication involving much hard work, to Adeline Wilson-Fox, who remained Hon. Secretary for close on three decades.

Shortly before Dio Crosthwaite-Eyre and I ceased our exploration of music for violin and piano, we had felt the need for some expert coaching. So we foregathered in London, where we were given potent injections: encouraging, though critical commentary by Adila Fachiri: more comforting, though less fiery counsel by Jelli D'Aranyi, those two brilliant sisters who were great-nieces of Joachim. During these sessions Adila had become fascinated by attempts to communicate with the spirit world. One day she greeted us in a state of overflowing and explosive excitement – 'Who do you think has been here – here in dees house? Schumann – SCHUMANN himself – come in, darlings, and I will tell you.' It seemed that Schumann had sent a message from Elysium, asking for the recovery of the score of his D minor Violin Concerto, said to be held by the Nazi custodians of culture. The work was to be released from detention and performed. Sadly for Adila the message appeared also to have been picked up elsewhere, for soon afterwards the role of Prince Charming fell to Hubermann: the Concerto had a brief reappearance befor subsiding once more into slumber.

At about this time a young violinist appeared like a meteor in the sky. The sisters attended a much-heralded recital, sitting side by side in the front row of the audience. Afterwards Adila whispered 'It is Oncle.' 'No,' said Jelli 'It is Christ!' I had the good fortune to perform with both sisters: Adila's playing of Beethoven was exceptionally exciting and brilliant: with Jelli I treasure the memory of a deeply expressive, eloquent and spacious account of the Brahms D minor Sonata, at a summer school in York.

Soon after the outbreak of war, two national organizations were inaugurated that were to bring music and drama to countless places that had become isolated. They were given an honourable, though wildly incorrect mention by a country parson when introducing a concert held in his church. 'I am sure,' he said, 'we all know what the letters C E M A stand for – and that is ENSA!'

For most of my generation September 1939 marks the abrupt end of our youth. It also brought to an end ten years during which Hervey, my black-and-white spaniel, had been a close and inseparable companion. Some neighbours returning one Sunday morning from church in the next village found him lying peacefully on a grassy bank at the side of the road, unharmed but lifeless. Being true countryfolk they naturally kept a sack in the back of the car, in which they brought him back to me. So he was buried in our cottage garden – and with his departure the world that we had both known and shared was fading away, never to return.

CHAPTER 21

In search of vision

The legendary fame of Herr Professor Vogt as an eye-specialist of world renown had been revealed to me, as to many, in Axel Munthe's *Story of San Michele*. Also impressive was the fact that among the names of many notable patients was that of De Valera. Best of all I saluted him for a truly democratic response to a command from Mussolini to come immediately to Rome to attend Il Duce. The reply stated that if Signor Mussolini would give himself the trouble to attend the Herr Professor's clinic in Zurich, an appointment would be forthcoming. So that when a friend urged me to consult the oracle, with an appointment made and hospitality proffered, I made my way to Zurich for the encounter. This was to be spread over two or three days, during which various tests would have to be undergone before the final confrontation.

The intermediary was the widow of another Herr Professor – Johann Kruse, violinist and colleague of Joachim. Frau Kruse, Polish by birth, retained a deep interest in music and musicians from early youth. Then she had first heard Joachim – and complained to her parents that he played out of tune. For this gratuitous piece of criticism she had been sent supperless to bed. Later, when she told Joachim of the incident, he said 'You were quite right, my dear; I have often wished that I did not play out of tune, but I cannot always help it.' When Bernard Shaw heard Joachim play the Bach Chaconne in London, he praised 'The perfect dignity of style and fitness of phrasing' as magnificent: he added, however, that it was given 'in the austerity of that peculiar scale which may be called the Joachim mode, tempered according to Joachim's temperament.'

After her marriage Frau Kruse had often travelled with the quartet when on tour. She compared the extreme variability of their playing during those journeys with the ever-growing technical mastery shewn by performers in more recent times. 'It is all technique now,' she said, 'When you have heard So-and-so play a certain work, you may be sure he will play it so wherever he goes. Like all the others he cannot afford to leave anything for the mood of the moment. Our quartet never played anything twice in the same way – it varied with the occasion. Sometimes we would arrive at a city where the hotel was comfortable, the hall warm and acoustics good. Then the playing would be lyrical, warm-hearted and glowing. At other times the hall would be cold, the hotel bad, so the playing would reflect the feelings of the poor, tired travellers.'

She had been present in Düsseldorf on the occasion when Elgar's music had first been acclaimed. It seemed that several influential sponsors who had made the occasion possible had never received a word of thanks from the composer. He had taken it all, she said, as his rightful due – and that was that.

Music apart, we talked of many things during my sojourn in Zurich during the winter of 1938–39. Of the inevitable coming of war, when the last and only hope of peace, my hostess claimed, lay in the banning of all newspapers and radio bulletins for a twelve-month. She had a shining belief in the potentially immortal life and indestructibility of the human spirit. Like many deeply religious people at heart, she was notably impatient over the narrow intolerance so frequently evident among those who cling to sectarian dogma. She would have whole-heartedly approved of a remark made by a former Master of Balliol College who, when a distinguished lady visitor, an agnostic, remarked with surprise at the number of theological books on his shelves, said 'My dear, you must continue to believe in God in spite of what the clergy tell you.'

This comment provides an opportunity to quote from some thoughts that Frau Kruse had noted, a copy of which she gave me during my visit to Zurich. It should be borne in mind that they are written in a language other than her native tongue.

'There was a spirit to whom God had given the power of creating. And he created Music. He wove it out of sunbeams and the heart-beat of the Universe, and music filled God's world with wonder. But he who created it was not content. He wanted to fill all worlds, so he went forth through space, leaving a trail of sublime melody. He was happy in his faith that he could stem the tide of evil, and with enchantment turn the wrath of Satan. But he was wrong, for demons followed in his steps and in derisive laughter drowned his godlike work by making a parody of it. So it was doomed. Then God recalled the spirit to His world where Music lived. Aeons passed, stars were born and perished, and the spirit waited . . .

'And he went forth once more and was a man. Not of this earth but of a glorious world far away in the immensity of the Almighty's realm. He was great and good and wore a talisman in his heart, but knew it not. He was a pilgrim in the Universe, and in his wandering he went from star to star in quest of Music. He did not find it, for all the time the treasure that he sought was in himself. When his life was ended he returned to God, and then he saw the talisman that he carried in his heart. His disappointment left him and he sang a song.

'In that song was the singing of a new-born power, with the ecstasy of freedom spreading wings and soaring to the sun. It told of rolling thunder and of raging seas: it caught the perfume of the trees and flowers and whispered of the gentle shimmering rain. It painted pictures of the fleeting clouds and fairy dance of silent drifting snow. It greeted with a hymn of praise the light of day and dreamed the mysteries of purple night. It glowed in rainbow colours strung together by a golden voice and touched the soul with tears and radiant joy. It poured in lavish streams a wealth of wonders. It sang the hope of Heaven, the despair of Hell. It was a prayer and it was a promise. It was the dawn of human genius and it was born to live. God heard the song and knew the forces that burst the prison of unconsciousness to rise as a clear and living flame above the fate of man. And He spoke thus: "Go forth once more, my son, take thy wondrous gift and spend it. And make thy path resplendent by showering it with blessings and with jewels too pure and fine for ruthless hands to spoil. Give and give, for in giving of thyself thy treasure grows and carries thee on waves of beauty to the Holy Circle, where there is no beginning and no end, and where the rhythm of creation beats the measure to thy golden songs.

'"And be thou deaf to the temptations of the demons who will assail thee with their promises of empty fame and wealth. Beware thy kingdom, O my son. It is the paradise of thine own making, a sacred refuge where none may follow thee, unless to give his soul into thy keeping and humbly serve the flame burning in the temple of thine heart. I will make thy gift a torch to light the way of those who walk in darkness. It shall be a charm to ease the heavy-laden, to dry the tears of suffering, shame and sorrow. It shall be a sword to slay the vipers of hypocrisy and scorn. It shall be a shield to hide thee from profane eyes: it shall be a crown of life immortal. It shall be My voice and with it I will speak of Hope, Faith and Love. May My blessing give thee strength to be true for ever to thy creation, to thyself and to Me."

'So the man was sent upon his mission. He heard that music ringing through the ages: to it he listened with his heart and spent his life in recreating what was given him to hear. Centuries come and go and still the music lives. Once again one will be born who hears it and with his heart-strings weaves the sounds together. Art never dies, it is eternal. It is the flame in God's creative hand, from which a spark is given to a few, though rarely. Some play with it, some pass it by, some throw it in the dirt. But once in generations a soul responds and tends the spark, and it becomes a light that shines through darkness, sorrow and despair, eternal consolation for him who keeps it clear like Truth. For Art aspires to Truth – and Truth is God Almighty. All the Arts are holy, but the holiest of them is Music, because it is the voice of God, because it says the things that only God can say. *Music is the essence of a language that has no need of words*. It must be heard in silence and in awe. Art is a trust; woe to him who touches it with unclean hands. He will not be forgiven. But much will be forgiven him who sins, and who can yet face his Maker, handing back the treasure he received unsullied.'

During my sojourn in Zurich a great deal of time was spent at the ophthalmic clinic, where kindly and rather baffled young women put me through various tests. One of these consisted of a stick being pointed at differently marked spots on a large board to see if my reactions, if any, might give clues for the forthcoming inspection. There was also a box, lit from within, revealing a red spot and a green line down the centre. With the red spot one had to play catch-as-catch-can on either side of the line. It seemed that I invariably landed up on the wrong side. After two days of these and other similar tiresome and tiring parlour games adapted to clinical usage, I was admitted to the inner sanctum where sacrificial victims were offered to the high priest: by this time I was in pretty poor shape for the ritual. In the shadows I had an outline impression of a short, broad figure of typical German-Swiss build. The Herr Professor was perusing the papers on which his satellites had recorded my all too evidently poor response to their blandishments. He looked up, frowning and indicating a chair. Then he turned his searchlights on me, growling in a rather disgruntled tone while he did so. Then we moved over to his desk again, where he said 'You – vot you do mit doze eyes?' 'Music' I answered. 'No' he said 'Zat I do not belief – es is impossible you do music mit dem. In a moment you must go: I can do nodding for you – nodding at all. But I tell you zat vot you haf will remain wit' you – it vill not get vorse – now go.'

Needless to say, my immediate reaction to this statement was one of considerable elation. If I had really been doing the impossible for 30 years, then, by all the Saints in Heaven, I would go on doing it. An old conviction, born of several equally pessimistic but less emphatic statements, convinced me that these fellows thrive on being proved wrong.

When sending a telegram the next morning to announce my return, I had addressed it to Wylye, Wiltshire, England. A stubby blue pencil crossed out the last two words with some vigour and disapproval. 'Vyle' I was told 'es enoff.' During the journey across France in the train I could scarce forbear to sing. A brisk and sprightly gale in the channel had whipped up a considerable turmoil, on which the boat danced hilariously during the crossing. Then I sang lustily to the wind and the waves while my fellow-travellers regurgitated their breakfast. I stood myself a celebratory lunch in the boat train from Folkestone. At Paddington there was considerable difficulty in finding a single ticket for Wylye. Search finally revealed a weather-beaten veteran with the serial number 0001: evidently every other traveller had come back again!

Six years later the help so abruptly withheld in Zurich was to be found in Bristol. To Anthony Palin a debt is owed that can never be repaid. Truly he has been a magician: he has been known to refer to me as 'my bloody miracle!' Be that as it may, he has given me the means to end a search for vision.

CHAPTER 22

Two Interludes: Downland Vigil

During the autumn of 1938 the shadow of things to come began to fall over our valley. The sad business of Munich had spluttered like a damp squib; we all knew what was coming. Flocks of unwelcome migrants in the shape of sandbags and gas-masks began to appear. As well as these harbingers of war there was an outbreak of foot-and-mouth disease at a nearby farm: during a spell of windless overcast weather the stench of burning carcases hung like a pall over the valley.

In the following spring we spent a few days at Aldbourne. Walking over the downs towards Ramsbury we came on three teams of horses at plough on a windy upland. The harness jingled and the brass facings gleamed in the chequered April sunlight. 'Take a good look at them,' I said to my wife, 'for you'll never see that sight again.' Early in September a freight train duly backed into the siding by Wylye station. Each truck held a tractor – one at least for each farm in the area. The horses disappeared – silently, overnight, leaving no trace at all. Fifty years earlier W. H. Hudson had watched, from Kingston Ridge in Sussex, one of the last teams of oxen at plough – and sadly recorded their imminent banishment from the landscape.

Meanwhile a Conservative government had been giving a more than usually convincing imitation of ostriches with heads buried in sand. Suddenly these heads were raised as a belated awareness of the situation registered, despite previous warning cries from a mere handful of colleagues that had gone unheeded. Clarion calls to volunteer for National Service were hurriedly sounded; I opted for night-duty with the Observer Corps. I couldn't see much but I could listen. There was to be a post on the down above Wylye, to which an assortment of local worthies rallied. Initially we were enrolled as Special Constables, though almost immediately transferred to the R.A.F., which paid us one-and-threepence an hour for time spent on duty.

The local C-in-C was Robert Newall, who lived in one of the three larger houses in our village. His passion in life was archaeology. Previously he had done some exploratory digging at Stonehenge, said then to have remained unexplored in this manner since the 18th-century. Those admirable gentry of a former age had obligingly left clues as to their operations, adding for good measure a buried bottle of port as a token of encouragement to their successors. Now Robert Newall was to find himself responsible for a motley bunch of rugged individualists, many of whom would have felt entirely at ease in the company of Falstaff at the *Boar's Head*. We all got on well together; in retrospect there seems hardly to have been a dull moment. During quieter nights there was ample scope for discussing every subject under the sun. True, it was to take some of us a bit of time to get tuned to the job. During one dark night soon after we had got under way, a deep stillness was broken by a solitary twin-engine plane on a training flight, zooming slowly and noisily across the valley, flying low. Silence was regained: the door of the hut opened, footsteps heard. Then a pause, followed by a voice that remarked in a rather petulant tone 'No, t'ain't, yer dam' fool!' However, we improved a bit as the months went by!

To watch the procession of the hours and seasons from such a vantage point was an unforgettable experience. Soon after our vigils began, in early October, old Orion appeared over the brow of the down, above a row of trees by Bilberry Farm. A phrase from one of Bliss Carman's 'realizations' of Sappho came into the mind like a well-loved tune:

> ". . . when the winter
> Huddles the sheep, and Orion
> Goes to his hunting."

Soon on the uplands shepherds would be making lambing folds, walled and partitioned by hurdles, carpeted by rich glowing straw from crops made tough and strong by natural manure – 'Little towns of gold' in Murray Allison's phrase. Then we would brace ourselves for the full fury of a Wiltshire winter. The Post faced north-east across the valley, beyond which lay Salisbury Plain, where the winds could gather strength and fury.

In early March we would look for the first intimations of spring. Little patches of young, fresh and vivid green would appear in the water-meadows, gradually spreading like a flush across each field, though not yet showing on higher ground. It was then that I would remember that magic shift from B minor into the key of G near the beginning of the first movement of Schubert's *Unfinished Symphony*. A long-held D in the horns heralds the transition, after it comes the modulation that prepares for the cellos to proclaim a new tonal climate – a crystallization in sound of what was happening in the valley below. Even as Dr. Johnson asserted that the man who is tired of London is tired of life, so would I claim that anyone who professed a love of music and who could resist that Schubertian blandishment must be suffering from a surfeit of over-indulgence.

Even in summer the breezes blew strongly as we plotted aircraft across our particular bit of sky. Meanwhile our telephonic colleagues in Bristol moved their tokens across the board. In quieter moments they and we resorted to games of chess, patience and similar devices to pass the hours of inactivity harmlessly by.

Particularly memorable were the dawns of early summer in 1940. During a prolonged spell of golden weather, a lark had nested near the edge of a field of barley that had been sown on the down behind our Post. Just before the sun came up over Yarnberry Camp this splendid bird would rise up, beginning to sing as it left the ground, spattering a silver shower of dew from its wings. Each day we expected to hear that the threatened invasion had begun; each day our skylark proclaimed that all would be well. Through the long anxious summer we waited, until there came a Sunday in mid-September when Goering's Luftwaffe received such a drubbing that it seemed likely we might escape from an ultimate horror, however hard and long the way ahead might prove to be. After such a hairbreadth escape, it was not surprising that a Labour government would – and did – replace the ostriches who had so nearly brought the country to the brink of a precipice.

It is time now to recall some of those erstwhile companions. Several, already elderly, had vivid memories of active service in the South African War. Nearly all had grown to manhood in a pre-mechanized England, for which they cherished a deep and abiding love, despite low wages, long hours and precious little in the way of compensations. They mostly belonged to the category of those described by A. G. Street as 'The Gentlemen of the Party' – those who, in Monk Gibbon's poem

> ". . . go home at dusk
> Along the lane."

There was Albert Simeon Bullock, retired signalman from the Great Western. He had spent many years at Sparkford in Somerset, where his box had been on the route of the Cornish Riviera. Bertram Carnell, a one-man coal merchant and eloquent advocate of duck-manure for everyman in his garden. Bill Carpenter (one of 'they byes' from the mill) had a roving brief at such times as he could be spared from home-duties, a kindly philosopher who gave people a hand as needed. Charlie Colborne, affectionately known as 'The Captain', arch-teller of tall stories, a splendid friend and companion during our joint vigils. Frank Davies, who delivered coal for Mr. Carnell's rival; 'Hayes'

Evelyn-Smith, retired schoolmaster and passionate bird-watcher. In quieter moments he would plot birds in flight, using the current aeronautic jargon as he did so – a quiet, infinitely kind and sensitive soul who bravely carried the stresses of active service in World War I and was shortly to enlist once more. Fred Still, landlord of *The Swan*, ex-Sergeant of musketry, moustaches curled at the ends, a champion spitter in bulk and distance – a skill effectively brought into play to denote a full-stop to sentences expressing contempt. Frank Taylor, who had manipulated steam-rollers in the service of the County Council, caring for them with paternal tenderness. He was also a dedicated choral singer, providing, often alone and unaided, a firm bass line. His great moment was the opening phrase of *Full Fathom Five* in Charles Wood's setting, a test-piece that seemed to be a perpetual stand-by as 'own choice' at local festivals. Eric Attewell, by tempera-ment an honorary member of Schumann's *Davidsbündler*, con-stantly bewailing the rude health of the philistines. He was a kindly idealist, my only contemporary in this elderly galaxy. George Imrie, architect and neighbour at Fisherton, having a constant and delightful flow of anecdotes and a keen interest and insight into the characters of our fellow-travellers.

One day Robert Newall came for a routine check on our vagaries, bringing a schoolboy, aged about 16, who was a member of the Junior Observer Corps. This pleasant fellow, sharing our duty, emitted a soft whistling sound that unquestionably re-sembled a tune in Mozart's *Eine Kleine Nachtmusik*.

'You seem to be interested in music; are you?'

'Oo – yes sir. I play the cello.' Thus began a lifelong friendship with Nicholas Gent, skilled physician, sporadic cellist and companion on many walks and sharer of mutual enthusiasms.

Stray echoes of conversational remarks from my companions still linger in the mind: here are a few of them.

(of a dairyman) 'Some'ow 'is life seems to be wrapped up in milk: I know mine ain't!' (spit)

'I see'd 'im wi' she walkin' up to'ards Groveley: What do'em want to go up there for – to look at sky? GAH!'

'Very expensive place Bournemouth; fourpence for a lettuce.'

'There was girls everywhere in Salisbury Saturday: hold up a shillin' an' they'd follow yer to kingdom come.'

'Our lorry, fully loaded, started backin' an' the rear wheel went right over me foot. I never felt nothin' but the tread of the tyre was marked clear on me skin for several days.'

'We 'ad a visitin' choir in church Sunday: R an 'twas a cantata they performed. Very pretty 'twere – jis' like music 'twas.'

(of a steam-roller) 'She were a lovely creetur – she were fast too. She'd do fully five mile an hour when in full steam: I know becos I timed her all the way from Wilton to Stoford Bridge – an' that's exactly five mile.'

'When I come 'ome and tak' off me shoen – an' me socks – an' if I were to walk across the floor, every step what I mid take 'ould be writ clear as writin' in a bloody book. But our Jim – 'e can wear a pair o' socks for a whole month, take they off – 'n shake the dust out of 'en as though they's taters in a sack.'

A widower, speaking of a kindly woman neighbour who gave a hand in his housekeeping, always alluded to her with warmth and appreciation as 'Thik-'oman-what-do-scrub-out-for-I-an'-who-do-cook-I-puddens.'

CHAPTER 23

What the teacup told me

In the early spring of 1941 our third son Antony was born: he lost no time in giving intimations of becoming a musician. Meanwhile a modified daily routine continued, with nightly vigils at the Observer Post.

Down the lane at Fisherton lived Dorothy Moore, tending an elderly mother. She used to come daily to the cottage to give us a helping hand, thereby becoming a firm friend in the process. An adept charmer-away of warts, she also told fortunes in teacups. One day she told mine: 'In a few weeks time you will be going on an unexpected journey. There will be a lot of people at the place; but you'll be all right. I see two men – one tall and dark, the other fair – they will help you.'

Sure enough I received my calling-up papers. They directed me to report at Boyce Barracks, Crookham, the training depot of the Royal Army Medical Corps. On a dark morning in late autumn I duly 'proceeded' to Fleet where, with several other conscripts, we were herded into a truck and taken to barracks.

This escapade was somewhat surprising, in that a previous Medical Board had intimated that it was unlikely that the Army would need me to give it a helping hand. The man who had been dealing with eyes had not troubled himself to examine mine, but a kindly doctor dealing with feet had spotted a possible problem. He had also noticed my name, proving to be a friend of my father, who was eminent in medical circles. So a halt was called to the proceedings while the assembled doctors and I had a cup of tea together, while fellow inspectees, stripped to the waist, grew restive in the wings.

On arrival at Crookham we were shoved around by numerous NCOs, some kindly, others seeming not to like the look of us at all. After which we were drafted to barrack-rooms, each containing about 25 beds. Several fellow-travellers had evidently been muted at home by the presence of wives and children: their initial response to release from bondage being a chorus of four-letter words, emerging with the pent-up pressure of uncorked bottles, though possibly intended as an affirmation of masculine potency. These characters were poised to explore nearby towns, in which – it had been softly intimated – alleviations for those in search of wine, women and song abounded in plenty. To the rest of us it seemed that the *modus vivendi* that accompanies four-letter worditis must be both monotonous and repetitive. By way of a more moderate approach it is hard to improve on Samuel Butler's admirable comment – 'It is the function of vice to keep virtue within reasonable bounds.'

We duly settled down to training, under the watchful eye of Sergeant-Major Martin, an admirable representative of the species. At the beginning of each working day we paraded outside the Company Office. Invariably it seemed that the rising winter sun would lurk behind a distant hillock until the moment when S/M Martin made his stage entry. While doing so he would roar the command 'D Company – CHORE,' that being the current pronunciation of 'shun' in Crookham circles. (A friend in another regiment was trained to respond to 'T'oop TOWE!') At the sound of that CHORE the sun would immediately breast the horizon. So the day's training would get under way, initially lectures, though with interspersed fatigue duties. The lectures, given by a galaxy of NCOs, were mass-produced, fourth-form little jokes and all, irrespective of whoever gave them. Sometimes a deputy would repeat yesterday's monologue, almost word for word. We found this very soothing, not a little reminiscent of talking parrots.

The sergeants, with one notable exception, were splendid fellows, the corporals extremely variable. We were generally pushed around by two of them. One was a large pink-faced example with thick rope-like fair hair and a lip that curled sardonically if innocently asked an un-military question. One day he ordered me to sweep out the barrack-room, indicating a brush for the job, but no receptacle. 'You won't find a dustpan here' he said 'You're supposed to be a soldier, not a bloody housemaid. Use an old packe' of Pl'yers to pu' the muck in.' Each morning I had to go into his cubicle to perform some trifling menial task: the lofty condecension with which he barely acknowledged my friendly 'Good morning, Corporal' was so comic that I found it hard to hide my enjoyment of this assumed *hauteur*. The other two-striped merchant was altogether less likeable; he was small in size with a reluctant moustache, green eyes and an incipient sneer. Somehow his loaded sallies failed to hit their mark, though anyone nursing a genuine chip on the shoulder could have been deeply hurt. He meant well but, try we never so hard, we were not really his type at all.

Being tall meant that one was apt to to be chosen as marker when undergoing marching drill. On the first and only occasion I was given the job, chaos ensued, since we had been ordered to keep some distant object in view that was invisible to me. The ensuing commentary, rich and fruity, made the diversion worth while for sheer entertainment value!

The Medical Boards had allowed some unlikely people to slip through their nets. One member of our intake was extremely hard of hearing. On the barrack square he would instinctively turn his head and put hand to ear to try and decipher each bark of command, even those emanating from Staff-Sergeant Blank, the one and only universally disliked man in the depot.

When a friend holding a commission arrived on the scene, diplomatic channels were improvised to make it possible for us to have an occasional brief outing during free time. The idea that a member of the humbler creation like myself could be on equal social terms with an officer caused mild astonishment, particularly in the breast of S/M Martin. He began to think I might possibly have some hidden qualities that had lain unperceived up to now. Subsequently he and I discussed poetry among other subjects, after he had discovered an anthology I had left in the communal locker in our barrack-room. He even confessed to having given way to the poetic impulse himself in youthful days. The anthology passed into his keeping during a locker inspection, officially confiscated as being unsuitable reading matter for the ranks!

There were two canteens, one at each end of the depot, identical in every way except that one possessed a more peaceful and friendly atmosphere than the other. It was interesting to discover that the Roman Padre celebrated Mass on Sundays and Saints Days in the canteen some of us found more congenial.

Sessions for religious instruction were held in various places, including the Garrison Theatre. This dark, cavernous and infinitely depressing building was allotted to Church of England types, they being the most numerous. During my few weeks sojourn we had three successive Chaplains. The first, from what must have been an upper-crust village in East Anglia, belonged to the 'Now chaps . . .' school of delivery. 'Come and listen to me burbling' he would say. In mid-burble one day he surprised us all by saying 'Now chaps, about the Resurrection – let's smoke, shall we?' He seemed blandly unaware as to the implication of this casual *non sequitur*! All too soon he was replaced by a diminutive fellow whom we summed up in about ten seconds. In his company we would settle down for a cosy chat while he worked himself into a frenzy at our total lack of response. He was barely audible and totally ineffective. The third specimen has left no trace in the memory. Not one of the trio ever dreamed of paying a visit to a barrack-room, since presumably the souls of officers had a higher value in the C. of E's spiritual stock-market than the likes of us. So we were handed over to the Church Army Captain. This dedicated and sincere fellow would appear on occasions, going through the motions of his kind, thumping the Bible and proclaiming it to be his shield and buckler. This was much to the liking of an ardent dissenter in our midst, though noisy, tedious and disturbing when we would be either reading, writing letters or just talking peacefully in the evenings. If any of the other professional clerics had possessed the inclination or the ability to communicate one iota of genuine, friendly goodness, the impact would have been considerable. But the C. of E. has ever been adept at dropping catches.

A soldier in the ranks is allowed to have a religion; it is almost his only unquestioned possession. One day we were being sorted into denominational groups for one of these RI comedies: all but one had been accounted, a solitary figure remained.

'Hey you, what religion are you supposed to have?'

'I'm a Christian Spiritualist, Sergeant.'

'Get over there double-quick with all those C. of Es – and don't be so dam' choosey another time!'

For our other possessions we had a kit-bag and a communal locker. Everyone else in our barrack-room bought padlocks; my own, tied by cord as issued, was the only one nobody ever tried to pilfer.

One afternoon some of us were marched down to a hut at the far end of the depot for eye-inspection. Curious to relate, there were two specialists at work there. One was very tall and fair, the other, also tall – and dark! For the first time during those weeks I remembered Dorothy and the teacup. These fellows proved to be kindly men. It was the dark one who asked me what I thought I was doing there; I told him I had often wondered myself, but that no clue had as yet emerged.

After that I had a charmed life for several days, during which even the Corporals who had tried to take hell out of me suddenly became kindly considerate human beings. So, by way of Kempston Barracks, the Army obligingly sent me back to Civvy Street.

CHAPTER 24

The Slow Train gathers speed

The Army's parting instruction was to lose no time in reporting to the Ministry of Labour. 'That's OK, feller' they said 'Run away and play.' An offer to rejoin the Captain and my other chums for Downland Vigils was similarly rejected. 'Better men than I' were now needed and, it seemed, forthcoming. So back once more to music.

Soon there came an invitation from St. Mary's School, Calne, to conduct a performance of my cantata *The Echoing Green*. This happy occasion became memorable on two counts: for the beginning of a friendship with the Headmistress Miss Matthews – 'Matt' of cherished memory – also because it led soon afterwards to my becoming the school's Director of Music. Though 'Matt' really preferred members of the male sex to be either Bishops or Admirals, she was none the less well-disposed towards musicians. Of these, during the three years when I visited the school regularly, none was more warmly welcomed than Reginald Jacques. He was persuaded to come every year to take charge of the annual concert. This took place in November by way of St. Cecilia Day celebrations. After we had brought the music to a gently simmering point, 'J' would bring it to the boil at a final rehearsal and concert. After the first of these occasions the singers were invited to take part in the Bach Choir's London performance of the *St. Matthew Passion* as a section of the ripieno choir. But the project was considered too rash for safety at a critical stage of the war. No one in my experience has rivalled 'J' in encouraging singers and players, particularly amateurs, to respond fully to the job in hand as well as to his exceptionally outgoing personality. Working with and for him has been an unforgettable and enriching experience that countless people remember with gratitude and affection.

Of other musicians who came to play to St. Mary's, memory recalls happy occasions with Bernard Shore (who succeeded 'J' as presiding conductor on these occasions), Julius Isserlis and John Ticehurst, the latter bringing his Kirkman harpsichord. Now that the makers of these instruments have gone in for intensive breeding, it is surely due in great measure to the pioneers of a previous generation that the present vogue has come about. These three musicians became and remained firm friends. Julius Isserlis has already made an appearance in this journey; Bernard Shore and I have shared an enthusiasm for railways in the days of steam, while John and I have walked together from his home on the edge of Romney Marsh. Two singers who won an outstandingly enthusiastic response at St. Mary's were Anne Wood and Mary Ross Macdougall, then operating as a duo.

Each week during term I would spend one night at Calne. Close to the school gates lived two elderly sisters, the Miss Antells, who took in the various people such as parents, lecturers and others, who came from time to time. The sisters belonged to a very strict religious sect that flourished in the town: texts and pamphlets abounded. They were blissfully unaware of geographical distances; after an air raid on Bath, they did not hesitate to attribute it to the Japanese. The Lord must indeed have provided for them, for they shared their meagre rations with their guests, or so they affirmed, without troubling to apply for extra provisions.

In company with many other musicians, I have visited countless schools, though none that responded with such happy spontaneity as St. Mary's in the now distant nineteen-forties. Shortly before I 'moved on' we did a broadcast from Bristol that included my setting of Rupert Brooke's poem *Day that I have loved*, set for three-part chorus and two pianos.

Meanwhile in Wiltshire, the Rural Music School had emerged from extremely modest beginnings and was expanding under the guidance of Katharine Marshall Jones, a soprano singer of charm and ability and an excellent musician. She was soon to exchange a career in music for marriage in Yorkshire. Since I was already connected with the Rural Music School and deeply interested in the work, I applied for the job of successor to Katharine and, to my delighted surprise, was duly appointed Director.

There is no doubt that the ever-growing interest in music and the arts was greatly stimulated during the turmoil of World War II. There was an increasing awareness of the part they were contributing to the everyday life of the nation. In Russia, during the siege of Leningrad, a directive was given that music and drama should be encouraged to continue as much as possible during those terrible days. In Britain the Carnegie Trustees inaugurated a five-year plan, by which counties willing to set up committees for the encouragement of both music and drama would be eligible for grants, to enable them to appoint organizers in both spheres of activity. Wiltshire elected for a variation on this theme, by which the Rural Music School became 'recognized' as the corporate music organizer, which meant that I, as Director, became linked with the Education Department at County Hall. Similarly for drama, Joan Yeaxlee was appointed to go out into the highways and byways to stimulate and encourage interest and participation in do-it-yourself productions. The Carnegie Trust urged co-operation between us, but this proved an impossibly tough nut to crack. It seemed that music and drama belonged to two different worlds, since those who supported one camp took care to keep well away from the other! Finally Joan and I devised a Words and Music programme that did, in the end, achieve a modest mingling between the separated faithful to one or the other arts. With the advent of the Butler Education Act, local authorities became under an obligation to take over the pioneering work that the likes of us were engaged in carrying out and in time became wholly responsible for it. It has been an exciting and rewarding experience to have lived and worked through a development of such far-reaching implications.

The RMS office at Trowbridge, at the time of my arrival, was over a butcher's shop in Fore Street. Through the windows came the encouraging aroma of beer being produced at Usher's brewery, while chimes from the parish church clock marked the hours of our working day. The shop below was run by two brothers, one of whom had written a hymn – in praise of water. He very kindly suggested that I might care to write a tune for it, but somehow I seemed unable to oblige. After all, I was very busy. But the dedication reminded me of Stravinsky, whose *Symphony of Psalms* is duly inscribed, not only to the Glory of God, but also to the Boston Symphony Orchestra. Here the Glory of God naturally took priority, though the runner-up was (by permission) The Trowbridge and Melksham Water Board.

Since secretaries in an office are as essential as signalmen to their boxes, this is the moment to recall with affection and gratitude Gilbert and Audrey Oakshott, devoted husband and wife, both amateur musicians as well as excellent secretaries, whose continuous and dedicated work for us in Wiltshire will be long remembered. Since they had been obliged to leave their London home, here they were – and how glad we were to have them. Audrey had been part-time secretary to Katharine Marshall Jones, so she was able to sort me out and indicate the general situation. Later when full-time help became essential, Gilbert took over, later generously providing office accommodation in his own house when an expiring lease threatened to put us on the streets.

Katharine, being a singer, had developed the choral side of the schools' work which, until her advent, had been mainly instrumental. The first and most daunting project I inherited was to conduct a series of massed carol festivals in various parts of

Wiltshire. As I lacked sufficient eyesight to drive, these had to be carried out by train and bus – and Wiltshire is a very big county.

Operation Carols began with a large assignment of boys and girls in Salisbury Cathedral. Here the atmosphere of the building and the efficiency of the vergers smoothed away the problems involved. Never has a visit there failed to bring a sense of benediction, though in the following year there was a near crisis on a similar occasion, this time for adult singers, mainly consisting of Women's Institute choirs. A local orchestral society had promised to provide accompaniments: ten minutes before we were due to start, not a single player had appeared. I was to conduct from the organ loft. As I watched the singers assemble, it seemed that the King of Instruments was watching me with a sardonic sneer, the ends of each manual curling slightly upwards. I had never coped with anything larger than organs normally found in village churches. At that moment a voice spoke behind me; 'Look here, le Fleming' it said 'Would you like me to play for you?' I turned thankfully; it was Canon Walter Ferguson, then the Precentor. So he played, bless him, though at his *tempi*, hardly ever at mine!

On the day after the first of these Salisbury occasions, which was one of December's gloomiest, hard, dry and sunless specimens, a bus took me to Malmesbury, where a similar operation was to take place in the Abbey. At the time the state of things ecclesiastical there seemed to be in rather low water, with only a Perpetual Curate in charge. He was elderly, ineffective and unhelpful. The young from the town and surrounding countryside were unresponsive and evidently allergic to carols. My heart bled for their teachers, who must have had an uphill struggle to persuade any sound to emanate from them. There was no heat in the Abbey, no sun outside – and a passive resistance to all my blandishments, while the Perpetual Curate ambled up and down the aisles with, it seemed, a Perpetual Sniff! Somehow we struggled through the morning rehearsal and the afternoon's so-called performance. The bus, standing in the market-square, that would take me back to Chippenham on the first stage of the homeward journey seemed a haven of comfort. How different was the impression when recently I visited the Abbey on a spring day to find how greatly the atmosphere within it has changed – from darkness, it seemed, to light.

Next came Trowbridge where, at the Tabernacle, all was alive, friendly, happy and responsive. Similarly, at the Parish Church at Bradford-on-Avon, the young singers co-operated splendidly. The final – and depressing – rally was in a cinema at Warminster.

Shabby plush, dim lights and atmospheric overtones of cowboys were not an exactly promising setting, nor were the lads and lasses eager to participate. We battled through the day; as a result it was a long time, even years, before I was able to look a carol in the face with anything approaching the 'comfort and joy' required by way of response.

'I must confess to a feeling of relief when New Year's Day comes round and the season of Decarolization sets in.' After the events just described I felt I had truly found a friend – in this instance the speaker was Sir Bruce Richmond who, with his enchanting wife Elena, had recently come to live at Nether-hampton. As editor of the *Times Literary Supplement*, Bruce Richmond had given encouragement to many writers and poets who subsequently achieved recognition and fame. Many musicians remember his interest, help and encouragement, not only the eminent but also those of us engaged in leading a village choir to the local festival, or inaugurating a modest instrumental group. Meanwhile the Richmonds were thoroughly enjoying their retirement. 'Oh yes' he said 'Elena is idly industrious while I am industriously idle.'

Meanwhile, as what has become known as a 'fringe body', I had established friendly relations with the Education Office at County Hall. The occupant of the hot Directorial seat was away on Active Service, so the department was presided over by his deputy, Dorothy Scott Baker. Like everyone else who came under her sway, I counted it a privilege to work with and for her. Behind her charm of manner there was a shrewd and realistic awareness of every implication in the many problems that came her way. She invariably detected true worth, however unpromising the situation might appear: mixed motives, attempts to impress and any sign of humbug received short shrift. She always found time to discuss a problem with any of us, however trivial it might appear in the general scheme of things. Later she became the first woman to be appointed a Director of Education.

There were others in offices down the long corridor who became real friends, such as Ted Littlecott, who looked after what was then known as 'further', now adult education and who later made a considerable impact in Hampshire. Youth (with a capital Y) had recently been highlighted: clubs were being set up all over the county under the guidance of Elizabeth Currey and her energetic and capable assistant Mary Royston. Incidentally where are they now, these clubs? We could do with them.

The long corridor of officers provides a suitable setting to introduce our Rural Music School Chairman, Alderman W. E.

Stevens, known as Willy, though not in his presence. When I was hurrying down this very corridor one day he stopped me, and with a gentle tap on the shoulder gravely said 'Di-rectors *never* run!' He was a kindly, dedicated character who later became vice-chairman of the County Council. Over our Governing Council he presided with a quiet and firm demeanour. As is often the case, there were the inevitable clashes of loyalties and personalities over one or two people who were said to be 'difficult' but who, none-the-less, carried out their jobs with unremitting patience, considerable success and precious little thanks. During a meeting when the situation over one of them had become tense, Willy Stevens said 'Now, ladies and gentlemen, we have discussed this matter very fully but we have not reached a decision. But there is one lady present this afternoon whose opinion we have not asked – I allude to My Lady Nicotine.' Then, taking out his cigarette case without waiting for a reply) 'Thank you so much – I feel sure she will enable us to reach agreement.' And she did!

CHAPTER 25

About People and Places

Since the modest salary I was earning in Wiltshire came mainly from the Carnegie Trustees, it was not long before there was an intimation that their music adviser, Dr. Sydney Northcote, would be coming to 'vet' the new boy on their books. The news seemed to cause an apprehensive flutter among the members of our executive committee; as it transpired, however, we arranged to meet in London. Within the first five minutes it was evident that all would be well: Sydney proved to be a musician of wide knowledge, a prolific teller of stories and an apt companion for the pub lunch that set a seal on our friendship.

I was taken to the National Council of Social Services office in Bedford Square. Since the N.C.S.S. was the channel through which Carnegie bounty flowed, our quarry was the Chief Rural Officer.

John Smeal was one of the last of a generation notable for the quality and quantity of truly individual characters. No one else in my experience so adroitly practised the art of gentle and harmless deception. In school days when in chapel, he and his confederates could be seen devoutly kneeling in their pew, heads bent in prayer, one hand over the eyes, the other gently engaged in passing cards to and fro in a truly reverent manner. 'Under the eye of God – yes' he said, 'But the Beak – No!' He shared with many other people the belief that flowers in the Garden of Eden were just as beautiful before they acquired elaborate names. He was once taking a somewhat gullible lady round his garden, who pointed to a shrub and asked its name. She had already revealed a complete lack of humour: with grave courtesy John replied 'Ah – now I can tell you the name; it is called schizophrenia immaculata!'

Back now to the moment when Sydney and I proceeded to our lunch. Later, when I too was working in London, the offices of the Carnegie music and drama advisers and the Rural Music Schools Association were next to each other at 106 Gloucester Place, in company with the British Federation of Music Festivals. There Sydney and I continued to exchange comments, stories and to discuss problems. When I became Editor of *Making Music*, a journal that was to flourish for thirty years, his constant help and advice were of the greatest value.

Into the office at Trowbridge one day came Dorothea Dalrymple, our principal string teacher, valiant and too little honoured pioneer. She said, 'Do you think we could have a summer school, so that my scattered pupils could have a chance to meet each other and play together?' In 1944 the chance of finding a suitable and available place seemed doubtful, but it happened that there was an evacuated convent school in a large house at Bratton, a pleasant village that lies under the northern boundary of Salisbury Plain, below the Westbury White Horse. The nuns welcomed the project, provided we arranged to come for a week at the end of the summer term.

The idea of a summer school of music for the young was then both new and exciting. The first had taken place a year earlier at Cowley Manor in Gloucestershire, organized by my opposite number in that county, Margot Hubert. Ours seems to have been the second, while a national venture, loudly proclaimed as the first, was in fact the third. So, at the end of a golden July, we moved in – at least the girls did, but since canon law forbade masculine presence at night, some of us were given hospitality in the village.

One of our committee members was the retired headmistress of a large girls' school in the North of England. She not only led the chorus of encouragement in the committee, but offered to come as a presiding matron of honour (a figurehead, one felt, and an example to us all). Somewhat rashly she insisted on our having a formal assembly each morning, duly inviting the local rector to come and give us a benediction. Since the community was totally Roman Catholic, his arrival was the signal for the nuns to hurry into chapel *en masse*. The simultaneous transmission on the same wavelength was further complicated by a group of Jewish students, who added their quota from a dormitory. The resultant clamour must have reached the celestial spheres in a very confused state: an equivalent in music might be envisaged as a combined performance of Bloch's *Sacred Service*, a Palestrina Mass and Stanford – in B flat of course. But in those days we still had beautiful minds – even the young, so nobody showed surprise. And nuns, bless them, are no strangers to the diverse ways of humanity.

It was a happy and successful week. For most of our boys and girls it gave a first experience of staying away from home and families and to consort with congenial companions. This, the forerunner of many similar occasions was a memorable experience.

The present job carried with it an invitation to spend a week each year at Dartington Hall, where a music teacher training project had recently been established with Imogen Holst as presiding genius. The Ministry of Education had recently 'recognized' the venture by giving an official blessing. (Many years past in *Punch* there was a series of drawings over the caption 'Entertainments at which we have never assisted'. A similar representation of the Department of Education and Science at the moment of recognition suggests possibilities for an imaginative illustrator.)

At Dartington, when I arrived, an early spring was giving the landscape a quality of dreamlike enchantment. It seemed that the ground was of a softer substance than elsewhere. In the early evening I went for a stroll when, coming round a corner, I encountered a middle-aged man, also in mid-stroll. 'Good evening' he said 'My name is Hugo; I am from Austria. Now I wish to ask a question. I haf been reading some of your English Restoration plays – and in dese plays it seems that many of the men greatly prefer their mistresses to their wives. Now you may perhaps be able to tell me – is dis true of Englishmen nowadays?' Just as a batsman might feel when he sees a ball coming straight for his middle stump, so I parried with something to the effect that while it is certainly true of some men, the majority, I was sure, naturally preferred their wives. The answer seemed to muddle him somewhat, so I gently led the way towards the *White Hart* and the conversation into easier channels.

This encounter was to be the first of many, equally unexpected and diverting. The students then in residence were predominantly feminine. Like everyone else they adored Imogen, who was taking them through the enchantments of polyphony, Schütz and on to JSB and Mozart – the period so aptly described by Alfred Einstein as the age of innocence in music. Then straight into the twentieth century, since for her the nineteenth evinced potent deviationist tendencies. As a foundation, people were being encouraged to write and to sing Rounds to words of their own choosing. Some of these I was later able to preserve in two books of assorted examples. The sound of part-singing by a group of young feminine voices seemed particularly apt in that gentle spring weather, over a soft undulating landscape. Imogen had just produced her sets of carols arranged for three-part unaccompanied voices. On a still and moonlit evening a group of students climbed to the top of the Tower to sing the Bedfordshire May Day Carol. The effect was sheer magic – the magic that belongs to Act V of The Merchant of Venice –

> 'Soft stillness and the night
> Become the touches of sweet harmony.'

Since that evening there have been two other occasions when
the sound of voices, unfettered by accompaniment, has revealed
the quintessence of sheer beauty. The next occasion, indeed both,
followed soon after that sojourn at Dartington. I was urged, in the
cause of 'further' education, to visit a lonely farm near Burbage to
'help' a young Jewish community with their music-making. These
delightful people had been given the promise of returning to their
native country after the war, on condition that they took over an
unoccupied farm to grow food. So, on an autumn evening, I was
met at Savernake station by an escort that led me along the
towpath of the Kennet and Avon canal, then across fields to a
farm. Furniture and fittings were minimal, but there was no
mistaking the generous kindness of the young of both sexes. The
décor would have made an admirable setting for a stage version of
Cold Comfort Farm, though here and now it seemed irrelevant.

After a meal of the High Tea variety, we all assembled, on
hardback chairs, in a circle round a glowing fire. The girls settled
down to sewing and mending, some of the men to their ploys. It
was the chief spokesman Reuben who said 'Now will you talk to
us about music?' 'But' I replied, 'won't you first sing for me?' The
response was immediate; an unspoken current of assent seemed to
flow round the circle – and someone started very softly to sing.
The others joined in – and soon they were away in full and
glowing harmony. Since the Jew has ever been a wanderer over
the world, his songs reflect many different traditions and cultures.
These voices at times simulated the effect of trumpets in strong
sunlight; at others they were as soft as an Austrian *Lied*, with
intimations of Schubertian grace and charm. At the end of a full
two hours I thanked them for their hospitality and for an
unforgettable evening. As we went towards our beds, the refrain
of one of the songs haunted me – and has continued to do so ever
since. In translation it runs 'It is the hand that sows – and the heart
that reaps.' Wherever those wanderers are now, I bless them for
one of the truly enriching experiences of a lifetime – and wish
them well. It was with gratitude that I informed the educational
source that it was I, not my friends, who had been 'helped'.

Another occasion when the sound of voices touched an
unexpected height of expression was during a holiday when, one
evening, we visited the old *Ship Inn* at Mevagissey. It was in the
days when the Barron family held sway and there was a homely
and cosy bar parlour. Round a table by the window sat a group of
fishermen, shortly intent on setting out for a night catch. They
were singing quietly together, completely unaware of the usual –
though now subdued – coming and going at the bar. Before

getting up to go, they broke into the ritual 'Good night, ladies –
we've got to leave you now. For we go sailing merrily – Across
the deep blue sea.' On the last phrase they lingered, the notes
swelling out in volume and finishing with a *diminuendo* to *niente* that
any professional group might envy. On the words 'Across the deep
blue sea' we, who were listening, felt a catch in the breath as we
recalled Homer and *The Odyssey* and all who have since gone
down to the sea in ships and occupied their business in great
waters.

By way of tailpiece, another chance encounter of a very
different calibre. On a brilliant Sunday evening in early summer I
was walking across Salisbury market-place towards the bus
station. The square was completely deserted, except for a
contingent of the Salvation Army in a corner by the Guildhall. An
evangelist preacher was in full spate, pouring out exhortations to
a solitary cat, two dogs, some pigeons – and me, pausing to listen
to him. The cat was thoughtfully stropping its back against some
railings, one of the dogs scratching, the other intent on a lamp-
post. The pigeons were alternately scouring the ground for
leavings from the previous day's market, or sitting on the eaves of
the houses discussing their own affairs. The bandsmen looked as
bored as they usually do when someone is talking, thus preventing
them from playing; they had doubtless heard this tirade many times
over. Eventually it came to an abrupt stop, while I, his solitary
human listener, felt impelled to offer a word of thanks. It had been
a splendid oration. The speaker's response was to give me what can
only be described as a very dirty look indeed: before stumping off
he said 'Well – I 'ope it will take effect, that's all!' I have since
learned that other sermonizers seem to get a nasty jolt when
thanked: perhaps after all such things are better said in music.

CHAPTER 26

Music in Religious Drama

When, in the period between the wars, Bishop Bell of Chichester appointed Martin Browne as Diocesan Drama Adviser, a far-reaching stimulus was given to an art-form that had not flourished since the middle ages. One of the first and most significant results was to provide occasions for writers such as T. S. Eliot and Dorothy L. Sayers to write plays for production in cathedrals and churches.

Following in the wake of so glittering a spearhead, other writers followed with a bewildering diversity of contributions. Soon the Religious Drama Society was born: like most pioneers it operated on a shoestring and was largely dependent on voluntary help. In contrast to the general attitude to music so often evinced by the world of drama, the Society was aware from the start of the part that music must play in the pioneering work it was so bravely undertaking.

All musicians know to their cost, none more so than composers, that the last ingredient that most producers and actors ever think about is the music. A typical instance was the occasion when Ealing Studios telephoned Vaughan Williams to request some music for a film in the final stages of production. V.W. expressed his pleasure in being asked to co-operate, but warned the voice on the telephone that he worked rather slowly. 'That's all right' came the reply, 'We don't want the full score till Wednesday.'

Legend has it that at the first summer school to be sponsored by the newly-formed R.D.S., a church musician was invited to give some ideas and suggestions as to the provision of music for plays. It seems, however, that he gave a very interesting talk that had little bearing on the purpose for which he had been invited to speak.

It so happened that a modest group called the Salisbury Diocesan Fellowship of Religious Drama decided to hold their own summer school at Uplyme in Dorset. Once again the beneficent name of Elena Richmond comes into these pages, since it was she who galvanized the local fraternity into action – and I was asked to undertake the job of advocate of music.

The organizers were a group of charming sisters who lived in The Close at Salisbury. Even in the mid nineteen-forties they still seemed to belong to the Edwardian age. When I asked for a gramophone on which to illustrate my talk, they replied in a letter as follows: 'We have searched high and low for a gramophone, since none of us seems to possess one. But the gardener at the house where we are going has offered to lend his instrument. It is contained in a sort of box – would that be suitable?' It transpired that the chosen victim was of a kind often advertized in journals of the period – £5 without lid (this can be supplied at slight extra cost). Fortunately there was a lid to subdue the surface noise too often emitted by 78 discs. Its lowest cruising speed, however, was around 85, so that the chosen illustrations emerged considerably quicker in tempo and at least a major third higher in pitch! Happily the general trend seemed to be what was needed, despite the unwonted jet-propulsion of delivery. The result of my effort was a booklet published by S.P.C.K. summarizing the kind of approach suggested.

It proved to be a truly enjoyable week. Again, like the music-making teenagers at Bratton, it was a completely new experience. Sedate and elderly ladies found themselves skipping along the passages, pausing to ask where the Group Work was in session; then, when told, hurrying away, as often as not, trolling snatches of the *Te Deum* in happy quavering *alto* voices. It was all very exciting.

News of my modest efforts with the gardener's jet-propelled gramophone must have penetrated to R.D.S. Headquarters. The two people responsible at the time for carrying out the job there were T. G. 'Jim' Bartholomew and Carina Robins, Secretary and Travelling Adviser respectively. Jim, sadly for all of us, was to leave this troubled world too soon: Carina continued for many years before undertaking similar explorations in Nigeria, where her pioneering brought rich rewards and many friends. It was she who conveyed the Society's invitation to come and 'do it again' at Bishop Otter College, Chichester, where the summer school was to be held in the following year.

So began a continued and varied annual visitation to summer schools in the various places in which they were held. Now that most colleges contain both men and women students, the standard of domestic amenities has greatly improved and become standardized. Formerly there would be a marked difference between institutions for one or other of the sexes. Colleges for women and girls' schools tended to be a little finicky. Curtains were apt to stray from hooks; there were few, if any, pegs on doors as well as the inevitable little notices. The occasion when an R.A.F. contingent found themselves billeted in a girls' school has passed into social history. These frustrated fellows were confronted in their sleeping quarters by bells, under each of which there appeared a notice – 'Please ring if a mistress is required.' Men's colleges, on the other hand, tended to omit essential adjuncts, a typical instance being an exhortation to leave the bathroom as you would wish to find it, without a sign of any equipment with which to comply.

At Chichester Jim and Carina excelled as host and hostess. Students came from far and wide. On that first occasion we were due to arrive on a Sunday. I had returned from another job in the north on the previous evening and so spent a night in London. In the morning I attended a Service at St. Martin-in-the-Fields. As nearly always there, I became deeply aware of a very special quality in the Service. Also by the striking contrast between the obviously well-to-do and the less fortunate people. It seemed that everyone had left their 'status' outside to become one united community. Soon after arriving at Chichester in the early evening I was talking to one of the Chaplains on the Course, to whom I mentioned casually that I had been to Church that morning, and added where. To my surprise he said 'Heavens, you didn't really go there, did you? Why, they do the most terrible things to the Liturgy!' Needless to say this padre was a splendid fellow, but like so many people in all the professions, it seems that diversity proliferates. It is certain that we musicians are no exception, particularly composers!

As it is impossible to recall at which of many gatherings certain events took place, still less to recount them, a few scattered fragments must suffice.

One of my duties was to organize a students' concert during the week. Every item was sympathetically auditioned beforehand; often unsuspected talent would emerge. There was always a rich harvest for the lighter side, though the more serious endeavours tended to vary in quality. An all-time high was reached when a group of young students from Northern Ireland offered to give a performance of Synge's *Riders to the Sea*. For sheer breath-taking sincerity and ability to go to the heart of the matter, the occasion was unforgettable. The group was led by Joan Barry, still remembered with deep and abiding gratitude thirty years on.

Another discovery was the poet Margaret Stanley-Wrench, whose work deserves to be better known, as well as some of the best of her poems published. To those who know them, few though they may be, her memory will be cherished.

Christopher Fry's *The Boy with the Cart* seemed particularly apt for the kind of performance our students were eager to give. Among lecturers Moelwyn Merchant was outstanding. When someone else failed to materialize, he proceeded to give an impromptu dissertation on *Macbeth* that revealed new depth and potency to all. When he came to a pause he said 'But of course all I've been saying is only at a level I would choose for a child of ten or eleven. With time to prepare this talk I would have been able to give you much more insight about this marvellous play.' Happy the parish in Dyfed that has had this dear man to talk to them every week.

Other people who made splendid and individual contributions include Kay Baxter, author of plays, one of which, *Your Trumpets, Angels* was commissioned for Southwark Cathedral during the Festival of Britain, for which I wrote the music. Doreen Woodcock, who was the producer on that occasion, also brought gaiety and inspiration to these festive summer meetings. Together we produced Kay's delightful 'morality' *Pull Devil Pull Baker*, based on nursery rhymes, which gave me a delightful opportunity to adapt these basic tunes in our heritage. Later I adapted it for narrator, children's voices and anything from one piano to full symphony orchestra. Sadly, after a few sporadic outings, it seems to have failed to hit the assortment of jackpots for which it was intended. Doreen was also the begetter of my *Smugglers' Song* to Kipling's poem in *Puck of Pook's Hill*. It was needed for a joint venture at Marcham, near Abingdon, where the Federation of Women's Institutes hold their Courses. Then there was Philip Turner, priest and playwright, former vicar of St. Matthew's, Northampton. For him I composed a setting of the Communion Service that has vanished without trace, as has the publisher who accepted it! And Stella Mary Pearce, illuminating the world of design and costume with rare imaginative insight – these and many more dedicated and gallant souls.

A long and happy association with this happy fraternity came to a natural end when the ubiquitous guitar began to twang and twitter, heralding a new approach to match changing attitudes to the eternal verities.

To glance for a moment at the reverse side of these high matters, there have been some aspirants to fame among the pious whose attempts at authorship have fallen a little wide of the mark. This was particularly true during the early days of revival. Two instances of 'how not to do it' provide notable examples. A play submitted opened thus: 'The Curtain rises in Abraham's Bosom. The Chorus enters to the tune of Comin' through the Rye!' Another, more complex, that came from a marine enthusiast, in which a symbolic treatment of famous ships of the line were to be represented by a group of ladies from the parish, each of whom was to be given a speaking part that would recall particular exploits of each ship. One unlucky lady, after naming her ship and recalling past glories, would be required to finish with this rather anxious-making statement 'I foundered off the Cape of Good Hope after being rammed amidships by a lusty man of war!'

The problem of adapting the right music for a particular situation is by no means simply resolved, particularly if the music is to avoid drastic surgery in the process. An occasion in mind is at a performance of Holy Night, a play in which part of the action is set in an empty church, after the congregation at an evening service has departed. Both the producer and the musician in charge had shown themselves at rehearsal to be equally iron-willed.

In the empty church the lights gradually reveal the Madonna depicted in the reredos to be alive and real. Near the front of the stage is set the Crib, with the Holy Child duly represented. We become aware that Mary is going to leave her 'frozen' position and to make her way down to the Child. Assuming that the time required for this manoeuvre might, at most, take about a minute in time, I waited with interest to hear some music that would provide a basis for this bit of action. So that when the celebrated Air in D from J. S. Bach's third Orchestral Suite began, played very softly beautifully, slowly and with both repeats on a memorable 78 disc, I watched with eager interest to see how the maternal journey could be stretched to accommodate the music. I knew that the musician who had chosen it was unlikely, to say the least, to allow any tampering with his choice, which on this occasion would take between three and four minutes. So the Holy Mother had to simulate both eagerness to get to the Child as well as, metaphorically, 'to go to Birkenhead by way of Brighton Pier!' There is always the danger that, despite the best intentions, something a little odd may happen – as in a very rapt village performance when a solemn elder, reclining on a rock, slid backwards on to the floor as the rock shot forward to reveal its natural identity as an upturned sugar crate. The elder's suppressed, but unmistakably bucolic laugh, created a welcome diversion, but fatally disturbed the raptus intended, perhaps a little too severely, for the frailty of that particular audience.

Religious Drama has by now proved a tough and well-tried art-form, triumphantly surviving these and many more serious mishaps. The name of Bishop Bell will long be held in thankful memory by countless numbers of people who have responded to the impetus that his foresight inaugurated.

CHAPTER 27

Oxford and Offley

My recently-completed *Suite for Strings* was given a first performance at a concert given by the Oxford Orchestral Society in the
Sheldonian Theatre. I had shown the score to Sir (then Dr.)
Thomas Armstrong who, bless him, seemed to like the work and
invited me to conduct it. The players and audience seemed to like
it too. The subsequent career of the score is one shared by all too
many other aspirants to performances. It went into hibernation on
the shelves of a publisher's hire library, emerged fleetingly once
or twice, before being adapted as a string sextet. Both versions
have now been accepted for publication in America, thirty five
years on. The music is in variation form, in which the real tune
emerges in the last section. It turns out to be *The Holly and the Ivy*,
thus making a potentially suitable ingredient for a programme
given during the festive season.

There must be countless musicians who think of Tom Armstrong with abiding affection and gratitude. As if it were not
enough to have been a brilliant organist, choir trainer and
conductor, administrator, teacher, writer, lecturer, water-colour
painter, it seems that in retirement he has taken to farming.

Nick Gent, who as a schoolboy had whistled Mozart during a
downland vigil, was now at St. John's College, where he was
reading medicine and playing his cello. I had been invited to stay
overnight in college. Shortly before going to bed I was given an
intimation that the ghost of Archbishop Laud was said to walk
along the passage outside the room where I was to sleep. I was not
to be surprised, should there be an encounter, if he appeared to be
visible from the knees upwards, as he walked on a lower level of
flooring, raised in more recent times. In fact there *were* some
heavy footsteps during the night, but they passed my door and
went their way, it seemed, straight through a wall, also
presumably of subsequent construction.

In the Long Gallery next day, while I was listening to some
music, there appeared the figure of a woman, elderly and
comfortably rotund and dressed in the apparel of a nineteen-
century domestic. After placing an invisible tray on a table, she
disappeared through a nearby wall. Grey must have been an
unlucky colour for women in past times, since these feminine
visitants almost invariably seem to wear it.

A few months later I visited Oxford again, to give a recital with

Audrey Piggott, a notable cellist, whose subsequent emigration to Canada and premature death was to prove a sad loss. Our programme included a Sonata by Herbert (John) Sumsion, of Gloucester and Three Choirs Festival fame. The Sonata has remained in my memory as possessing a truly lyrical 'flow' from first to last, through which it seemed that golden-brown autumn leaves drift slowly to the ground on one of those still, misty days that mark the fall of the year. Sadly, the work seems to have remained unpublished, known only to those few of John's friends who have persuaded him to release it on bail for occasions such as this.

A notable encounter was to meet and talk with that venerable music historian, Dr. Ernest Walker. He was then living in the house of the Deneke sisters, who treated him with deference and with strict formality. They invariably addressed him as 'Dr. Walker', though the friendship must by now have been of many years standing. I had recently come across Tennyson's comment on musicians who had set his poems to music. 'You damned composers, who make me say two or even three times something I only said once.' When I asked the great man whether this oft-quoted remark was authentic, he replied in characteristic manner. His speech was crisp, clipped and clear, tending to produce falsetto overtones – 'Yes, O yes indeed – and what is more he said it to me.'

Before leaving Oxford, here is a brief wartime anecdote by way of tailpiece. Hitler, it was said, had an eye on becoming Chancellor in the University, so the Luftwaffe were instructed to avoid it. In consequence there were few air-raid warnings. However, at about 1.30 a.m. on a cold winter night the sirens sounded. At a Post in Carfax the Wardens on duty were two sedate denizens, one living up the Banbury Road, the other in the Woodstock Road. The Post was below the point where these roads converge. Two silent figures met at the junction, coat collars turned up, fell into step and made their way to the Post. There they waited; still no word was spoken. As soon as the All Clear sounded, they locked up and set off towards their homes. It was only at the point where their ways diverged that the silence was broken. One of them said to the other 'Damned cheek those fellers coming over here at this time of night!'

Another and more tenuous link with Tennyson was made in boyhood days at Brockenhurst station. On journeys to and from school we had to change trains there. In the Waiting Room on the down platform there are still somewhat faded photographs of Victorian men of letters, given years ago to the London and South

Western Railway in memory of the Bard. He also frequented the station on journeys from Faringford to Haslemere. On one long past occasion I commented on the photographs to an elderly porter.

'Yus, young guv' he said with great solemnity 'Alfred Lord Tennyson – I remember 'im, remember 'im well. 'E 'ad a large, wide-brimmed black 'at 'e always used to wear: 'e 'ad a beard too and was very partial to 'is pipe. 'E used to change trains 'ere, on 'is way to 'Aslemere. 'E could get to 'Aslemere b'train in them days a darn sight quicker than what you can now. That's progress I s'pose – any road that's what our Company seems to think it is.'

And so to Offley, a pleasant peaceful village in north Hertfordshire. In 1940, Sir Walford Davies, Master of the King's Musick, had the happy idea of suggesting the appointment of a small band of musicians. They were each to be given a region in which to travel, their mandate being to foster and encourage the arts during the difficult years of war. Until an office could be not only found, but afforded, the Rural Music School based on Hitchin undertook the necessary administration. Thus a firm *entente* was created, duly celebrated by a holiday week in which the scattered fraternity could meet, discuss problems, plan for the future and, best of all, make music together. So we foregathered at Offley Place, a pleasant country house, then in use as an outpost of the Froebel Institute, later to become a Teacher's Training College. It was here that Hester Thrale, Dr. Johnson's 'Leading Lady' spent her girlhood days.

When some people arrived for lunch one day, they very quickly found themselves taking part in a performance of Haydn's *Toy Symphony*. One of their number, Eric Walter White, was confronted with the nightingale's part, for which the simulated sound requires a saucer of water with the inevitable flotilla of bubbles. This assignment was carried through with an expression of startled gravity on the player's face. Other newcomers reacted in similarly characteristic ways. Arthur Alexander coaxed some remarkable sounds from a rather inhibited resident small grand piano, that one suspected of having the instrumental equivalent of tonsil or adenoid trouble. George Parker, who lived near by, delighted us with his singing.

Each day after breakfast people played, sang, or both for about twenty minutes before discussions began. On one sunny morning Rose Morse gave a group of *Geistliche Lieder* with a ringing sincerity that still echoes in the memory.

The C.E.M.A. Traveller operating from Cambridge into East Anglia was another singer, Ursula Nettleship. Into her geo-

graphical fold, back to his native Suffolk, came Benjamin Britten.
Many choirs had been reduced to members on the distaff side.
Ursula lost no time in asking for something new for them to sing.
Britten's response was to produce *A Ceremony of Carols*, some copies
of which she brought, hot from the press, for our sopranos and
altos to sample. The sequence of words, running through
Christmas into spring, illuminated by such sensitive, original and
yet approachable music, has retained this quality of freshness
through the years – an inviolate quality that no amount of rough-
hewing seems to damage.

Ursula also brought with her, from a nearby depot, a young
soldier with a truly remarkable voice; his name was David
Franklin.

The Vaughan Williams *Benedicite* was still new and not as yet
well known. This we took to our hearts. V.W. had evidently
taken his basic D major aura from Bach, as have others. Here he
gives the key a glowing resonance that recalls a lifelong reverence
for the music of J.S.B.

One evening we performed another recent piece by this
composer – his *Magnificat*. The eloquent flute part was played by
another musician who was all too soon to leave this world – Eve
Kisch. Vaughan Williams, like Monteverdi and Bach, lifts the
Magnificat out of the liturgical thicket in which it has become
enmeshed. After hearing it some of us strolled out into a summer
night, in which the stars seemed to be 'not far up' and
exceptionally bright. Walking with me through the peaceful
landscape was Maurice Jacobson. Contemplating 'The Infinite
Shining Heavens' with the music we had just heard in mind,
Maurice said that certain special and particular works of art made
him feel that somewhere, in the furthest reaches of the cosmos,
away and beyond the ultimate range of all religious faiths, isms
and the rest, there must be a centrepoint where lay the secret of
ultimate truth.

With René Soames as tenor soloist, we performed my *Singing
Friar* with our small chorus and orchestra. These were settings
made after a visit to Fallodon, described earlier, and hearing Lord
Grey quote some verses from Peacock's *Maid Marian*. These I had
subsequently made the basis of this cantata. In addition to a
sensitive and exceptionally responsive voice, René was a superb
raconteur – in all colours of the spectrum! It was surely he who
sowed the seeds of the recent and welcome revival of interest in
the music of Peter Warlock, a composer with whom he must have
felt an affinity.

On Sunday morning the weather brought one of those rare days when the end of summer is tinctured by a foretaste of September gold. A group of us sat in the garden, looking across a paddock to Offley church, framed in trees. Under the guidance of Mervyn Bruxner we sang Kodaly's *Jesus and the Traders*, another piece that had recently become available. Mervyn had left a teaching post at Eton to become Music Organizer for Kent, a gigantic undertaking, though one for which, at the time, he was admirably suited. In the gradual assimilation of responsibility by local government for such assignments, he and other Organizers became known as Advisers – and their successors Inspectors. Of such is the jargon of officialdom.

The week passed all too quickly, though many seeds sown in discussion were to mature. Among them, to give one instance, the forming of Music Schools in Kent and Dorset. In another and far more spacious pipeline, plans were being formed in which C.E.M.A. was to become The Arts Council of Great Britain.

A year later the war ended: the Rural Music Schools Association decided to re-open a London Office. A good deal had been accomplished in Wiltshire, so that when Mary Ibberson offered me the job of Assistant Director, based on London, a new and exciting part of my journey lay ahead.

CHAPTER 28

Andante and Rondo Capriccioso

The London Office of the Rural Music Schools Association was in Gloucester Place. It consisted of a small, sunny and comfortable room overlooking York Street. The main part of the building was occupied by the British Federation of Music Festivals, firmly entrenched on the ground floor. A nomadic school of dancing made sporadic forays immediately above them; we shared the top storey with the Carnegie Advisers for music and drama – Sydney Northcote and Leo Baker, welcome and congenial neighbours.

For many years Mr. Fairfax Jones had been in charge of the Federation: he was then on the point of retiring. In his place came Stanley Harper, fresh from the hive-like activity of Boosey and Hawkes in Regent Street; changes followed swiftly. A general air of tasteful, though faded, décor gave place to brighter colours. A former atmosphere of sedate calm gave place to brisk and business-like bustle as the Federation got into gear for a rapid post-war revival of competitive festivals.

This was to be the base for many and varied operations for the next six years. For a short time Norman Hearn shared the office. He had been appointed with a mandate to bring music to youth clubs – then much in people's minds – though mainly to start a centre in Bermondsey on R.M.S. lines to become a 'pilot scheme' for urban exploitation. To provide a metaphorical *basso continuo* for such contrapuntal activities, we were extremely fortunate to have Rosalind Borland, also a musician, but who became an admirable custodian and secretary to keep both of us, as well as the office files, in reasonable order. Her advent was to prove the beginning of a long and happy association, to be continued when we both became involved with music in Kent.

For the first few weeks the tempo remained at *andante*, while plans were drawn up and contacts made. The ensuing *capriccioso* was to be sustained at a brisk pace, a steady *allegro con brio*, infinitely varied and greatly rewarding.

Everyone was eagerly getting back to a normal existence after the frustrations of the war years. Our days were full of surprises, no one as yet knowing exactly where people, firms or commodities had landed up. The first telephone call we received came from someone at the B.B.C. who seemed to have mislaid a harpist and asked our help: Rosalind proceeded to find one for him. Someone else at the Ministry of Education asked the Association if 200 qualified string teachers could be available in six weeks time!

Soon the *capriccioso* was under way. The journal *Making Music* was launched on a thirty years' career. Days of music were planned, took place and were duly cleared up at the finish, the latter often being the most tedious part. One or two people invariably went away with a hired orchestral part or choral piece in their music cases: two or three more would leave something behind them to be retrieved, identified and returned. Summer schools and shorter courses came and went, books and records were reviewed, the training centre at Hitchin regularly visited. Conferences and committees were attended, people wanting jobs interviewed, education officers and music organizers visited in various counties, staff meetings held, scores and parts collected from, and returned to publishers. In those happy days these elusive fellows clustered round the centre of London. One could even buy or hire music at a reasonable cost as and when needed. Now one would have to apply to a distant computer for a permit, wait at least three weeks, only to discover that the piece required is probably out of print, or if available, at a cost that has increased by at least 200 per cent.

Then there were organizations whose operations were complementary to our own. These involved a good deal of to-ing and fro-ing, the result almost always being mutually helpful. Various people who were interested in what we were trying to do would come to the office when we were particularly busy, taking a disproportionate amount of time. Our Headquarters were at Hitchin; there Mary Ibberson and Helen Wright initiated policy and planned manoeuvres, though allowing time for deployment should the need arise. Three occasions when we sponsored musical events in London must find a mention here.

Pride of place must go to the 21st birthday celebration of the R.M.S. movement at the Royal Albert Hall. This was the occasion for which Vaughan Williams had written his Concerto Grosso for our special needs, as described in an earlier chapter.

Later in the evening some members of the chorus came with me to take part in the B.B.C.'s once-popular programme *In Town Tonight*. We found ourselves in a large and semi-compartmented studio. There, among a richly-assorted motley, was Irving Berlin. It was a privilege indeed to shake the hand that had penned so many memorable tunes. There is a legend that, in somewhat similar vein to our open string players, this great man prefers to play only in the key of C. Rather than submit to the tedium of further explorations, he is said to have acquired a piano fitted with a sliding mechanism, by which he was able to achieve the full chromatic range from the white notes of the keyboard. A great man, whose music has the ring of deep sincerity and true inspiration.

We also arranged the first London performance of Britten's *Saint Nicholas* in Southwark Cathedral, with the composer conducting and Peter Pears as principal soloist. As companion pieces to begin the programme we chose a string fantasia by Byrd and the Purcell *Bell Anthem*, which were conducted by Reginald Jacques. Our President, Lord Harewood, escorted Queen Mary to this concert; she cherished a special affection for the building, its history and welfare.

At the Musicians' Church, St. Sepulchre in Holborn, we gave a programme of Music for Candlemas. This happy Festival, on February 2nd, marking the end of the winter solstice, has been unduly neglected in recent times, with its coming as it does when the days are lighter and longer. Spring, heralded by the first snowdrops, seems truly getting nearer. Not only does Candlemas commemorate the Presentation of the Infant Jesus in the Temple, when Simeon made the memorable statement that we know as the *Nunc dimittis*, it is also the day when candles are blessed as an act of thanksgiving for Christ as the Light of the World.

There is an old country rhyme about the weather on Candlemas Day, wich I have set as a Round in a published collection.

> "When Candlemas Day is bright with sun,
>   Then the winter's but half begun;
> But when Candlemas Day is dark with rain,
>   Then Winter's power is on the wane."

According to a Hungarian friend, it is on this day that the bear comes out of his cave: if he can see his shadow on the ground, he quickly retreats back into it.

The two main works in our celebration were the Bach Cantata (82) *Ich habe genug* and Britten's *A Ceremony of Carols*. While the Cantata provides an incomparable meditation on Simeon's encounter in the Temple, the Britten sequence merges winter into spring. For it a group of young singers entered from the back of the church, each carrying a candle, to be placed in the Sanctuary during the performance. I think it was Adrian Bell who said that if he ever found the way to heaven, this would be the only light by which he could find the way.

Towards the end of my six years spent working for the Association, the property of Little Benslow Hills at Hitchin came into its possession, through the generous bequest of a member of the Seebohm family. Also a grant that had made our work in

London possible completed the span allotted to it. Rosalind was soon to become assistant music adviser to Mervyn Bruxner in Kent, while I became involved in music publishing.

Paying a visit one day to Chesters, and discussing a project we had in view with Douglas Gibson, the presiding genius of the firm, I happened to mention my predicament. At once he said 'Look here – you ought to be doing this kind of thing for us.' Since the firm had already published a number of my pieces, I was particularly glad to be able to work among friends in familiar surroundings.

J. and W. Chester Ltd. occupied part of a gaunt building in Great Marlborough Street otherwise dedicated to textile merchants. Sometimes we had to pick our way over bales of cloth in order to win through to the upper floors. There were long stone corridors that separated the various sections of activity. After the fluid régime of Gloucester Place, from which each job required a different schedule, it was hard to adjust to a rigid 'nine to five' working day. The commuter train that brought me from Tonbridge was apt to linger at London Bridge *en route* for Charing Cross. The cause was the inability of the engine – a Bulleid Pacific – to get a grip on the rails when wet and to move a heavy train from a standing start on an upward curve. So we waited for a shove in the rear from an incoming electric train, thus a precious ten minutes was lost. On the first occasion, in response to a loud and disapproving sniff from the Company Secretary, I rashly offered to stay on at the end of the day. 'Don't be ridiculous' he said 'We close at five.' That's how it was. My main assignment was to develop and expand the firm's growing interest in educational music. Somehow I never seemed to get the priorities right, one of them being that imprint takes precedence over contents. The general atmosphere of the building, the deployment of those who worked in it, had a distinctly Dickensian atmosphere. It was not unlike reading a nineteenth-century novel and finding that one had become a character in the story. Taking my turn in the showroom one day, I was a trifle bemused when a customer came in to ask for some of my music and for details about the composer!

After two years it seemed that my talents, such as they were, would be better employed elsewhere. Happily a long and enduring friendship with Douglas Gibson has survived this commercial 'incompatibility of temperament'. Let it be said that the firm of Chester has since achieved a total change of climate and atmosphere, cosily tucked away among the labyrinthine purlieus behind Faringdon station.

So, at the age of forty seven, I decided to become my own

master once more. An admirable bank manager urged me on, saying 'now or never'. Since we were living in Kent, there I would set up my standard. Apart from many brief forays elsewhere, including an adjudicating tour across Canada, Kent was to become the centre of operations for another twenty five years. The slow train had brought me to London. Another shorter trip would bring me to a new beginning.

At the same time two encouraging prospects came into view, unfortunately proving to be beckoning in opposite directions. Through a meeting with Dr. Greenhouse Allt, then Principal of Trinity College of Music, I became an examiner for a brief spell. Some happy forays in Scotland and the Fens were about to develop into overseas tours.

Shortly after I took on this interesting and varied work, there was a tempting opening at Sutton Valence School, where the Music Master had died, suddenly and tragically, leaving an aching void within a week of the beginning of term. Despite a rather shaky state of diplomatic relationship with the organ, the Headmaster, C. R. Evers, encouraged me to take charge of the school music. A fortnight after settling into the job there was a telephone call from Trinity College, asking if I would go to Ceylon for three months 'next Saturday'. This proved to be a moment of decision. As it was impossible to relinquish duties only just happily begun, I realized that examining on a global scale and teaching could only mix under exceptional circumstances, which were far from within reach for me at the time.

For six months life at Sutton Valence proved exceedingly happy. But when Ronnie Evers asked me to confirm my appointment as a permanent one, the call of the outside world beyond the school gates was too strong to be resisted. Perhaps the best achievement during those somewhat monastic months was to revive the school orchestra (that had disappeared under the previous régime) and to give a complete performance of *The Yeomen of the Guard* that went with a considerable *brio* from beginning to end. With male soloists from the school, notably Richard Horn, we were lucky to be able to have Brenda Bentall and Ruby Hope as admirable exponents of the soprano and mezzo solo parts. Memory recalls a last minute replacement of a lost black tie by a substitute 'clip-on' specimen which developed such a determined list to starboard that I was obliged to detach it from inadequate moorings and throw it in fury towards the wholly innocent second violins.

Happy memories abound of that sojourn at the school, from the windows of which the Weald of Kent spread out below into a distant haze. Taking glowing and rewarding memories with me, I returned happily to the larger world beyond.

During the previous two years, when I had become involved in music publishing, I had rediscovered, among buried treasure, the songs of C. W. Orr. The firm then published a house journal called *The Chesterian*. An opportunity came to write an article about these admirable settings of A. E. Housman and other poets. The result was a warm response from the composer, followed by a friendship that culminated in a joint recital at what was then called The Recital Room at the Festival Hall. This duly happened shortly before the emergence of the Purcell Room and the Queen Elizabeth Hall. We persuaded Wilfred Brown and Gordon Clinton to sing for us, each accompanying our own part of the programme.

The two Wilfreds – Brown and Orr – have been sadly missed since their deaths. Wilfred Brown's singing remains a cherished memory for all who ever listened to him, recalling another singer – Eric Greene – who gave help and encouragement to Bill Brown in earlier days. Many still recall Eric's superb gift as a *raconteur*, in addition to his fine singing and warm-hearted, generous personality.

Wilfred Orr was a more elusive and detached character. Like many of his generation his experiences in World War I had taken their toll. He lived quietly in Gloucestershire for many years, regarding the world with a kindly though cynical gaze. For me he became the Badger of Painswick Hill and signed his name in letters with a symbolic drawing! He had been greatly influenced by Wolf and Delius, seeking to inject his songs with a range and potency that few, if any, of his fellow-countrymen have mustered. It is good to know that his songs are beginning to attract the recognition they so richly deserve.

Since the main rondo theme of this chapter has been concerned with occasions for music in London, it may happily end with a final statement that revives memories of a particular friendship as well as the echo of a modest personal contribution.

CHAPTER 29

Kentish Coda

Just as a farmer, moving to another district to make a fresh start, needs to consider such factors as quality of soil, facilities for marketing his produce, so a musician must cast a weather-eye on the prospects for deploying his skill.

In Kent the welfare of music and musicians had already received considerable encouragement by the mid-nineteen fifties, when I began to add a modest quota. The County Music Committee, with Rollo Russell Scott as Chairman and Mervyn Bruxner as Music Adviser, were formulating developments that were in process of being implemented by a responsive County Council. Already there were days or week-ends of music as well as the annual summer school, by now firmly established at Benenden. Towards the end of Gloucester Place days we had taken a hand in the founding of a Kent Rural Music School. It had begun with an inaugural concert given by Antonia Butler, Norman Greenwood and Ronald Smith. To get to their seats the audience had to pass the newly-appointed Honorary Treasurer, Mr. Cornwell, who held a begging bowl in his hand! This event, together with an initial grant of £200 from the County Council, unleashed an organization that, in a few years, would be giving lessons to more than 6,000 pupils each week.

So meteoric a success was due to two factors: the organizing ability and enthusiasm of the School's first Director, Muriel Anthony and the increasingly generous support from the County through the Education Committee.

Another venture sponsored by Mervyn Bruxner was to establish the first Saturday morning school outside London for young music students who showed exceptional ability and promise. Auditions were held each year, tuition given in two instruments as well as the essential background of orchestra, chamber music, chorus and training in aural and theory, these in particular being frequently and inexcusably neglected in school curriculae. For this venture the teachers, as well as pupils, were to be the best available.

Mervyn's final achievement was to persuade the Authority to acquire and maintain a Music Centre. There was an unused building in Maidstone that dated back to the fourteenth century. Originally it had been a College for Priests and a resting-place for pilgrims on their way to Canterbury. The house had been bequeathed to the town Corporation, who were evidently unable to find a use for it. One solitary old man and a cat had been occupying it; the old man had died, though the cat seemed still around. So the County Council were persuaded to acquire a lease and to adapt the interior as a centre for music.

After Mervyn's departure Kent was fortunate enough to secure as successor Bèla de Csillèry, a musician of international repute and outstanding ability. A new addition to all that had gone before was the formation of a County Youth Orchestra that, under Bèla's expert training and conducting, has become outstandingly proficient, as an annual invitation to appear at the Royal Festival Hall gives eloquent testimony.

Another development has been the emergence of a Kent Sinfonia, basically a chamber orchestra, though capable of expansion for special occasions. This project was initiated by Bèla to provide an opportunity for teachers, advanced students and proficient amateur instrumentalists to give concerts in towns and villages where such events were either rare or non-existent.

By a happy coincidence the first appearance of the Kent Sinfonia coincided with Bèla's marriage to Gillian Sansom, the violinist. Her playing, as well as her personality and teaching ability, have combined to enrich the welfare of music in the county.

In this hive of activity it has been exciting and rewarding to have had some part – as teacher, composer, committee member, writer – in fact a potentially useful busybody. It was a special privilege to follow Rollo Russell Scott as Chairman of the County Music Committee and to undertake the same responsibility for the Kent Music School Board of Governors – the 'Rural' had by this time sunk without trace, though the same spirit of pioneering activity remained and was fast turning towards consolidation. Since such schools direct their efforts towards ultimate absorption into the provision made by local authorities, it is good to know that the process is well under way in Kent. Such a transfer has the added advantage of giving security beyond the ability of any voluntary organization to provide.

Perhaps Bèla's greatest achievement has been to set a new standard in performance and to combat with considerable success a former tendency, all too prevalent, to be satisfied and even gratified by second rate standards. Such a tendency has hung like a cloud over far too much amateur music-making. During my years in Kent it was heartening to see the cloud showing clear signs of breaking!

On a more personal note the greatest reward has come from

giving tutorial classes for adult music students, first for the Workers' Educational Association, later for the School of Continuing Education under the auspices of Canterbury University. This wholly congenial undertaking materialized through the good offices of a fellow composer, Jasper Rooper, then operating from Oxford and responsible for the vagaries and deployment of music tutors over a large area. To pay weekly visits through the winter months to groups of music lovers, to break down prejudices and to fan – and share – their enthusiasms has been infinitely rewarding. Initially one would encounter such comments as 'I can't stand this modern stuff – I turn it ORFF!' Such cases, except perhaps the most virulent, can be gently, firmly and patiently treated – and even alleviated. The Wagner complex arose frequently. One or two staunch devotees would be overshadowed by a numerous opposition when discussing the next season's syllabus. 'Not Wagner surely?' 'MUST we have Wagner?' 'O yes, please, do let's have some.' It was a great moment when, rather against the tide of opinion, I had gently insisted on some sessions about *The Ring* when, a few weeks later, some members of the class came to tell me they had acquired tickets for the complete cycle.

The different atmosphere of places visited was also intriguing. In all save two – of which more in a moment – firm friendships have been made and many kept. Christian names developed spontaneously, though there were always a number of shy and reserved members who expected and received formal treatment.

Particularly happy were classes at Tunbridge Wells, Folkestone, Shoreham and Cranbrook. In retrospect the Shoreham class, later migrating to nearby Sevenoaks, became the best of all. The two failures were at Maidstone, proving a tougher nut than I could crack, and Uckfield in Sussex. This was virtually a feudal occasion. I would come into the Hall by a side door while the class members made their appearance through the main entrance. Apart from a class secretary who confined her observations entirely to the matter in hand, not a soul spoke to me. While I would be getting ready to begin, a masterful feminine voice would say 'I see the lecturah has arrived.' After the session I would make my humble way back to a nearby café for a much-needed cup of tea – and so home.

Back (thankfully) in Kent there were occasional sessions in which a literary colleague and I would join forces. In company with Katharine Moore, we contemplated Falstaff, through Shakespeare, Verdi, Nicolai, Vaughan Williams and Elgar. With Monique Raffrey we happily combined words and music in relation to aspects of nature. Classes in different places would provide a totally different atmosphere, so that a varied approach to the job in hand would be adjusted to the prevailing climate. An example comes to mind in comparing Petts Wood with Cranbrook. Since the student days at Chislehurst described in chapter 14, when happy bands of squatters forgathered in semi-rural pubs, Petts Wood had emerged as a pleasant suburb of south-east London, not unlike Valley Fields in stories by P. G. Wodehouse. It had grown on land associated with the Willett family, one of whom, Sir John, had been responsible for the introduction of summer time during World War I. Fittingly the hostelry round which the place clusters commemorates the association in the name *Daylight Inn.* Here a pleasantly informal atmosphere prevailed, as befitting a quiet corner of commuter-land. By contrast Cranbrook, with the farming community strongly represented, a less serious-minded and considerably more extrovert group never failed to encourage the occasional spiced anecdote, sprinkled over such commentary and information as I could muster.

Apart from the Uckfield penitential, there were various forays into Sussex, of which the most exacting was a year of acting as caretaker Director for the Sussex Rural Music School. This emergency arose through the untimely death of Ronald Harding, a brilliant musician and greatly loved man. When my stint had been completed, the School was gently and happily taken into the care of the local authority.

There were also visits to schools to take singing classes in the days before that gentle art had been swamped by instrumental developments. At one prestigious establishment I also gave piano lessons. A typical attitude to such 'frills' was that of a pleasant young maiden who, at the end of term, said 'Oh, Mr. le Fleming, I'm afraid I shan't be able to do any practising during the holidays. The thing is that although we've got a house in London, another in France, a marvellous yacht, hi-fi – you name it – but we haven't got a *piano.*' At another school the girls were delightful, but tended towards a kind of gentility that goes with an inability to open the lips more than the merest crack when they either speak or sing. So I used to make up phrases by way of exercises to improve diction. Getting out of a train one day a notice caught my eye – 'Passengers must cross the line by the footbridge: All Season Tickets Must Be Shewn – By Order.' So the words became a Round. The object was to sprinkle vowels with as many consonants as possible. A strange story attaches to one of these exercises. I had made up the phrase 'I left my pink parasol on the upper deck of a Hammersmith bus – O Bother.' This evolved into another Round. Three months later I met a friend who had been to a summer school in Scotland. She said 'While I was there we learned a splendid new Round; it was made up by the man who conducted our chorus.' Then she sang my Pink Parasol to me! Needless to say I could hardly resist claiming it, in the manner of Touchstone for his Audrey as 'a poor thing but mine own.'

So my two collections of Rounds were assembled, a venture that gave an opportunity to preserve some of those heard at Dartington many years earlier, when Imogen Holst held sway over that delectable training ground for musicians.

In all the countless journeys made between Kent and Sussex, I have never ceased to be aware of a totally different atmosphere between the two counties. Even the weather would frequently change as the train emerged from either the Crowborough or Mountfield tunnels. It was G. K. Chesterton who once asserted that the true boundaries of England were not to be found on any map: that they were the Heptarchy of old – the seven kingdoms into which this land was once divided. Then Kent and Sussex were separate kingdoms: in many ways it seems as though an echo from that distant past still lingers. It is surely not only the soft speech that gives a unity to the ancient kingdom of Wessex. Despite the differing characteristics of counties in the south-west – excluding Cornwall as unique and strongly individual – there seems to exist an underlying consonance in the country that lies between Winchester and Exeter, extending northward to Marlborough and Hungerford.

Now, for me, these slow train journeys are over. From a cottage in Devon it is pleasant to look back on things done well. On others, done less well and even ill, memory has a way of dredging up sludge that makes one wish it were possible to jump off 'time's winged chariot' to return and to do them better, in the light of experience gained, bringing patience and understanding. That the gains outweigh the losses remains a steadfast hope. We can but pin our faith on being given a second chance, somewhere, some time, perhaps in 'another world than this.'

(Tonbridge – Woodbury: 1976–1981.)

PART TWO
'MEDITATIONS'

CHAPTER 30

Composers and Communication

The complexities of our time tend to encourage the occasional nostalgic backward glance. To choose an example at random, there was an occasion when Louis (or Ludwig) Spohr, having acquitted himself with honours at an evening concert and tucked heartily into the supper that ensued, proceeded to join the dancers at a nearby party. There he took part in a quadrille and was delighted that the band chose to play tunes – doubtless suitably adapted – from his friend Mozart's opera *The Magic Flute*. Then there was simply – music.

Nowadays we have become enmeshed in categories. Passing lightly over the diversification of pop, jazz, the blues and other manifestations of a similar nature, we arrive at popular, light and (so called) serious music. For composers near the apex of this pyramid – the numbers diminishing on each successive layer – there is the Songwriters' Guild, the Light Music Society and the Composers' Guild of Great Britain, each providing a rallying point for those who produce the appropriate commodity. It is, however, the Composers' Guild that seeks to care for the welfare of those who have an urge to communicate something of more than ephemeral value. It is this category that will be the focal point for what follows here and now.

Earlier in these pages the reader may have noticed several occasions when gallant pioneers have been encountered, full of zeal and enthusiasm, though invariably with scant financial support for their cause and effort. The Guild is of their number. Up to the mid-nineteen forties composers of this calibre were included, by way of tailpiece both in title and operations, in the Society of Authors and Playwrights. As such the organization must have presented an image strangely reminiscent of The Three Bears, before the smallest of them decided to opt for independence.

Despite the economic handicap, the Guild has succeeded in establishing a Music Information Centre, containing a comprehensive collection of tapes, discs and scores of twentieth-century British music. At 10 Stratford Place, in the centre of London, is a haven where conductors, performers, programme-builders and music-lovers can find a wealth of assembled music of our time. Such a provision is one which is normally regarded by any government as a national obligation. Many have included as an essential adjunct facilities for composers who can, if they choose, be available to give additional information to those interested. Needless to say, no British government has as yet even considered the possibility of such a venture. So the Guild sought and found assistance from charitable trusts and one or two helpful organizations. Initial grants were based on a three year period and the Centre became a reality in 1967.

In 1970 the present writer had the honour to be elected Chairman of the Guild. His first confrontation was a reminder that these grants were about to flicker and die: that unless somebody took immediate action, the Centre would vanish without trace before the end of the year. It was an added concern that many music publishers were no longer able to afford to display their wares in London, with the exception of those whose founders had secured a permanent stronghold, before rapacious landlords demanded exorbitant sums for the renewal of leases.

Now, after a dozen years or so, the Centre is very much alive, though as a non-profit-making concern it is particularly vulnerable to inflation. Increasing numbers of visitors come to discover treasure-trove that would otherwise remain in obscurity. It has become virtually the only place where a composer can show the result of his labours.

Apart from depositing the score of a symphony or choral work that has just been completed, what else can be done to send the work out into the world? The first move will doubtless be towards the B.B.C. There, provided the score comes safely through an initial scrutiny, it may be accepted with the proviso 'if offered.' Alternatively it may join a very long queue for transmission 'in the near future.' In that case it may have to face considerable delay; one composer recently encountered had waited nearly ten years for the happy ending – or perhaps beginning might be more apt. Meanwhile there will have been the inevitable ding-dong between potential publisher and performer for the first move. There is an apocryphal story that illustrates this predicament.

A worthy young man who had courted the daughter of an eminent peer asked permission to pay his addresses. The noble Lord replied 'Certainly not – and get yourself out of this house at once and never dare to enter it again.' Whereupon the young man said 'Well, before I go, would it interest you to know that I have just been offered a Directorship in Blinkham's Bank?' At which the irate parent said 'Sit down, young man, and tell me more.' So the suitor made his way to the Bank, gained admittance to the inner sanctum, where a similar curt request to leave greeted his gambit. At which he said 'Before I go, would it interest you to know that I have just become engaged to the daughter of Lord Blank?'

The moral here is that it is more likely than not that the publisher will say 'Get two or three performances fixed and come back again; we couldn't consider the work at present.' Equally a potential concert-promotion organization or established conductor (or group) will tell the composer to get his work published, after which they will hope to be able to think again. There is also the added hazard that new works need extra rehearsals, which cost a lot of money, coupled with the undeniable fact that they create what is known as bad box-office.

Now comes the hardest nut to crack. To achieve communication it is desirable, if not essential, to elicit a response at the receiving or consumer end. In these islands, with the honourable exception of Wales, where contemporary composers have achieved a remarkable integration in the cultural heritage, the majority of music-lovers retain a habit of blandly knowing what they like and liking what they know. For every ten people who will go to a concert to hear a new work, it is probable that at least one hundred music lovers will stay away.

A major difficulty that besets, thwarts and delays the assimilation of new music is that most people in their earlier years have been so heavily indoctrinated with diatonic tonality that the adjustment to fresh idioms, as they grow older, becomes harder to achieve. It is curious that many people who care deeply for music refuse to adapt themselves to a different tonal climate. Similarly an alarming number of amateur choral singers, with years of participation in these operations, have never troubled to master the rudimentary principles of sight-singing or aural training. Yet these same people would not dream of visiting another country without a sufficient knowledge of the language to make adequate contact with those around them.

In the deeper waters of contemporary music it is not without significance to recall an occasion when a select number of *avant-garde* composers were listening to each others' recent products. During one of the pieces a composer sitting next to a colleague, whose work was being played, whispered the admonition 'Take care, dear boy, your triads are showing.'

Here perhaps is the crux of the matter. The triad – the three notes of a major common chord – arise as part of the natural harmonic series, described by Hindemith as 'rooted and grafted in nature.' From these three notes music begins, to them it returns. Here is a basic factor intuitively recognized by countless people to whom the mechanics of music mean nothing. An instinctive search for a recognizable tune is another symptom of normality, despite the earnest endeavours of the *avant garde* to dismiss such foibles as 'old hat.' In this sense it is not without interest to note the steady decline of interest in serial music, with the exception of a few memorable masterpieces. Equally it is significant to note the increasing acceptance and acclaim accorded to Shostakovich and Britten, in large measure because they communicate in a basic language instantly recognizable as such. The same can be said of composers such as Bartok who, though disclaiming key usage as such, base their concepts on a selected note as a tonal anchor.

Sometimes the obstacle to appreciation lies in an incomplete awareness of the imaginative impulse from which music has been written. As an example there is a great deal of English music, composed during the earlier decades of the present century, that has now achieved a wide recognition and acclaim. Such men as Bax, Finzi, Ireland and Moeran have recently received recognition denied them during their lifetime. The process seems at last to be accelerating so that Tippett, Berkeley and Rubbra have been able to receive due appreciation while still in the same world as their hearers. Indeed it would seem that audiences are at long last beginning to acquire a taste for exploration.

Even when a composer has achieved both publication and performance, his problems are by no means over. If his piece is of the kind that requires a number of choral copies or string parts, it is probable that one of each will be bought and the rest incubated by one of the fertile devices of modern photographic technology. If copies are available from a public library, one set will be acquired to cover a large area and even be loaned elsewhere to other libraries in other districts, thus ensuring that any hoped-for returns by way of royalties are effectively strangled in infancy. Similarly, it is also likely that a modest number of purchasers for a recording, if and when it might appear, will have previously made a tape of a broadcast performance. The recording will then achieve a total sale of 439 copies in a full year and disappear into oblivion as a write-off.

At one stage in the preparation of that promised, though costive alleviation, the proposed Public Lending Right, it had not dawned on those responsible that composers, as well as authors, should be included in the scheme. So that anyone wishing to borrow the libretto and vocal score of an opera under copyright would be required to pay a fee to the librettist, while the vocal score, over which the composer had laboured long and hard, would have been 'for free.'

In the light of these – and other – considerations it is hoped that anyone still under the illusion that a composer's path is strewn with roses will have a more realistic conception of the matter. Meanwhile let us be thankful that, despite the hazards, so much music is still being written and that a great deal of it continues to survive and flourish, despite the whims of fashion, the hidebound reactionaries, the pirates and the plagiarists who continue unchecked, unabated, to take their toll of the just rewards that belong by right to the long-suffering composer.

CHAPTER 31

Organists and the Clergy

Now that the various denominations of the Christian Church are overcoming their reluctance to draw closer to one another, there is, within each fold, an aspect of the trend that offers scope for investigation. It is the relationship of the clergy to their organists – and vice versa. Since the present writer has been a fringe body in both camps, there have been many opportunities to observe a fascinating aspect of human relationships at close range.

From the outset it has been clear that there are different, sometimes conflicting loyalties, even a great gulf fixed. Dedicated musicians in continuous contact with music in worship are apt to be given a rather distorted view of Abraham's Bosom, while the arts do not invariably provide an attractive vista from the ecclesiastical side of the gulf. This impression has arisen from having been a recipient on countless occasions of commentary from both participants on the shortcomings of the other.

The dichotomy first presented itself when, during boyhood days, we were spending a holiday with an uncle who was the parish priest at a seaside town in the Isle of Wight. His church organ was a Harrison that produced brilliant and exciting sounds under the hands of the resident musician. A moment of revelation came in a performance of *Finlandia* as a concluding voluntary after Evensong – a truly memorable experience for a boy with an all-consuming passion for music. A request made on the following day to meet this superb exponent of Sibelius met with a somewhat cold reception. The summer breeze seemed to turn distinctly cooler; after a pause came the reluctant reply, 'Very well – I'll have a word with him.'

The meeting duly took place, to reveal a fine musician who, over the years that followed, patiently shared a tithe of his wisdom and experience with an eager and probably exasperating youth. But any mention to him of my uncle was received in stony silence!

The same uneasy truce was evident in our home town. There for a time my father became a member of the choir and obtained for me a permit to sit in the organ loft during Services. Throughout the sermons the organist would show signs of impatience, clearly disassociating himself from the exhortations emanating from the pulpit. This was the staunch isolationist previously mentioned, who absented himself from the town in a marked manner when Sir (then Dr.) Sydney Nicholson came to seek affiliation to the newly-formed School of English Church Music. According to my father it was his habit during choir-practice to walk down into the nave of the church, listen to the singers, and shout 'Perfectly horrible' when they desisted!

A later attempt to establish diplomatic relations with the King of Instruments was made during student days at the Brighton School of Music. There was an occasion then when, during a lesson, Dr. Alfred King, old and venerable after years of office at the town's parish church, happened to mention a recent incumbent of the living. A defiant fist thumped the organ stool – 'The Clergy' he growled, 'They little know what they are up against when they come to ME!'

Organists – alone in their job, thinking their own deep thoughts, while enduring the interminable drone of endless sermons. Stories abound of evasion tactics, such as the almost, though not quite, legendary story when, during a lengthy oration, a strange pattering sound seemed to come from the organ loft. It transpired on investigation that the occupant had been catching up with arrears of correspondence on a portable typewriter. Fauré in younger days had been dismissed from similar post for smoking a cigarette in the porch. And the author whose book you are now reading, once a humble village organist (at £6 a year!), found his patience so sorely tried by weekly rhapsodies on the splendours of St. Paul's character, that he had the happy notion of raising the intoning note by a semitone each week. At the fourth rise there was a distinct flicker in the vicar's response, followed by a summons to the vestry after the Service. 'The organ,' said the dear man, 'seems to be getting rather out of tune.' He was assured that recent severe weather conditions had temporarily affected the instrument, but that when Spring came he would be sure to notice an improvement. So the note was lowered week by week; snowdrops appeared in the churchyard. The vicar responded to the regained familiar note like a homing pigeon: 'You were quite right,' he said 'The organ seems much better now!'

So much for instances that reveal a considerable degree of separatism between the arts and the way of salvation. In the former there are no specific frontiers to limit the scope of subject-matter. But he who takes the pilgrim's way, staff in hand, must needs resist the blandishments of Vanity Fair, a town in which many artists have found both interest and stimulus. While a great deal of music is written to the glory of God, a great deal more has come into being with no such intention. None the less there are countless church musicians who have managed to solve a difficult equation, whose lives and music-making have been totally devoted to the service of Almighty God.

Meanwhile, what of the clergy? Here a very deep root has to be tapped, going back in time to the early Fathers of the church. These men were deeply conscious of the power of music. They realized how easily it could be used to divert the minds of the devout from prayer and worship by sheer beauty of sound. With the exile of the old gods so close behind them in time, it was Orpheus 'the great deceiver' and Apollo, with ravishing and sensual song, that caused these holy men grave disquiet. To them it was essential that music should be kept on a fairly tight ecclesiastical leash, so as to become a handmaid, decorously robed in sober clothing. It seems unlikely that any candidate for Holy Orders should not be given some inkling of this tendency and even, perhaps subconsciously, be aware that the modest handmaid might at any moment appear in glamorous array to reveal her shapely and distracting form!

The church, as distinct from cathedrals and a few other honourable exceptions, once the patron of music as of the other arts, appears now to be neglecting her precious heritage. Choirs that formerly took pride in the singing of set services, anthems and motets, are no longer permitted to do so. Many of the clergy seem to be fighting a rearguard action, clamouring for maximum congregational involvement at the cost of jettisoning a precious heritage. Such changes have obviously been adopted to meet the wishes of many churchgoers. Fortunately the humanists and agnostics, untroubled by these internal problems, have taken over the custody of treasure-trove, now largely disregarded and abandoned by those for whom it was specifically intended.

Perhaps the core of the matter may be summed up in the words of Albert Einstein*:– 'In earlier days there was no audience in the modern sense. The church was the only place where a musician was able to reach a fairly large audience – and it cannot be said that the congregation was a real audience with an interest in musical or aesthetic values. A church musician serves the church. A churchgoer is there for edification and *music is only a means to an end*' (my italics).

Evidently that was why my uncle did not entirely approve when, for one member of his flock, the highlight of an Evensong

---

*Albert Einstein: *Essays on Music*, W. W. Norton & Company Inc., New York.

long ago was not the Service, but the *Finlandia* that followed, after the altar candles had been extinguished. The spirit of Orpheus was present in Finland then – and could still claim at least squatters' rights in an English parish church.

CHAPTER 32

Music, Places – and Silence

I

'That nature imitates art,' said Oscar Wilde, 'I don't think even her worst enemy would deny now. It is the one thing that keeps her in touch with civilized man.' In this sense it is diverting to imagine Dedham Vale and the Stour Valley, where John Constable lived and worked, giving themselves a shake-up to try and look a little more like those superb paintings. And sunsets doing their best to emulate Turner. But if painters and writers have done much for particular places and districts, what about musicians? Surely they have given some tunes for the wind to whistle?

What tunes, for example, did they carry over the Malvern Hills before Elgar wrote some for them? And how much more exhilarating are the Atlantic breezes on the north coast of Cornwall now that they can ring the changes on Wagner, Bax and Boughton round the walls of Tintagel Castle. In Gloucestershire the air is richer in quality for intimations of Holst, Howells, Gurney, C. W. Orr and Vaughan Williams. Echoes of Finzi still linger over the Berkshire downs –

> "Poets (like angels) where they once appear,
> Hallow the place, and each succeeding year
> Adds reverence to't."

'In some mysterious way a countryside, the look of a landscape can reveal the secret of a composer's attraction.' So wrote Sir Arthur Bliss. He goes on to say 'During a walk along the shores of Lake Constance I felt I was penetrating the charm of some of Liszt's pictorial music. And a visit to the Benedictine Abbey of Melk seemed to offer a clue to the appreciation of Bruckner. Neither of these composers had hitherto meant much to me. Perhaps seeing with one's own eyes what they must have seen gives rise to a sympathetic understanding.'

Thayer records how, on a bright sunny day in April 1823, Beethoven took Schindler for a long ramble through the scenes in which he had composed his fifth and sixth symphonies. Schindler continues – 'after we had looked at the Bath-House and its adjacent garden at Heiligenstadt and he had given expression to agreeable recollections touching his creations, we continued our walk through the Kalenberg . . . passing through the pleasant valley . . . which is traversed by a gently murmuring brook that hurries down from a nearby mountain and is bordered by high elms, Beethoven repeatedly stopped to let his glances roam, full of happiness, over the landscape. Then, seating himself and resting against an elm, Beethoven asked me if there were any yellowhammers to be heard in the trees around us. But all was still. He then said "Here I composed the scene by the brook and the yellowhammers up there, the quails, nightingales and cuckoos round about, composed with me." To my question why he had not put the yellowhammers into the score, he drew out his sketchbook and wrote an ascending arpeggio on the chord of G major as played (in bar 59) by a flute. "That's the composer up there," he remarked, "hasn't she a more important role than the others? They were meant only for a joke."'

The pleasant valley through which Beethoven and Schindler walked, talked and sat is a landmark in more senses than one. Not only is it a place to which a piece of symphonic music can be directly related, but also one in which the composer and his birds are alone and undisturbed by any other human activity – no dancers, no other figures in the landscape, not even the suggestion of a shepherd's pipe.

A new awareness of nature was becoming a dominant feature of the Romantic movement, particularly in central and northern Europe. It was said of Weber, for instance, that 'as he sat in his travelling-carriage, the country through which he passed would present itself to his inner ear as music.' Human activity, even when present, was no longer an essential ingredient as a focal point, around which the landscape would obligingly provide a suitable backcloth. Anyone who enjoys walking alone in solitary places can become aware of sights and sounds in a totally different way than when shared. Then the pleasure can be as great, sometimes greater, though at others either diminished or even totally dispelled.

The sounds and silences of a landscape can be heard as clearly in music as seen in painting. Before Beethoven such scenes were usually general rather than specific; nor has the human element, apart from the composer, been eliminated. In Corelli's *Pastorale ad libitum* from the sixth *Concerto Grosso* and in Handel's *Pastoral Symphony* from *The Messiah*, to take two examples, the stillness is intensified by faint though distant intimations of a shepherd's pipe. Also both pieces owe their inception to an incident in the story of Christ's Nativity.

In the music of J. S. Bach it is impossible not to become aware of the sturdy footsteps of that inveterate walker. When listening to the *Sinfonia* that sets the scene for Cantata 42 (*Am Abend aber dessellbigen Sabbats*) there is both the feel and the sound of evening, with sunset clouds trailing through the woodwind as well as the elation felt by the disciples converging through the glowing twilight towards their secret and pre-arranged meeting-place. Nor is it of any consequence whether the landscape is that of Palestine, Thuringia or the Weald of Kent.

No composer more consistently reveals the true countryman at heart than Haydn. As such he shows himself to be the antithesis of Mozart, of whom it was said that rarely, if ever, did he look out of a coach window when on his numerous journeys. His music, detached from external stimuli, seems rather to emanate from air and light. On the other hand when, in the operas, he is concerned with human joys and sorrows, these become touched with an enchanted wand of luminous sound, from which can be heard precisely where the composer's sympathies lie as the drama unfolds. Perhaps the nearest approach to a pastoral feeling in Mozart's instrumental music may be found in the Oboe Quartet, often associated with the first poem in Blake's Songs of Innocence – "Piping down the valleys wild . . ."

In the same year as that in which Beethoven and Schindler took their walk Schubert was composing *Die Schöne Müllerin*. As in that supreme masterpiece, his landscapes are frequently characterized by the implied sound of flowing water. It is the absence of this quality that accentuates the desolation of the rejected lover in *Die Winterreise*, throughout which the river is frozen. Instead of the familiar reassuring sound there is a stark, icy stillness.

The landscapes of Mendelssohn and Berlioz have in the main been amply plotted by these composers, though in the latter's *Symphonie Fantastique*, the young artist and the two shepherds can be placed anywhere at will, provided the scene is rural on an evening when there is thunder in the air.

Schumann, apart from Manfred and the Rhine, is less specific. Brahms, like Bach, returns from long country walks with glowing intimations of his delight in forests, lakes and hills. Dvorak is another complete countryman; like Beethoven he is ready to encourage any bird within earshot to add a phrase or two when preparing a score. Whatever may be said about the *New World Symphony*, that stalwart and original masterpiece had a strong influence on the earlier music of Charles Ives, though it was not long before he began to fill his tonal canvas with noisy crowds, whose hymns and ditties frequently obliterate the natural background.

With the advent of the various Nationalist groups, the spirit of place begins to acquire homegrown characteristics. In more recent times such sounds have become less recognizable as such. Returning once more to birdsong in music, the responses have become exciting, though totally different. Examples such as those revealed by Messaien after bird-listening in the French Alps, or Jim Fassett who, in musique concrète, puts American birds through their paces in a surprising manner, provide apt illustrations.

Ever since Debussy brought Mallarmé's Faun into the concert-room, the animal world has been deprived of an erstwhile and endearing innocence. No longer are the sounds of the countryside transmuted in their former freshness: rather have they tended to become symbols of human aspiration and frustration. Typical of the changed aspect is the amorous lizard watching a goldfinch as in *Le soleil des eaux* by Boulez. Animals have in fact become anthropomorphous: gone are the carefree days when any bird was glad enough to toss a phrase to the composer passing below.

> "We'll to the woods no more,
> The laurels are all cut,
> The bowers are bare of bay
> That once the muses wore."

Fortunately the testimony of time past lives on. Its high summer is recalled in the sad, haunting and autumnal strains of Delius and many others who have eloquently lamented the passing of a long and enchanted day.

II

So far the relationship between music and the natural world has dominated this meditation. Music that recalls or stems from the busy world of cities, seaports, circuses and even, as for Varèse, the Paris Metro, requires another and a different approach. But behind all music there exists the basic, if elusive, reality of silence – incidentally as intense, one would imagine, as anywhere at night-time in the purlieus of the Metro.

It has been said of Webern that his music lies nearer to silence than that of any other composer. A personal experience as to the truth of this statement, as well as a vivid revelation of the potency of silence, require a modulation in the style of presentation for what follows.

On an evening in late summer we had stopped at the summit of the Simplon Pass. Leaving the car, we wandered away from the road. On one side the sun still shone on a snow-capped peak, rose-coloured against a deep blue in the eastern sky. To the west a dark face of jet-black mountain jutted into the sunset glow. Far below the distant lights of Brig showed like pin-points of yellow-gold in a cauldron of deep purple. There was no breeze, no sound other than the occasional passing of a car on the road. Sometimes, during a lull, nothing at all. Nothing – except a vast, deep silence.

I found myself wondering what music, if any, could suitably illuminate such a moment. Then I realized – this was pure Webern, the Webern of the Orchestral Pieces. Since then the mists that formerly swirled between this music and my understanding have thinned, leaving clear patches through which has come a glimmering of the scope, intensity and power contained in it.

There is a poem by Siegfried Sassoon in which the phrase "Stillness, man's final companion" occurs. In this sense it places stillness as an ante-room of silence. Such mysterious regions held a particular attraction for the writers and poets of the Celtic Twilight. Fiona Macleod (William Sharp) for one –

"Behind the little windless leaves of the wood
The sea-wastes of the wind-worn Hebrides,
With thunderous crashes falling wave on wave
Are but troubled sighs of a great silence."

In the *Immortal Hour* the same poet sets the opening scene in a moonlit wood at the edge of the world. In it the wandering King Eochaidh encounters Dalua, the god of shadows. This encounter symbolizes a situation and experience common to many people who, either in fact or in imagination, find themselves suddenly aware of hitherto unknown, unexplored and unfathomable mysteries, lying beyond human reach. Such intimations are usually attended by complete silence. Nor does Dalua confine himself to the world's edge: I am certain he once crossed my path many years ago – of all unlikely places in a small parish church in Wiltshire where I once was organist.

During the second world war Evensong was held during the pre-blackout hours of afternoon. The proceedings on such occasions tended to assume a dream-like character, notably during the winter months, when the sermon merged into the falling twilight. Then the building assumed a strangely unsubstantial quality, as though constructed of echo and shadow. The organ was placed in an apse, where the blower and I presided by ourselves. There was no choir in this hamlet of less than one hundred souls.

One particular Sunday remains in the memory. The Rector was

nearing the end of his sermon, well past his spiritual Tattenham Corner and coming down the final stretch towards the tape, but taking his time. 'And so, my brethren,' came his gentle voice, the owner almost invisible in the shadows, 'let us ever be mindful of the duality that exists throughout the whole of God's creation.' This naturally led into the usual clerical embroidery – good and evil, light and darkness etc. etc. I began to muse about all this and nearly missed my cue for the last hymn. Words of poems were running in my head, one by Rupert Brooke in particular "Further than laughter goes, or tears, further than dreaming . . ." a line from *Day That I Have Loved* that I happened to be setting to music at the time.

Suddenly I heard the Rector giving out the number of the last hymn. After the Blessing I played again, while the small congregation emerged from the church and vanished into the dusk. Daylight had almost gone; there had been a breeze blowing across the valley from the south-west all day, bringing soft and gentle rain. Now all was still. I played on for a moment or two, then stopped. Peter, the young organ blower, scampered quickly off towards home while I collected the bits of music, blew out the candles and shut the organ case. Then, it happened. Suddenly, just before the verger came out of the vestry, in that intense stillness, a shadowy figure stood on the chancel steps. Like Dalua he seemed, gentle, kindly, sombre in black hood and mantle, very tall and infinitely silent.

In that brief moment something I had never known before came to me in the gloom, wrapped in strangeness and mystery, after the last sigh of wind from the bellows had subsided. Silence.

Then with a clatter of rustic boots, the verger joined me. 'Dark in 'ere,' he said, 'and so quiet it quite gives you the creeps. I thought you'd gone 'ome – I might've locked the door on you.' Together we left the church, bidding each other 'good night' at the churchyard gate.

On the way home I kept thinking of silence filling that little church in a remote corner of our valley. I imagined that dark figure smoothing out the jagged edges of sound we had made – a cipher during the last hymn and the strange contribution made by the self-appointed leader of the singing – a golden-hearted alto with a voice like tin. Even in that quiet church there would be those sudden little noises of the night that sound so formidable in the surrounding stillness. Harold Monro describes them thus:

"A distant engine whistles, or the floor
Creaks, or the wandering night-wind bangs a door.

Silence is scattered like a broken glass;
The minutes prick their ears and run about,
Then one by one subside again and pass
Sedately in, monotonously out."

All this may seem a long way from Webern and *Ce qui l'entend sur les montagnes* or from the edge of the world. Yet it is closely linked in imaginative experience. Webern very neatly disposes of Oscar Wilde's argument. And the passing breezes bring with them sounds that are very close to the heart of music.

CHAPTER 33

Music and Railways

Towards the end of the steam era there appeared in *The Railway Magazine* a letter from Mr. E. T. Coxon, in which he noted a particular enthusiasm for railways among organists. 'A partial explanation,' he says, 'may be that both organist and engine-driver are in a position of control over a large and complicated machine, with the sense of power that it gives. . . . It seems to me, therefore, that there may be a relation between the sense of power of a man who can "drive" his organ through, say, Bach's *F major Toccata* and the man who knows he can drive a 'King' from Paddington to Plymouth.'

A similar duality of interests is also evident among members of the clergy. A month or two after the appearance of Mr. Coxon's letter, the same journal recorded the untimely death of the Rev. J. S. Caddick-Adams, whilst photographing trains on the former L.M.S. line between Crewe and Shrewsbury, adding that he had recently appeared as the soloist in a performance of Grieg's *Piano Concerto* in Hanley Town Hall.

Could it be that a fundamental link might be found in the lines of a stave? A small boy decided, one wet afternoon, to write some tunes. Like the monks of old, he seemed to prefer four lines to the more usual five; instead of tunes, there appeared trains. What, then, is the connection between the stave (or staff) in music, the permanent way on which run trains, musicians, some assorted clergy, a small boy – and a poet or two for good measure? The mixture invites investigation.

In his journal for the year 1836 Tom Moore records a trip by train from an unspecified point of departure to Liverpool, 32 miles distant. He is impressed by the comfort of a journey that occupied one-and-a-half hours, 'The motion so easy I found I could write without any difficulty *chemin faisant*.' But a subsequent journey, three years later, with a change to coach and back, was another matter. On that occasion the passengers were unduly hustled by station staffs, so that we find a complaint 'There is a tendency to *Americanize* in the whole course of the world to-day.'

Like many another ultimately successful relationship, not all such beginnings have been auspicious. Somewhere around the middle of the 19th-century Rossini paid a visit to his friends the Rothschilds in Frankfurt. From Paris he travelled by way of Belgium and the Rhine, being much fêted en route. While in

Brussels he made a trip to Antwerp and, for the return journey, decided to sample the new railway. The result was disastrous since, as a result of being whisked along at an unprecedented speed, he fainted. That journey, however, was to find an echo among the delightful collection of pieces called *Péchés Vieillesse* (Sins of my Old Age). Among them is one for piano called *Le Petit Train du Plaisir (Comique-imitatif)*. It has various sections: The Devilish Whistle, Sweet Melody of the Brakes – but wait – The Terrible Derailment, First Wounded Man, Funeral Ode – and finally – Amen.

It is interesting to find Wagner, in company with his first wife Minna and Robert – a large stray Newfoundland dog that had attached itself to the Meister – in London. They had recently arrived after a terrible crossing from Norway, a sea voyage that blows and rocks its way through the score of *The Flying Dutchman*.

In *Mein Leben* Wagner recounts how 'We shuddered through a ghastly London Sunday and wound up with a train trip (our first) to Gravesend Park.' (Or might it have been Greenwich?) They must have made the journey from London Bridge Station, then jointly and uneasily shared by the rival Croydon and Greenwich lines. That uncomfortable partnership was soon to be eased by the opening of a new terminus at Bricklayers' Arms. The latter was heralded as a 'Grand West-end Terminus' despite being situated in the Old Kent Road, but so called on account of being an interchange point for coaches from the west country.

When approaching the metropolis these same coaches would halt at Notting Hill Gate, where the driver would announce 'Next stop London.' Near this point, at No. 1 High Row, lived William Horsley, Bachelor of Music, composer, organist (at a nearby Asylum for Female Orphans and later at The Charterhouse). He and his family established firm friendships with visiting musicians, among them Mendelssohn, Chopin and Joachim. His eldest daughter Mary was to become the wife of Isambard Kingdom Brunel. As well as being beautiful, she was said to be dignified and somewhat aloof. But we catch a glimpse of her playing an uproarious game of Ghosts in the garden with Mendelssohn and others. Though the link is tenuous, it seems likely that the paths of Brunel and Mendelssohn may have briefly converged at the home of the Horsley family.

London Bridge Station was soon to become the city terminus of the London Brighton and South Coast Railway. It was that company which, in dire need of increased locomotive power, placed an order with the firm of E. B. Wilson and Co. for a new design. This was duly carried out by the company's chief draughtsman, David Joy. The result was a batch of single-drive 2–2–2 type engines, the first of which was named Jenny Lind. So successful were they that other companies lost no time in evolving variations of the class, all of them associated with the name of a singer then enchanting audiences in London as elsewhere.

No musician was a more dedicated railway enthusiast than Dvorak. This great and – in company with Schubert – most heartwarming of composers was a lifelong lineside addict. He is said to have caught the chill that led to his last illness from lingering overlong, watching shunting operations on a cold day. One of his New York pupils has told the now legendary story of how, when she arrived for a lesson, the great man's question was 'Did you come by train?' If the answer was 'yes' the number of the engine was instantly demanded. If it were given correctly the lesson went well! It was useless to invent a number if a pupil had forgotten to note it, since Dvorak was fully aware of types, classifications and other relevant details of the various lines converging on the city.

In more recent times it seems that the majority of dual enthusiasts are to be found within the ecclesiastical fringe of music, particularly among the Broader and Higher sections of the Anglican fraternity, though noticeably rare in Evangelical circles. Add for good measure a liberal sprinkling of composers, singers and instrumentalists. For the majority the focal point remains the steam locomotive, together with the surrounding mystique in which it lived, worked and *sounded*. That it has become a nostalgic interest seems, if anything, to have given an added stimulus. Many people still living can claim first-hand contact with what might be called the railway age of innocence – in these islands the pre-1923 era of infinite variety under the sway of the old companies, each with coat of arms proudly emblazoned, different designs, liveries and buildings – almost all of them taking inordinate pride in appearance and cleanliness.

The contrasting splendour of Midland red, Caledonian blue – different from either Great Eastern or Somerset and Dorset blue – differing shades of green, bright on the Great Northern, middle green on the Great Western, dark for the Great Central. For the latter add black and white linings and, for the splashers, cylinder casings and underframes, dark red with vermilion lining. As though such splendours were not enough, there was always 'the firm next door' where an entirely different aura awaited a visit.

A major attraction for the musically-minded was the contrasting sounds, not only of whistle or hooter, but in the variety of response from engines. At Euston there would be columns of steam ejected from the safety valves of comparatively small engines being worked to capacity and the 'tink' of Crewe valve-gear as a station pilot brought in a train on the departure side of that now vanished 'train shed.'

At nearby St. Pancras, crowned by William Barlow's splendid roof, one immediately became aware of a general air of dignified seemliness in the demeanour of trains, resplendent throughout in that unique Midland red. Graceful clerestoreyed coaches were moved sedately by engines with the deep-throated exhaust that characterized Derby compounding.

Paddington presented a strange duality: on one side of the station there was an almost ceremonial handling of the arrival and departure of trains. On the other side crates of flowers and an unmistakable smell of fish evoked visions of Cornwall and the Isles of Scilly. Here also, long after the virus of piped music had infected other London termini, The G.W.R. Staff Band, resplendent in uniform, would play on the station forecourt on Sunday mornings. To crown all, there was the unforgettable Swindon 'bark' as train after train departed with unfailing dignity, seldom, if ever, troubled by slipping driving wheels, 'setting back' or any of the other hazards that might occasionally be found elsewhere.

Then there was Liverpool Street, gateway to East Anglia and the Fens, murky under a cavernous roof, but facing an eastern sky, bright with intimations of country that was the special preserve of the Great Eastern Railway. Here one noted the continuous sound of Westinghouse brake pumps on stationary engines, panting away, sometimes with frantic urgency, in the manner of an athlete who has just completed a marathon. At others a gentle sigh of contentment, like an elderly gentleman settling into his favourite club armchair and dozing over a leisurely perusal of *The Times*.

At Victoria the unique golden-yellow, officially described as Mr. Stroudley's Improved Engine Green, had given place to the dark umber introduced by his successor Douglas Earle Marsh. It none-the-less provided a good background on which the letters L.B.S.C. still gave an intimation of former golden glory. One of William Stroudley's habits, when in office, had been to walk the platforms at Brighton station, remove a glove and wipe a finger on a stationary engine. Woe betide the driver if a trace of dirt or grime was revealed.

These and other characteristics, even such details as lineside fences, became linked with the different landscapes through which each line penetrated. Memories such as these confirm the validity of a broadcast comment once made by Patrick Hadley about the composer E. J. Moeran, that 'he belonged to the Romantic School of railway enthusiasts.'

In those halcyon days the different companies acquired favourite lineside vantage points, from which their devotees frequently and lovingly set up their cameras and took out their note-books. Brentwood Bank for the Great Eastern – then semi-rural and with only double track – Potters Bar or between the Welwyn tunnels for the Great Northern; Sonning Cutting for the Great Western – and so on.

Returning to the ecclesiastical fringe, the present writer once found Sir John Dykes Bower reading *The Railway Magazine* within the precincts of St. Paul's Cathedral. Sir Sydney Nicholson was another dedicated subscriber to that journal, a link that has been maintained by his successors at the Royal School of Church Music. At Salisbury, Sir Walter Alcock built scale-models that ran in his garden, to the delights of his friends and for their builder's pleasure. Dr. Henry Ley at Eton knew many top-link drivers at the Royal Oak Depot and could recount their exploits – one might say cadenzas – in detail.

A large number of devotees are time-table addicts. Since their interest might be broadly described as contrapuntal, they could be said to belong to the Polyphonic School, as distinct from the romantic or technical groups. Here are two instances of time-table addicts in action.

A Canon of the Anglican Church was recently encountered, coming away from his station bookstall in rapt, almost processional manner. Under his arm was a newly-acquired, large and comprehensive time-table. His response to a friend's greeting was 'I say, have you seen what they've just done with the 8.57?' It transpired that 'they' had cut two minutes off the previous schedule, while adding another stop en route.

Another instance is that of a missionary who returned to these shores after an absence of twenty years. He arrived at Dover on a Saturday afternoon, where he was met by a relative, then living at Walmer. 'If we hurry,' said the relative, 'we can just catch the 3.28.' The missionary put down his luggage and pondered. 'But,' he said, 'The 3.28 doesn't run on Saturdays.' He was right – it still maintained that elusive habit.

The railways have occasionally reciprocated the interest shown by musicians. There was a Great Western engine of the Bulldog Class, built in the early 1900s and named Edward Elgar, the 'Sir' being added when the composer received his knighthood. After it was sent to the scrapyard in the 1930s there was a hiatus over the name until after the end of World War II. Then there appeared a brand new Castle Class engine with the composer's name once more displayed above the central splasher. Shortly before this 'happy event' the first postwar Three Choirs Festival had been held at Hereford. Over tea one day there was a conversational lament over the disappearance of the Elgar nameplate. Various people, notably E. J. Moeran (whose Sinfonietta was being performed) expressed the hope that something might be done to rectify the omission. That conversation was reported in the local press, in a diary column about notable people attending the Festival. It seems possible that someone connected with Swindon read the column and took appropriate action.

A reference to Moeran inevitably also recalls his friend Peter Warlock. Hamilton Ellis has written of a train journey to Oxford, during which he and a fellow-traveller talked of railways in Wales, a subject on which his companion displayed detailed knowledge. Subsequently he discovered that it was Peter Warlock who had revealed such considerable expertise.

No commentary such as this would be complete without a reference to Honegger and his Pacific 231. Since the wheel arrangement of this type is invariably that of 4-6-2, the composer's explanation, that he only counted the wheels on one side of the engine, sets the record to rights.

In retrospect it seems that the steam era and diatonic tonality merge happily together. If, in future, any diesel or electric locomotives are to be given a composer's name, the choice should surely be made from those who specialize in serial or electronic idioms.

Some musicians have in their time been in the railway service. Balakirev, for example, though one cannot help wondering whether he gave his whole mind to the job. Among English composers, both Rubbra and Eric Thiman spent some time as railwaymen though not, in the light of later achievements, with any noticeable intention of remaining as such. The father of George Butterworth was at one time General Manager of the North Eastern Railway. Most notable of all must surely be Sir George Grove, within the folds of whose Dictionary so many musicians have found a place. Trained as an engineer, he worked during early years with Robert Stephenson during the construction of the railway at Bangor and in the building of the Britannia Bridge that carries the former London and North Western line over the Menai Straits. In addition he was also a notable biblical scholar as well as a lifelong participator in the world of music. He provided programme notes for concerts at the Crystal Palace for forty years, while his studies of the life and work of Beethoven,

Schubert and Mendelssohn have secured for themselves a permanent place in our archives. To him belongs the distinction of becoming the first Director of the Royal College of Music. Best of all was a memorable journey to Vienna when, in company with Sullivan, he was able to discover the part-books for the whole of Schubert's *Rosamunde* music.

On the other hand there are men in the railway world who have given proof of their love for, and knowledge of, music. Cecil J. Allen was a masterly exponent at the organ. Hamilton Ellis has revealed a deep and abiding love for music in his writing. Others, such as Kenneth M. Leech, have acquired considerable skill and ability as composers – and they are but three of many.

So, with a backward glance at the small boy whose tunes turned into trains, the time has come to end a necessarily brief and imcomplete survey. Except in the field of private enterprise, the age of steam has passed. As a legacy we have an abundance of books, paintings and photographs. Also, thanks to Peter Handford and Argo Transacord, the sounds as well. With these in safe keeping our grandchildren will be able to catch a glimpse of the splendour that once was ours.

With diesel and electric motive power the railways may be said to have gone dodecaphonic. The time-table addicts, at least, will be kept on the alert. But when diesels fail, as still too often happens, the seasoned traveller will recall the gallant efforts of engine crews to 'nurse' an ailing steam locomotive to journey's end.

By way of coda, another poet to keep Tom Moore company. It is midsummer on the Great Western; the poet Edward Thomas. An express draws up 'unwontedly' at Adlestrop –

> "The steam hissed. Someone cleared his throat.
> No one came and no one left
> On the bare platform. . . ."

The hissing steam must have emanated from one of George Jackson Churchward's Star Class engines. The coaches would almost certainly have had clerestorey roofs. The long-familiar chocolate and cream livery had temporarily given place to maroon; the familiar erstwhile décor was to be restored after the end of World War I.

Through the carriage window, secured by a notched leather strap, not only "Willow-herb and grass and meadowsweet" were visible, but also –

". . . a blackbird sang
Close by, and round him, mistier
Further and further, all the birds
Of Oxfordshire and Gloucestershire."

Yes, we remember Adlestrop – and surely there will be a corner in Elysium where the age of steam still flourishes.

CHAPTER 34

The Piano – in Sickness and in Health

If you happen to possess a piano, you will be aware that, at more or less regular intervals, a tuner will materialize on the doorstep bearing a bag containing every requisite for his trade, except a duster which he will immediately request. This little ceremony (obviously desirable in the interests of hygiene) holds a certain fascination for the donor. It suggests an imaginative picture of the culminating point in an apprentice's training – the moment comes for the final inspection of the tools needed on the qualifying tuner's life journey and it is tempting to think that he then takes a solemn oath that never, never will he . . .

Following this traditional declaration of his status, the tuner will then proceed to perform his skilled and dedicated task. As likely as not, his opening gambit will bear a remote, though recognizable, likeness to the phrase in which a lone flute sets *L'Après-midi d'un faune* in motion, but in a strangely truncated, emphatic and questioning manner.

What of your tuner? Is he middle-aged or elderly? Who will succeed him? The chances are, if you are lucky, another tuner who has recently retired and who needs a little private practice to supplement his pension. And when he too folds your duster for the last time? Who then?

Very few school leavers are becoming apprentices to the piano trade now. Of the few that do, how many will have taken this step despite discouragement from parents, teachers and even the trade itself? A friend, incidentally a qualified musician as well, spends the most part of his time restoring, tuning and maintaining pianos. He finds it a fascinating life, particularly as he is able to take part in music-making also. The careers master at the school he attended thought his wish to enter the piano trade and to study at a college of music quite absurd – so much so that almost anyone else would have been effectively put off for life. This of course was in the past, for he is now middle-aged, but it would be interesting to know how many other careers masters at the present time actively discourage the musically-minded pupil, with insufficient opportunity or ability to become a professional musician, to think of the piano trade as a possible means of livelihood. Once qualified he could become his own master, find time for some music-making and be assured of as much work – or more – as he could undertake.

A difficulty not unknown to the aspiring apprentice seeking

training is that many firms have strong family connections. A boy who recently applied to a well-known source was asked, in a cold, distant manner 'Let me see now, how many other members of your family have we had here?' It would surely take more than the usual quota of youthful self-confidence to survive such an unpromising opening.

A good many people, particularly representatives of education authorities, persist in regarding the piano as a piece of furniture or what they describe as equipment. To attempt to persuade them into considering it a musical instrument strikes them as slightly comic, and even quaint, which is charming if they happen to like you personally, misguided if they don't. So it would seem that betwixt the closely guarded piano industry, departments of local government and the unenlightened parent-householder there are considerable gulfs fixed. And into one of them has very probably fallen the man who might have tuned your piano when the present visitant retires.

A growing preference for the cheapest estimate does little to establish a good reputation for the piano trade workers. It is strange that many people have yet to discover that a good piano by a reputable maker is a good investment only if it is cared for and regularly maintained.

There is a growing superstition among the lesser-informed that the craft of tuning has become the monopoly of sightless persons. It is a matter for praise and gratitude that so much skill can be acquired in overcoming a major disability. Indeed, it is impossible to over-estimate the achievements and courage of many who have become expert tuners, despite difficulties that seem insurmountable to those who do not share so heavy a handicap. But, tuning is only a part of the care that is needed.

Surely it is time for attitudes to this skilled job to change. It combines a full and varied training with the value and prestige of craftsmanship which must be a better way of life in the long run. It is said that some young tuners now emerging have taken, in a mechanized age, to working with the aid of electronic devices. Judging from the comments of musicians who have experienced this treatment, the results are not encouraging. Are not even simple skills better than the lure of immediate high wages for unskilled monotonous jobs with little, if any, promise of promotion or satisfaction?

To me, at least, it is all too clear that unless or until the various experts make a combined effort to bridge the existing gulfs, the future prospect for tuning and maintaining our pianos is very bleak indeed.

CHAPTER 35

Bach's '48',
Dr. Ebenezer Prout and others

The gradual acceptance of the clavier music of J. S. Bach among pianists was heralded by such staunch advocates as Liszt and Busoni. At a time when keyboard virtuosity was regarded as an essential ingredient, notable Bach transcriptions frequently appeared in concert programmes, in which the clear flowing water from a seemingly inexhaustible spring was diverted through pianistic grottos and artificially contrived waterfalls, from which additional clusters of notes fell on the ear like tonal spray. At a more modest level, students were given some of the smaller pieces as part of a basic diet. The moment of revelation was yet to come.

In Britain the names of four pioneers will ever be held in grateful memory. Largely through their patient endeavours, the wide range of Bach's clavier music, shorn of decoration, embellishment and well-meaning but impious editing, has emerged unscathed. Meanwhile the 48 preludes and fugues had been the constant companions of Mozart, Beethoven, Chopin, Schumann, Wagner, Brahms and countless others.

Formerly English audiences tended to be too easily dazzled by brilliance from overseas. They could also be a little 'slow on the uptake' about anything different. So it was not until the 20th-century was well under way that programmes, devoted to Bach's clavier music (apart from the organ), such as draw audiences to-day, became established.

Among pioneers, the name of Edward Danreuther (1844–1905) claims priority. Incidentally a friend and host to Wagner in London, he was a staunch advocate of Bach and the writer of a book on ornaments of that period. Later, when he was a Professor at the Royal College of Music, Harold Samuel was one of his pupils. It was the latter's series of recitals at the Wigmore Hall in 1921 that firmly and finally set the seal on the rehabilitation of this music. By that time the full tide of Romanticism had retreated sufficiently for Harold Samuel to achieve this triumph. His totally dedicated and lifelong advocacy is commemorated in a well-known and much-used edition of the 48 preludes and fugues, with the valuable addition of wise and illuminating commentary by Donald Francis Tovey.

Of Tovey it was said that not only could he, in company with Chopin, Harold Samuel and others, play all the 48 from memory, but that he could transpose any of them into other keys, to the delight of his friends and pupils.

At the Royal Academy of Music Dr. Ebenezer Prout (1835–1909) is remembered for a notable book on orchestration. He was also among the first to remove from the orchestral score of *The Messiah* then in general use, the additional accompaniment gratuitously supplied by Mozart. By way of encouraging his pupils to explore and study the 48 preludes and fugues, he had the ingenuity to apply catch-phrases to all the fugue subjects. They have now become something of a curiosity, incidentally giving a glimpse of post-Dickensian humour. It should be borne in mind that they emanate from a period when 'good clean fun' proliferated, at a time when the young were much addicted to the word 'jolly'.

On the original autograph copy of Book I, part of the composer's inscription reads: 'The Well-tempered Clavier of Preludes and Fugues through all tones and semitones . . . are . . . for the Practice and Profit of Young Musicians desiring Instruction as well as for the Enjoyment of those already versed in the Study.'

Before proceeding further, a warning must be given. Some dedicated Bach addicts regard such verbal descants as a form of sacrilege. The reason given is that, having once known Prout's commentary, they are unable to disassociate it from the deeper content of the music. Familiarity, they say, permanently mars their appreciation. For the greater majority, however, they are easily detachable, except when recalled with pleasure. The present writer's enjoyment of No. 11 (Book I) in F has been permanently enriched by the shade of the Bishop of Exeter! For the serious-minded there is always an antidote at hand in the commentaries of Tovey, Cecil Gray and many others.

Here then is Prout: his attachments are as given, during youthful days in Brighton, by a loved and valued teacher, Emma Lomax. She has already appeared in these pages and, when young, actually encountered the great man.

Book I

No.

1 in C   He went to town . . . in a hat that made all . . the people stare.

2 in C minor   John Sebastian Bach sat upon a tack, but he soon got up again . . . . with a howl.

3 in C sharp   (The Mistletoe) O what a very jolly thing it . . is to kiss a pretty girl.

4 in C sharp minor   Broad . . . . beans and ba . . con.
(Counter-Subject 1) Make an excellent good dinner for a man who hasn't anything to eat.
(Counter-Subject 2) With half a pint of . . stout.

5 in D   Gie a body meet a body
           Com . . in' through . . the rye,
(Answer)   Gie' a body kiss a body
           Need . . . a bo . . . dy cry!

6 in D minor   He trod upon my corns with heavy boots – I yelled!

7 in E flat   When I get aboard a channel steamer, I begin to feel sick.

8 in D sharp minor   (Pears' Soap) You dirty boy, just look at your face! Ain't . . . . . you ashamed?

9 in E   Hullo! Why what the devil is the matter with the thing?

10 in E minor   Half a dozen dirty little beggar boys are playing with a puppy at the bottom of the street.

11 in F   The Bishop of Exeter was a most energetic man.

12 in F minor   The slimy worm was writhing on the footpath.

13 in F sharp   Old Abram Brown was plagued with fleas, which caused him great alarm.

14 in F sharp minor   (The Organist) As I sat . . . at the or . . . gan the wretched blower went and let the wind out.

15 in G   O Isabella Jane! Isabella Jane! Hold your jaw! Don't . . . make such a fuss! Shut . . . up! Here's a pretty row, what's it all about?

16 in G minor   (The Prodigal Son) He spent his money, like a stupid ass.

17 in A flat   Put me in my little bed.

18 in G sharp   How sad our state by nature is – what beastly fools we be.

19 in A   There – I have given too much to the cabman.

20 in A minor   On a bank of mud in the river Nile, upon a summer morning, a little hippopotamus was eating bread and jam.

21 in B flat   A little three-part fugue, which a gentleman named Bach composed, there's a lot of triple counterpoint about it, and it isn't very difficult to play.

22 in B flat minor   Brethren – the time is short.

23 in B   He went and slept . . . under a bathing machine at Margate.

24 in B minor   The man was very drunk, as to and fro, from left to right, across the road he staggered.

Book II

No.

1 in C   Sir Augustus Har . . ris tried to mix a pound of treacle with a pint of castor oil.

2 in C minor   Old Balaam's donkey spoke like an ass.

3 in C sharp   O here's a lark!

4 in C sharp minor   Hey diddle diddle the cat and the fiddle
The cow jumped over the moon!

5 in D   To play these fugues through is real . . . jam.

6 in D minor   (The Cockney) 'Ark to the sound of the 'oofs of the gallopin' 'orse! I 'ear 'im comin' up Regent Street at night. (Counter-subject) 'Is 'oofs go 'ammer, 'ammer, 'ammer 'ammer, 'ammer, 'ammer on the 'ard 'ighway.

7 in E flat   Mary, my dear, bring the whiskey and water in, bring the whiskey and water in.

8 in D sharp minor   I went to church last night and slept all the sermon through.

9 in E   I'd like to punch his head.
(Counter-subject) If he gives me any more of his bally cheek.

10 in E minor   As I rode in a penny bus, going to the Mansion House, off came the wheel – down came the bus – all of the passengers fell in a heap on the floor of the rickety thing.

11 in F   Needles and pins! needles and pins! When a man's married his trouble begins.

12 in F minor   I told you you'd have the stomach-ache if you put such a lot of pepper in your tea.

13 in F sharp   Great Scott! What a trouble it is to have to find the words for all these subjects!

14 in F sharp minor   She cut her throat with a paper-knife that had got no handle.
(Bar 20) The wound was broad and deep.
(Bar 36) They called the village doctor in: he put a bit of blotting-paper on her neck.

15 in G   The pretty little dickybirds are hopping to and fro upon the gravel walk before the house, and picking up the crumbs.

16 in G minor   O my eye! O my eye! What a precious mess I'm getting into to-day.

17 in A flat   I passed the night at a wayside inn, and could scarcely sleep a moment for the fleas.

18 in G sharp minor   Two little boys were at play, and the one gave the other a cuff on the head and the other hit back.
(Counter-subject) Their mother sent them both to bed without their tea.

19 in A   In the middle of the Hackney Road to-day I saw a donkey in a fit.

20 in A minor   He that would thrive must rise at five.

21 in B flat   The noble Duke of York he had ten thousand men, He marched them up the hill and marched them down again.

22 in B flat minor   O dear – what shall I do! It's utterly impossible for me to learn this horrid fugue: I give it up!
(Counter-subject) It ain't no use – it ain't a bit of good! Not a bit – no, not a bit – no, not a bit.

23 in B   See what ample strides he takes.

24 in B minor   The wretched old street-singer has his clothes all in tatters and toes showing through his boots.

List of Music by
Christopher le Fleming

Op. 1. Cradle song for Christmas (Eleanor Farjeon) Unison   *O.U.P.*
1929   Hymnus (God be in my hede) Sarum Primer 1550   *Anglo-*
      a. for high voice with acc.   *American*
      b. SATB unaccompanied.

2. Songs with pf: mezzo or baritone (Medium Voice)   *Chester*
      The Hills of Heaven (Mary Webb)
      In a Sleepless Night (W. H. Hutton)
      To an Isle in the Water (W. B. Yeats)
      Sheep-shearing (Dorset folk song)

3. Songs with pf: *See* Op 44 for final versions   *MS.*
1932   Moonlight on the Door (William Barnes)
      The Blackbird (William Barnes)
      Singer within the little streets (Monk Gibbon)
      Lovers be patient (duet) (Monk Gibbon)

4. Piano pieces: *Chester*
1933   Nocturne 'Tweon-ea'
      Bramshaw Folly (also arr. pf and strings)   *Chester*

5. The Echoing Green   Cantata for S A Chorus with
1933   piano and strings   *Chester*
      Words by William Blake, Monk Gibbon, Thomas
      Hardy, Shakespeare, Murray Allison & R.H.B.
      (First performed Mary Datchelor School by
      Mary Donnington 1935)

6. The Peter Rabbit Music Books   *Chester*
1935   1. Pf solo: 2. duets
      Book 1 revised and re-named Beatrix Potter Suite
      Book 2 revised for wind quartet as Homage to Beatrix
      Potter

7. Light Opera Penelope Anne: Libretto by S. H. Hamer   *MS.*
1936   and J. C. Gent. Revised 1953

8. Songs: The Bright Messenger (Mary Cecil)   *MS.*
1936   Cap Finisterre *See* Op 44 (Robert Cecil)   *MS.*
      The Birthright (Eiluned Lewis)   *Cramer*
      When Wintry Weather's all a-done   *Cramer*
      (William Barnes)
      Burn not the sweet apple tree (Gaelic trans)   *MS.*

9. The Singing Friar: Cantata for Tenor solo.   *Chester*
1937   SATB Chorus and small orchestra. Words by
      Thomas Love Peacock (from Maid Marian)
      (First performance S. African Broadcasting
      Service 1940)

10. Five Psalms for soprano solo, SATB chorus and full
1939   orchestra. Also arr. pf and strings   *Chester*
      (First performed Three Choirs Festival,
      Gloucester 1947 with Elsie Suddaby as soloist)

11.	Day that I have loved S S A with either 2 pfs or 1 pf with	
1939	strings. Poem by Rupert Brooke	*Chester*
12.	Songs: Her Song (Thomas Hardy) *See* Op 34	*MS.*
1939/42	When I set out for Lyonesse (Thomas Hardy)	
	See Op 34	*MS.*
	Egypt's Might is Tumbled Down	
	(Mary Coleridge)	*Chester*
	If it's ever spring again (Thomas Hardy)	*Chester*
	I love all, beauteous things (Robert Bridges)	*Cramer*
	(either unison with descant or SATB)	
	Lighten our darkness (Collect) Duet	*Anglo-American*
	Springtime (Grace Armitage)	*O.U.P.*
13.	Song cycle Earth and Air (Final version for S A	
1937	Chorus with pf) (Walter de la Mare)	*Cramer*
14.	Sonatina for violin and piano	*MS.*
1943		
15.	Suite for Strings: *See* Op 42	*Chester*
1943	(First performance in Sheldonian Theatre, Oxford 1944 by Oxford Orchestral Society)	
16.	Songs: O Mortal Folk (Stephen Hawes)	*Curwen*
	Unseen Comradeship (Monica Sinclair)	*Cramer*
various	A Smugglers' Song (Kipling)	*O.U.P.*
times	A Children's Te Deum (Barbara Godlee)	*Cramer*
	Strings in the Earth and Air (James Joyce)	*Elkin*
	Let Folly Praise (Medieval Hymn)	*Elkin*
17.	Pilford Suite for Elementary String Orch.	*Cramer*
1939		
18.	Song cycle A Quiet Company Walter de la Mare	*Cramer*
19.	Songs: Hilaire Belloc (*See* Op 33)	*MS.*
1947	O my companion, O my sister Sleep	
	Han'acker Mill	
	Twelfth Night	
	Tarantella	
20.	Your Trumpets, Angels: Score commissioned by the	
1951	Provost and Chapter of Southwark Cathedral for Festival of Britain Play by K. M. Baxter	
20a.	The Progress of Love: Suite from Op 20 of choral songs	
1952	and dances.	*MS.*
21.	Sinfonietta for Chamber Orchestra	*MS.*
1952	Written for a Wiltshire Summer School of Music 1953	
22.	Evening Service in D (Mag and Nunc) for the Choristers'	*O.U.P.*
1953	Guild of Liverpool Cathedral to mark the 21st anniversary of the Dean's office (F. W. Dwelly). (Printed) for the Choir, later reprinted O U P and accepted for further publication by the Dolphin Publishing Co. (York)	
23.	Orchestral Suite: London River (from Southwark Music)	
1954	Performed by Bournemouth S O with Charles Groves: the final distillation (1976) remains as Overture for a Southwark Festival	*Ashdown*

24.	Air and Dance (formerly Air Poppels) for either vn, viola, cello, fl or oboe with pf.	*Chester*
	April Serenade for orchestra	*Francis Day & Hunter*
25. *1956*	Sutton Valence Suite for School Orchestra	*Boosey*
26. *1958*	Rune for small orchestra	*MS.*[3]
27. *1958*	Te Deum and Benedictus for Choir and Organ (Commissioned by Liverpool Cathedral)	*Novello*
28. *1959*	Four Pieces for flute, violin and Pf. (For the Dunedin Trio and broadcast B.B.C. Scotland)	*Anglo-American*
29. *1959*	Tenax et Fidelis – Festival March for School Orchestra. (Commissioned by Dartford Grammar School and Kent Ed. Committee)	*MS.*
30. *1960/64*	Songs: St. David's (Eiluned Lewis) either SA or SATB with pf.	*Novello*
	Praise be to God (Ethel Towner)	*Elkin*
	Four Songs from the Canterbury Tales	*Novello*
	Jubilate Deo	*Cramer*
31.	Variations for pf on Annie Laurie in the manner of	*MS.*
32.	Four pieces for piano:	
	Soliloquy & Rob's Round	*MS.*
	Sunday Morning: Whistling Tune	*O.U.P.*
33. *1961*	Valley of Arun: Cantata for baritone solo, SATB chorus and orchestra. Revision of Op 19 with the addition of 'Lift up your hearts in Gumber'. Commissioned by Kidderminster Choral Society.	*Novello*
34. *1962*	Six Country Songs (Thomas Hardy) Cantata for Soprano and tenor solo, chorus and orchestra. Commissioned by Kent County Music Committee for Benenden Summer School 1963.	*Novello*
35. *1964*	The Silver Dove: Morality (K. M. Baxter) for Narrator, childrens' chorus and acc. by anything from pf to full orchestra. (This is an adaptation of a former mime with music published by SPCK under the title of *Pull Devil Pull Baker*).	*Belwin Mills*
36. *1965*	Communion Service in D St. Matthew Commissioned for St. Matthew's Church, Northampton	*MS.*
37. *1966*	Music for Alcestis (Gilbert Murray) commissioned by Mayfield Convent School	*MS.*
38. *1966*	Christmas Triptych SSATBB unaccompanied I sing of a maiden The Changing Night (Grace Armitage) Cradle Song (Arthur ffords)	*Robertson*
39. *1967*	Suite for Brass Quintet	*Anglo-American*
40. *1968*	Trees in the Valley 8 part songs (Grace Armitage)	*Boosey*

41.	Squirrel Nutkin – music for an adaptation by Beatrix	*F. Warne*
	Potter	
42.	Suite for Strings in G (*See* Op. 15)	*Anglo-*
1969	(also arr. Sextet for strings)	*American*
43.	Three Pieces for Piano	*Anglo-*
1972	The Frozen Lake	*American*
	Whitemill Bridge	
	Rolling Bay	
44.	Songs of Youth and Age	*Roberton*
1976	1. The Inland Gull (Frank Baker)	
	2. *Cap Finisterre see* Op. 8	
	3. The Blackbird *see* Op. 3	
	4. Singer within the little street *see* Op. 3	
	5. Lovers be patient *see* Op. 3	
	6. Moonlight on the Door *see* Op. 3	
	7. The Life of a Man (Traditional)	
	8. The Wanderer (Thomas Hardy)	
45.	Motet: Since we stay not here (SSATB) (Jeremy Taylor)	*Roberton*
1977	Commissioned by Friends of Cathedral Music	
	for St. Albans.	

Christopher le Fleming – Arrangements and transcriptions

1933	Blue Danube Waltz Piano solo	Chester
1934	Mortify us by thy Grace (Bach) for 2 pfs.	Chester
	Jesu source of our desires (usual title already OUP copyright)	
1938	Organ Prelude and Fugue St. Anne for 2 pfs.	Chester
	(Dedicated to and played by Cyril Smith and Phyllis Sellick)	
1938	Blue Danube and Tales from Vienna Woods Waltzes for 2 pfs.	Chester
1940	Sleepers Wake & Sheep may Safely Graze Piano solo	Chester
1950	The Wraggle Taggle Gypsies, O. SATB unaccompanied	O.U.P.
1955	O Waly waly SSA unacc.	Boosey
	Spring has now unwrapped the flowers	
	Spring carol SSA unacc.	Cramer
1957	Agincourt Hymn for SAB Chorus with string acc.	Elkin
1960	Three Traditional Tunes for string Quartet	Novello
1961	Rounds and Canons	Belwin Mills
1964	More Rounds and Canons	Belwin Mills
1974	The Mikado for SSAA.	Cramer

Index (Persons)

A

Alcock, Sir Walter   181
Alexander, Arthur   145
Allen, Cecil J.   183
Allen, Inglis   34
Allison, Mrs.   30
Allt, Dr. W. Greenhouse   152
Anthony, Muriel   154
Armstrong, Sir Thomas   143
Ashdown, Hugh (Bishop)   21
Atkins, Sir Ivor   44, 46

B

Backhaus, W.   22
Bairstow, Sir Edward   74
Baker, Constance   43
Baker, Frank   70, 74, 84, 92–3, 101
   102
Baker, Leo   148
Bantock, Sir Granville   19, 45
Barnard, York   25
Barnes, Harry   70, 71, 74–6
Barry, Joan   140
Bartlett, Ethel   87
Bartholomew, T. G. 'Jim'   139–40
Batten, Liza (Elizabeth)   96
Bax, Sir Arnold   28, 164, 170
Baxter, Kay   7, 21, 141
Bedford, Herbert   26
Beecham, Sir Thomas   8, 17, 29, 34,
   45, 82
Bell, Bishop   138, 142
Benison, Rev. E. D.   58
Bentall, Brenda   152
Birch, Montague   39
Bliss, Sir Arthur   28, 170
Borland, Rosalind   148, 157
Boughton, Rutland   37
Boult, Sir Adrian   64–5, 82, 102, 109
Boult, Olive   89
Brailsford, Henry Noel   49
Brent Smith, Alexander   25
Brewer, Sir Herbert   44, 46
Britten, Benjamin   24, 146, 150, 164
Brooke, Rupert   128, 175
Brown, Wilfred   109, 153
Browne, E. Martin   139
Browne, Roger 'R.H.B.'   53, 89
Bruckner, Anton   20, 29, 170
Brunel, Isambard Kingdom   178
Bruxner, Mervyn   147, 151, 154–5

Brynley, David   41, 75, 96, 98
Busch, Wilhelm   7
Butler, Antonia   103, 154
Butt, Dame Clara   22
Buzzard, Sir Farquar   55

C

Cameron, Basil   19, 23
Capper, Alfred   20
Card, Cicely   102
Carson, Violet   76
Churchward, G. J.   183
Clarke, Rebecca   77
Clayton, Rev. 'T'   109
Clifford, Julian   19
Clinton, Gordon   153
Coates, John   46, 77, 104
Cole, Maurice   109
Collins, Gertrude   64
Cooke, Rev. Herbert   52
Crosthwaite Eyre, Dio   88, 103, 111
Crosthwaite Eyre, Sir O.   88, 103
Currey, Elizabeth   131

D

Danreuther, Edward   187
D'Aranyi, Jelli   84, 111–2
Dalrymple, Dorothea   110. 133
Davies, Sir Walford   28, 145
De Bary, Rev. R.   57
De Bary, Anna Bunston   57
De Csillèry, Bèla   155
De la Mare, Walter   6, 108–9
Delius, Frederick   34, 35, 75, 153, 173
Del Mar, Norman   62
Donnington, Mary   89

E

Eardley, Violet   30
Earp, Herbert E.   32
Eaton, Sybil   110
Edrupp, Canon   58
Eisenberg, Maurice   81
Elgar, Sir Edward   17, 18, 28, 43, 44,
   85, 114, 156, 170, 181–2
Ellis, C. Hamilton   182, 183
Elwes, Gervase   15, 16, 85
Evers, C. R.   152

F

Fachiri, Adila   84, 111–12

Farjeon, Eleanor 42
Fellowes, Canon E. H. 9–10, 25–6, 75
Ferguson, Canon Walter 130
Finzi, Gerald 164, 170
Flecker, James Elroy 21
Fletcher, Mary 85
Fleury, L. 26
Forsyth, Edward 77, 80
Fox Strangways, A. H. 45
Frank, Alan 64
Franklin, David 146

G

Gent, Dr. Nicholas 121, 143
German, Edward 16
Gibbon, Monk 41, 75, 77, 89, 120
Gibson, Douglas 155
Ginn, E. M. 18, 49
Godfrey, Sir Dan 19, 23, 27–38, 60, 88
Gomer, Ronald 42
Grant, Eric 109
Greene, Eric 76, 153
Green, Leslie 70
Greenwood, Norman 154
Gresley, Sir Nigel 96
Grey of Fallodon, Lord 96–8, 111, 146
Grove, Sir George 182
Gurney, Ivor 25, 170

H

Hadley, Patrick 46, 180
Hamer, Sam 93–4, 96
Handford, Peter 183
Harding, Ronald 157
Hardy, Thomas 3, 37, 41, 46, 49–51, 89
Harewood, Lord 65, 150
Harper, Stanley 148
Harper, Sydney 31
Harris, Joan 21
Harris, Richard 83, 84
Harty, Sir Hamilton 25, 82
Hathaway, Joseph 43–4
Havergal, Henry 10
Hayes, Dr. 43
Hayter, Mr. 53
Hearn, Norman 148
Heelis, William 94
Hewitt, Godfrey 70
Hewson, Mrs. 30
Hibberd, George 52–3
Hislop, Joseph 22
Holst, Gustav 24, 28, 46, 50, 67, 170
Holst, Imogen 134, 135, 158
Hope, Ruby 152

Horn, Richard 152
Horsley, William 178
Housman, A. E. 16, 18, 89, 153
Howard Jones, Evlyn 34–36
Howden, Lilias 86
Howells, Herbert 25, 170
Howes, Frank 65
Hubert, Margot 134
Hull, Sir Percy 108
Hutton, Dean W. H. 74

I

Ibberson, Mary 62–3, 65, 102, 147, 149
Imrie, George 106, 121
Ireland, John 16, 25, 31, 64
Isserlis, Julius 103, 104, 127

J

Jacobson, Maurice 146
Jacques, Reginald 111, 127, 150
Joseph, Harry 21

K

Karpeles, Maud 60
Kaye, Miss 7
Kaye Smith, Sheila 63
Keith, Charlton 22
Kelly, Cuthbert 75–6
Kelly, Nellie (Carson) 76
King, Dr. Alfred 31–3, 167
Knapp, Father 57
Knight, Gerald 70
Kruse, Johann 103, 113
Kruse, Frau Professor 103, 113–4

L

Lamb, Henry 39–40
Lambert, Constant 28
Law, Hamilton 37
Leech, Kenneth M. 183
le Fleming, Canon Hugh 56
le Fleming, Michael and Daniel 104
le Fleming, Antony 123
Lehmann, Liza 16
Leighton, Clare 48–9
Leslie, Sir Shane 56
Lester, John 15
Ley, Dr. Henry 25, 181
Littlecote, Ted 131
Löhr, Hermann 16
Lomax, Emma 32, 188

M

Maclean, Alick 19
Macleod, Fiona 174
MacDougall, Mary Ross 128
McInnes, J. C. 85

McKenna, John   104
Marsh, Douglas Earle   11, 180
Marshall Jones, Katharine   128-9
Martin, S/M   124-5
Matthews, Miss   127
Menges, Madame   32
Merchant, Moelwyn   140-1
Miles, William   58, 60
Milne, John   108
Moeran, E. J.   7, 78, 164, 181, 182
Monro, Harold   175
Moore, Dorothy   123, 126
Moore, Katharine   156
Moore, Tom   177, 183
Moore, Vera   85, 87-8, 96, 98
Morse, Rose   145
Mühlen, Raimond von Zur   80
Mukle, May   77

N

Nettleship, Ursula   145
Newall, Robert   118-9, 121
Newman, Ernest   28, 85
Nicholson, Sir Sydney   25, 66-73, 167, 181
Noel, Rev. G.   101
Notley, Norman   75
Northcote, Dr. Sydney   17, 109, 133, 148

O

Oakshott, Gilbert and Audrey   129
Olivier, Edith   106
Orde, Valentine   103
Orr, C. W.   153, 170
Ouseley, Rev. Sir F. Gore   74

P

Paderewski, I.   22
Palin, Anthony   117
Palmer Stone, Tony   30
Parker, George   145
Parry, Sir Hubert   16, 24, 83
Peacock, Thomas Love   97-8
Pearce, Stella Mary   141
Pears, Sir Peter   76, 150
Peel, Graham   40
Pemmel, Charlie   21
Piggott, Audrey   144
Potter, Beatrix   93-96
Powell, Anthony   88
Powys, Theodore   51-2
Prout, Ebenezer   32, 188

Q

Quilter, Roger   16

R

Rachmaninov, S.   81
Raffrey, Monique   156
Raynor, John   70
Reed, W. H.   22, 43, 44, 46
Reeves, George   36, 80-2, 84
Reeves, James   24
R. H. B. – see Browne, Roger
Richards, A. N. G.   41
Richmond, Sir Bruce   108, 131
Richmond, Elena   131, 138
Richmond, Robin   70
Ridout, Herbert   68
Robertson, Rae   87
Robey, George   34
Robins, Carina   139-40
Ronald, Sir Landon   16, 17, 26, 27
Rooper, Jasper   156
Rorke, J. D. N.   13
Royston, Mary   131
Rubbra, Dr. Edmund   34, 164, 182

S

Sale, James   22
Salter, Rev. G.   67
Sammons, Albert   111
Samuel, Harold   25, 187
Sanderson, Wilfrid   16
Sansom, Gillian   155
Sargent, Sir Malcolm   19
Sassoon, Siegfried   105, 174
Scott Baker, Dorothy   131
Scott, C. Russell   154-5
Sellick, Phyllis   87
Sharp, Cecil J.   24, 26
Shaw, Geoffrey and Martin   69
Shaw, George Bernard   113
Shephard, Rupert   77-9, 83, 90
Shore, Bernard   127
Shutler, Miss   30
Silk, Dorothy   46, 76
Smeal, John   133
Smith, Cyril   87
Smith, Ronald   154
Soames, René   146
Somerset, Lord Henry   16
Somervell, Arthur   19
Spencer, Stanley   40
Spencer Watson, Hilda and Mary   41
Stanford, Sir Charles Villiers   16, 25-6, 62, 85
Stanley Wrench, Margaret   140
Stephen, Sir Harry and Lady   102
Stevens, Horace   46
Stevens, Alderman W. E.   131-2
Stocks, Mabel   39
Strafford, Charles   109

Strauss, Richard   62
Stroudley, William   11, 52, 180
Sumsion, H. W. (John)   44, 144
Sutherland, Helen   96, 98
Sutton, Joyce   76
Szigeti, J.   82

T

Tanner, Phyllis   88
Terry, Sir Richard   78
Thayer, A.   170
Thrale, Hester   145
Thiman, Eric H.   182
Thomas, Edward   183
Ticehurst, John   127–8
Toscanini, A.   68
Tovey, Sir Donald   187–8
Trew, Arthur   64
Trotter, Dr. Yorke   27, 88
Tunnard Moore, Thomas   51, 84
Turner, Rev. Philip   141

V

Van der Velde, G.   32–3
Vaughan Williams, Adeline   60–1
Vaughan Williams, Ralph   16, 19,
   24–5, 28, 45, 60–5, 67, 108–9, 138,
   146, 149, 156, 170
Vaughan Williams, Ursula   65

Verey, Rev. Lewis   56
Vogt, Herr Professor   113

W

Walker, Dr. Ernest   26, 144
Walton, 'Mr W. T.' (Sir William)   28
Warlock, Peter   78, 146, 182
Warner, Sylvia Townsend   9
Webb, H. B. L.   77
Webb, Mary   76–7
White, Eric Walter   145
White, Maud Valerie   16
Whyte, Marjorie   21
Wilde, Oscar   170, 176
Williams, C. Lee   44
Wilson, Christopher   83, 87
Wilson, Sir Steuart   46, 65, 76
Wilson Fox, Adeline   111
Wood, Dr. Thomas   62, 111
Wood, Anne   128
Woodcock, Doreen   141
Woodford Finden, A.   16
Wotton, Louise   86
Wright, Helen   149

Y

Yeats, W. B.   26, 77
Yeaxlee, Joan   128
Young, Kenneth   22